Visit us at

www.syngress.com

Syngress is committed to publishing high-quality books for IT Professionals and delivering those books in media and formats that fit the demands of our customers. We are also committed to extending the utility of the book you purchase via additional materials available from our Web site.

SOLUTIONS WEB SITE

To register your book, please visit **www.syngress.com**. Once registered, you can access your e-book with print, copy, and comment features enabled.

ULTIMATE CDs

Our Ultimate CD product line offers our readers budget-conscious compilations of some of our best-selling backlist titles in Adobe PDF form. These CDs are the perfect way to extend your reference library on key topics pertaining to your area of expertise, including Cisco Engineering, Microsoft Windows System Administration, CyberCrime Investigation, Open Source Security, and Firewall Configuration, to name a few.

DOWNLOADABLE E-BOOKS

For readers who can't wait for hard copy, we offer most of our titles in downloadable e-book format. These are available at **www.syngress.com**.

SITE LICENSING

Syngress has a well-established program for site licensing our e-books onto servers in corporations, educational institutions, and large organizations. Please contact our corporate sales department at corporatesales@elsevier.com for more information.

CUSTOM PUBLISHING

Many organizations welcome the ability to combine parts of multiple Syngress books, as well as their own content, into a single volume for their own internal use. Please contact our corporate sales department at corporatesales@elsevier.com for more information.

Next Generation SSH2 Implementation: Securing Data in Motion

Dale Liu Lead Author and Technical Editor

Max Caceres
Dario V. Forte
Devin L. Ganger
Wipul Jayawickrama
Jan Kanclirz, Jr.

Tim Robichaux
Eric S. Seagren
Brad Smith
Christopher Stokes

Unique Passcode

75285725

PUBLISHED BY
Syngress Publishing, Inc.
Elsevier, Inc.
30 Corporate Drive
Burlington, MA 01803

Next Generation SSH2 Implementation: Securing Data in Motion

Printed and bound in the United Kingdom
Transferred to Digital Printing, 2010

ISBN 13: 978-1-59749-283-6

Publisher: Laura Colantoni
Acquisitions Editor: Andrew Williams
Developmental Editor: Matthew Cater
Technical Editors: Dale Liu,
Max Caceres, Justin Peltier

Page Layout and Art: SPI
Copy Editor: Jill Batistick, Judith H. Eby and Michelle Huegel
Indexer: SPI
Cover Designer: Michael Kavish
Project Manager: Andre Cuello

For information on rights, translations, and bulk sales, contact Matt Pedersen, Senior Sales Manager, Corporate Sales, at Syngress Publishing; email m.pedersen@elsevier.com.

Library of Congress Cataloging-in-Publication Data

Liu, Dale.
   Next generation SSH2 implementation: securing data in motion / Dale Liu.
      p.   cm.
   Includes index.
   ISBN 978-1-59749-283-6
   1.   UNIX Shells. 2.   Computer security. 3.   Data encryption (Computer science)
   4.   Computer networks--Security measures. I.   Title.
   QA76.9.A25L59 2008
   005.8--dc22

                                                                                    2008040375

Lead Author and Technical Editor

Dale Liu, (MCSE Security, CISSP, MCT, IAM/IEM, CCNA) has been working in the computer and networking field for over 20 years. Dale's experience ranges from programming to networking to information security and project management. He currently teaches networking, routing and security classes, while working in the field performing security audits and infrastructure design for medium to large companies. He currently resides in Houston TX with two cats. He enjoys cooking and beer brewing with his girlfriend and live-in editor Amy.

Dale wrote chapter 1, "Introduction," *chapter 4,* "SSH Features," *chapter 6,* "SSH Client Basics," *and chapter 11,* "SSH Command Line and Advanced Client Use." *Dale also technically edited Chapters 1, 2, 3, 5, 6, 7, 8, 9, 12 and 13.*

Contributing Authors

Max Caceres is director of research and development for Matasano Security, an independent security firm specializing in providing software and services to help organizations and vendors improve their security postures. Max has over 14 years of product development and security research experience, and is one of the security industry's leading experts on penetration testing. Before joining Matasano, Max led the team responsible for creating the first automated penetration testing product CORE IMPACT and co-invented several now patented technologies including system call proxying and exploit automation.

Max lives in New York City and enjoys spending time with his wife Gabriela and jumping out of airplanes.

Max wrote chapter 10, "Mac SSH," and technically edited chapter 11, "SSH Command Line and Advanced Client Use."

Dario V. Forte, CISM, CFE, is Adj. Faculty at the University of Milano at Crema, and Founder of the IRItaly Project at DFlabs. Dario, a former police detective and founder of DFLabs, has worked in information security since 1992. He has been involved in numerous international conferences on information warfare, including the RSA Conference, Digital Forensic Research Workshops, the Computer Security Institute, the U.S. Department of Defense Cybercrime Conference, and the U.S. Department of Homeland Security (New York Electronic Crimes Task Force). He was also the keynote speaker at the Black Hat conference in Las Vegas. Dario also provides security consulting.
Dario graduated in Organizational Sciences at the University of Torino, with a PGd in Computer Security from Strayer University and an MBA from the University of Liverpool.

Cristiano Maruti, Thomas Orlandi, and Michele Zambelli, are security consultants at DFlabs, Italy, and are in the development team of the PTK, the advanced opensource forensic interface. Graduated in Computer

Science at the University of Milano, Cristiano, Thomas and Michele have written several publications and have contributed to many research projects worldwide. Their research interests are (but not limited to) Digital Forensics, Information Security, Log Analysis, and Information Security Risk Management.

Dario wrote Chapter 7, "The SSH Server Basics," along with Cristiano Maruti, Thomas Orlandi, and Michele Zambelli, of The IRItaly Project at DFlabs

Devin L. Ganger is a Messaging Architect for 3Sharp, Microsoft Exchange MVP, Battlestar Galactica fan, Call of Duty 4 addict, writer, speaker, blogger, husband, father, and geek. He is a lover, not a fighter, despite venturing into karate for health and fitness. His current plan of record is to retire from IT "real soon now", become a dilettante and science fiction novelist and settle down to the challenging second career of ruling a small country with an iron fist.

Devin wrote Chapter 08, "SSH on Windows."

Wipul Jayawickrama is the Managing Director of Infoshield, a company bringing together the skills, knowledge and expertise in information security to serve clients across Australia, Fiji, Sri Lanka, and Papua New Guinea.

Wipul is a Certified Information Systems Security Professional (CISSP) with over 16 years of experience in the IT industry. During this period, he has held diverse roles in both technical and management capacities. As a consultant he has worked with government, financial and corporate clients from a wide range of industry sub sectors.

His specializations include SCADA systems vulnerability assessment and audits and risk management. His recent engagements include the establishment of the Sri Lankan National Computer Emergency Response Team and several Lead Security consultant roles in Critical Infrastructure Computer Network Vulnerability Assessments.

Wipul is currently reading a Master's Degree in Information Security and Intelligence, and holds several Industry certifications in information security. He has presented at many national and international conferences and information security interest group conventions.

He is also a SANS GIAC Certified Systems and Network auditor (GSNA) and was recently accredited as an International Information Systems Security Professional Certification Scheme Practitioner (ISSPCS) status.

He has been published in the Lecture Notes in Computer Science Series and is also the coauthor of a forthcoming book to be published by British Standards Institute on Integrated Management Systems for Information Security and IT Service Management.

Wipul wrote Chapter 3, "An Introduction to Cryptography."

Jan Kanclirz Jr., (CCIE #12136-Security, CCSP, CCNP, CCIP, CCNA, CCDA, INFOSEC Professional, Cisco WLAN Support/Design Specialist) is currently a Senior Network Information Security Architect at MSN Communications. Jan specializes in multi vendor designs and post-sale implementations for several technologies such as VPNs, IPS/IDS, LAN/WAN, firewalls, content networking, wireless and VoIP. Beyond network designs and engineering, Jan's background includes extensive experience with open source applications and Linux. Jan has contributed to several Syngress book titles on topics such as: Wireless, VoIP, Security, Operating Systems and other technologies. When Jan isn't working or writing books he enjoys working on his security portal and exploring outside adventures in Colorado.

Jan wrote Chapter 13, "SSH Port Forwarding."

Justin A. Peltier is a Senior Security Consultant with extensive experience in firewall and security technologies. Mr. Peltier currently holds ten certifications in an array of technology and security products and is the author or co-author of several security books, including "Information Security Fundamentals" and "How To Manage a Network Vulnerability Assessment" and is currently working on "Security Testing: Practices, Guidelines and Examinations".

Mr. Peltier has been involved in implementing, supporting and developing security solutions and has taught courses on many facets of IT security including, Vulnerability Assessment and CISSP preparation.

He has also directed the security practice development and trained at the corporate level with companies like Suntel Services and Netigy.

Justin has taught classes for a variety of training institutes and companies all across the United States, Europe and Asia.

Justin technically edited Chapter 4, "SSH Features, " and Chapter 10, "Mac SSH."

Tim Robichaux is a consultant with over 10 years of experience in Linux and Microsoft Windows integration. Currently working as a Unified Communications Consultant, he continues to provide technical expertise in the field of system integration and administration. He has his MCSE and CCNA and is a former United States Marine. Tim currently lives in the Seattle area with his wife Julie, and three cats.

Tim wrote Chapter 9, "Linux SSH."

Eric S. Seagren (CISA, CISSP-ISSAP, SCNP, CCNA, CNE-4, MCP+I, MCSE-NT) has twelve years of experience in the computer industry, with eight years spent in the financial services industry working for a fortune 100 company. Eric started his computer career working on Novell servers and performing general network troubleshooting for a small Houston-based company. While working in the financial services industry, his position and responsibilities advanced steadily. His duties have included server administration, disaster recovery responsibilities, business continuity coordinator, Y2K remediation, network vulnerability assessment, and risk management responsibilities. He has spent the last few years as an IT architect and risk analyst, designing and evaluating secure, scalable, and redundant networks.

Eric has worked on several books as a contributing author or technical editor. These include; Netcat Power Tools (Syngress), How to Cheat at Configuring Open Source Security Tools (Syngress), Secure Your Network for Free (Syngress), Designing and Building Enterprise DMZ's (Syngress), Firewall Fundamentals (Cisco Press), Configuring Checkpoint NGX (Syngress), Hacking Exposed: Cisco Networks (McGraw-Hill), Hardening

Network Security (McGraw-Hill), and Hardening Network Infrastructure (McGraw-Hill). He has also received a CTM from Toastmasters of America.

Eric wrote Chapter 12, "SSH Server Advanced Use."

Brad Smith, RN, ASCIE, MCNPS, CISSP, NSA-IAM, Director and Principal Owner of Computer Institute of the Rockies, began working with computer technology in 1972. His Computer the Computer Institute of the Rockies was named the 2005 Microsoft Small Business Partner of the Year. Brad was the first Registered Nurse (RN) / Microsoft Certified Professional (MCP), and is currently the only RN / Certified Information Security Systems Professional (CISSP) in the country. Brad maintains a private practice as an informatics nurse, specializing in information security.

From years of nursing practice and with a degree in Clinical Psychology, Brad has an indelible ability to use and understand persuasion techniques and the practice of influence. Brad is a frequent presenter, trainer and lecturer on Neuro-Linguistic Programming, informatics and security topics at a variety of national conferences, including Computer Security Institute, DEFCON, HIMSS and INFOSEC.

Brad wrote Chapter 5, "SSH Shortcomings."

Christopher Stokes currently works as a network engineer with the Hewlett-Packard Corporation. As an engineer, he has been involved in building many large scale dmz's and security zones. His IT and security experience spans over 14 years with many high profile companies and engineering firms. He has extensive knowledge in the areas of OS hardening, sniffer analysis, firewall technology and vulnerability assessment. In his spare time, he performs research into Internet threats such as viruses, spyware, botnets, application exploits and attack techniques. He has presented the results of his research to many local and federal law enforcement agencies. His interest in security has been driven by the addiction to understand the latest techniques used by hackers. Chris currently holds the following certifications: CCNA, CEH, CNX, NCA, CST, NANS, A+ and Network +.

Christopher wrote Chapter 2, "OSI Model and Then Some."

Contents

Acknowledgments

I would like to dedicate this book first to the Staff, Publisher and Editors at Syngress:

- Laura Colantoni, Publisher
- Matt Cater, Developmental Editor
- Gary Byrne, Developmental Editor

And to all of the other contributing authors, editors and copy editors, without these people this project could not have succeeded!

To Tommy and the entire staff of the ***Bull and the Bear Tavern and Eatery,*** in Houston Texas! Especially Table #1 where a lot of the book was created and edited, you really have a great place to work!

And finally and most importantly to Amy Mitamura, my Muse, Inspiration, Support and in house Editor, your continued support and understanding were vital for this process to come to completion!

I thank you all!

—*Dale Liu*

## Chapter 1

Introduction

Solutions in this chapter:

- Why Is There a Need to Use SSH?

- What SSH Does and Does Not Do

- Comparison Between SSH and SSHv2

- What Are SCP and SFTP?

- SSH and the C-I-A Triad

☑ Summary

☑ Solutions Fast Track

☑ Frequently Asked Questions

Introduction

The purpose of this book is to explore the needs and functions of Secure Shell (SSH). We will endeavor to explain the history of the networks we use today and how they developed and expanded to a point where tighter security became increasingly more important.

We will look at how the OSI (Open Systems Interconnect) model and SSH relate to each other and also how to use the OSI model for troubleshooting network connectivity. Then we will look at the role of cryptography and the various methods of encryption from which we can draw. Once we understand the cryptography, we will then look at the actual SSH standards and how this protocol can aid in the secure transmission of controls and commands across the network. Then the various SSH platforms will be discussed and documented. The later chapters will round out the book with topics on port forwarding.

So let us embark on our journey with a brief history and introduction to SSH; all aboard!

Why Is There a Need To Use SSH?

In the beginning there were main frame computers. These large computers allowed programmers to input large mathematical formulas that would take hours or days to solve by hand. These computers could take the same formula and datum and solve it in seconds or minutes. As these computers became more flexible and could handle not only mathematical datum but also text and numerical information, people began to use them to manage more and more business and research data. Computers became more than just a tool for college and government organizations, as they started to be able to manage business data. As they became smaller and more powerful, tools to input and store data came into being and costs became more reasonable.

More customers were in the business world. These computers stored massive amounts of data and people could access these machines in a controlled environment. The topology of the network was called the Centralized Data Model; in this model all the data was stored on one central computer and access was through "dumb" terminals. The terminals themselves had no computer processing power or storage. This protected the data from loss, damage, theft, and spying. In this model encryption was not necessary as the data was never vulnerable to the outside world. People could see only what the administrators allowed through the "green screen," or dumb terminal.

As computers became more powerful and a need to share data across diverse and distant locations became more prevalent, wide area connections were established. At first these connections were done over analog phone lines using modem (Modulator/Demodulator) technology. There were two types of modems, synchronous and asynchronous. Synchronous modems used a special timing bit in the stream to keep the communications channel operating smoothly. In asynchronous modems, instead of a constant timing bit, the technology used a start and stop bit for each part of the transmission, ensuring each piece of data was received consistently. These analog connections were point to point and it was not easy for people to "listen in" on these connections.

As communications technology progressed and a shared, or interconnected, network of networks developed and more and more "private" data was being transmitted over these open links, the need for encrypted transmission become necessary. In addition, with the wide areas of transmission, personal computers also brought about internal or Local Area Networks (LANs). These internal networks allowed computers to transmit and receive data from other computers and servers within the building. The data traffic of these devices became subject to eavesdropping by other individuals inside the network. The eavesdropping, also known as packet capturing, allowed internal people to view data they might not otherwise had the privilege of viewing. These two scenarios increased the need for data encryption.

Are You Owned?

Data Loss, an Inside Job

Survey after survey shows that data loss and data exposure are most likely done by people inside the organization. Check out some of the statistics:

- 61% of respondents think data leakage is an insider's job. 23% believe those leaks are malicious.

  McAfee and Datamonitor's Data Loss Survey, 2007 (requires registration)

- 85% of organizations surveyed reported that they have had a data breach event.

  Scott and Scott LLP and Ponemon Institute LLC, May 15th, 2007

- One third of companies surveyed said a major security breach could put them out of business.

  McAfee and Datamonitor's Data Loss Survey, 2007 (requires registration)

- More than 90% of the breaches were in digital form.

  2006 Annual Study: The Cost of Data Breach. Ponemon Institute, LLC, 2007

  These statistics can be found at: http://www.absolute.com/resources/ computer-theft-statistics-details.asp

For each type of remote connection, there are options on how to secure it. In this book we will focus on remote login/control from a client to a server. In the early days, we had two options. The first was remote login, or RLOGIN (TCP port 513); it allowed us to open a session on a UNIX server and issue commands. The second option was telnet (TCP port 23); both of these protocols use a clear text channel to send and receive information. Any user with a packet capture program like Wireshark™ will be able to see the entire session, including usernames and passwords. As networks became more vulnerable to these types of attacks and data leakage, we needed to protect the sessions. For this connectivity issue, SSH is the answer.

SSH employs strong industry recognized encryption methods to protect your data from exposure. It makes no difference if you are using SSH across your local area network or the Internet from a remote location; your data will be secured in these encrypted channels. This software replaces telnet and rlogin as your connectivity method and offers protection to your data. Continued use of rlogin and telnet could be considered a violation of your organization's security police and in some cases a violation of law; Sarbanes Oxley, for example, mandates that all communications containing financial data must be encrypted. If you are using telnet to create a remote session to a UNIX computer that contains your financial application, you are not in compliance with Sarbanes Oxley.

What SSH Does and Does Not Do

Is SSH a complete encryption solution for all your network needs? No! SSH is a method of connecting to a remote system and creating a console session for the issuing and executing of commands in an encrypted channel. It is not a remote access method for connecting to a LAN over a wide area connection; it is not a protocol that will encrypt your e-mail over the Internet. It provides for the ability to do the functions of rlogin and telnet with the added protection of encryption.

If you were to connect to a remote network (LAN) from a remote location, you would need Virtual Private Network (VPN) technology; to protect your e-mail with encryption, you would need PKI (Public Key Infrastructure), also known as digital signatures. Each type of data and connectivity will have its own type of encryption and protection. If you do not employ some method of protection, you will increase the risk to data exposure and loss.

Notes from the Underground...

Types of Attacks

Throughout this book you will be introduced to a number of data attacks; these include man-in-the-middle, replay, packet capture, spoofing, and data manipulation. Each of these attacks can be stopped by adding encryption. This protects your data from view and manipulation, but only if the encryption is strong and implemented properly!

It is important to know the limitations of any type of security solution. SSH's major purpose is to establish encrypted shell sessions between your client machine and a server of some sort (that server could be an actual Linux, UNIX or Windows server, or it could be a router, firewall or switch).

It also gives you the ability to securely copy files from machine to machine. It does not, however, protect data sent outside the encrypted channel. You can use some aspects of SSH to create encrypted tunnels between your e-mail server and a spam filtering system. Once you get past the spam filtering system, you are back to clear text data!

Comparison Between SSH and SSHv2

The major differences between the original SSH and the second version are the added encryption and security features. According to the US Computer Emergency Response Team (US-CERT), there are, at the time of this writing, at least 50 known vulnerabilities with SSH in their database. Over time any protection standard will be weakened by attacks. It was not long ago that the 3DES block encryption standard was unbreakable; now it cannot be used on federal and military networks because it has been breached.

NOTE

The URL for the US – Computer Emergency Response Team is http://www.kb.cert.org. You can search for SSH Vulnerabilities there.

SSH Version 1 was developed by Tatu Ylönen in 1995, which was the year the Internet was first opened to the general public. It was a response to attacks that he detected to his data sessions. Ylönen was a researcher at the Helsinki University of Technology; he gathered a group of researchers to come up with a protocol that would replace the unsecure methods, such as telnet and rlogin, of connecting to shell sessions and stop the exposure of usernames and passwords in clear text. In July of 1995 he released his first version, now known as SSH-1, and by December 1995, the user base of SSH-1 had grown to over 20,000. In 1996 a revised SSH was release by Ylönen; this was called SSH-2 and had increased security by adding stronger hashing algorithms created by Whitfield Diffie and Martin Hellman. These algorithms not only strengthened the protocol, but also, by incorporating industry recognized technologies, made the protocol more compatible across divergent technologies. In 2006 the SSH-2 protocol became a proposed industry standard by having been submitted as an RFC (Request For Comment) with the Internet Engineering Task Force (IETF). See Chapter 4 for references to the RFC's documenting SSH-2 or SSHv2.

The volunteers at the OpenBSD Foundation, a Canadian not-for-profit Corporation who do not fall under US encryption laws, took the open source standards created and created OpenSSH, which was derived from code originally released as OSSH. This has become one of the most popular releases of SSH in use today due to its open source license. Figure 1.1 shows the current website of the OpenSSH foundation.

Figure 1.1 OpenSSH Homepage

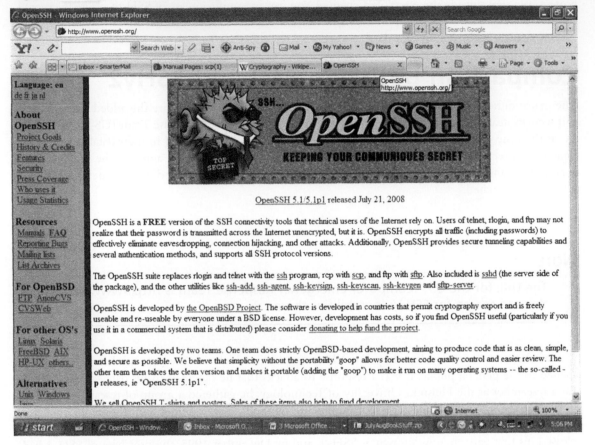

Encryption Standards

If you are talking VPN, SSH, digital signatures, and PGP (Pretty Good Privacy), you are talking about encryption and hashing algorithms. In this book we will talk primarily about the algorithms that pertain to SSH. However, most of the technologies and algorithms we discuss will be similar, if not the same as, protocols used in other secure protocols.

Some of the protocols we will discuss in future chapters are as follows:

3DES (Triple Data Encryption Standard)

ARCFOUR (Alleged RC4)

Twofish symmetric

Serpent

Blowfish

AES, the Advanced Encryption Standard

These protocols are industry standard protocols that are currently included in the SSH protocol and in other associated commands such as SCP and SFTP. As other protocols are accepted by the industry at large, they will be added to the SSH standards. See Chapter 4 for more information on these protocols.

> **NOTE**
>
> For more historical information on cryptography, check out this URL from Wikipedia:
> http://en.wikipedia.org/wiki/Cryptography

What Is SCP and SFTP?

SCP (Secure Copy) is a command defined by the IETF in cooperation with SFTP (Secure File Transport Protocol). SFTP has in the past been confused with Simple File Transport Protocol as both have been referenced by the SFTP acronym. These two utilities allow us to move files and data from one machine to another in an encrypted manner. SCP allows files from one directory on the source machine to be copied to a directory on the remote machine in a scripted, or batch file, structure. See the chapter on command line and advanced SSH for the options and functions of this command. IETF RFC (Request for Comment) describes these protocols.

Both SCP and SFTP operate on TCP Port 22, like SSH itself. However SFTP is not just FTP (File Transport Protocol) over SSH; it is a totally new program developed from the ground up.

Table 1.1 compares FTP, SCP and SFTP.

> **NOTE**
>
> The Command Line Manual Pages for SFTP and SCP (OpenSSH Standard) can be located at these locations:
> http://www.openbsd.org/cgi-bin/man.cgi?query=sftp&sektion=1 and
> http://www.openbsd.org/cgi-bin/man.cgi?query=scp&sektion=1

Table 1.1 Comparison of FTP, SCP, and SFTP

FTP (File Transport Protocol)	SCP (Secure Copy)	SFTP (Secure File Transfer Protocol)
Utilizes Ports 20 and 21 TCP	Utilizes port 22 TCP (SSH)	Utilizes port 22 TCP (SSH)
Clear text interactive file transfer	Encrypted point-to-point file transfer	Encrypted interactive file transfer
High speed/low security	Medium speed/high security	Low speed/high security
64 bit file space (large files over 4GB)	64 bit file space (large files over 4GB)	32bit file space (files less than 4GB)
Not easily used in batch files	Easily used in batch files	Not easily used in batch files
No hashing	Diffie-Hellman hashing	Diffie-Hellman hashing
No industry encryption support	DES, RC4 or AES, 3DES, ARCFOR (and other industry recommended standards)	DES, RC4 or AES, 3DES, ARCFOR (and other industry recommended standards)
Supports anonymous support	Requires Key Pair (PKI)	Requires Key Pair (PKI)
Not supported in OpenSSH	OpenSSH support	OpenSSH support

SSH and the C-I-A Triad

Figure 1.2 C-I-A (Confidentiality, Integrity and Availability)

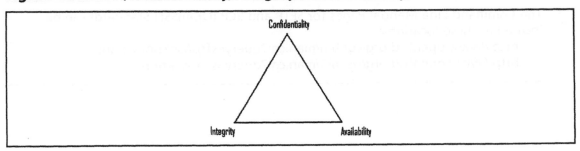

The C-I-A triad (Figure 1.2) is a balance between confidentiality, integrity, and availability. If any of these are compromised, the data we are trying to protect can be affected in a negative and costly way. Let's take a look at each of these three parts, how the effect the data, and how we protect them.

Confidentiality is keeping the data secret from people who have no "need to know." The data is the property of your company and only those people in the organization that have to use, update, modify, or analyze the data should be allowed to have access to the data. However, there are people out there both inside and outside the company that want to know your information. These people could be disgruntled internal employees, competitors, teenagers with too much time on their hands, or just people who stumble onto the information due to inadequate protection processes and controls. To protect the confidentiality of your data, you incorporate different layers of protection, and you put the people and the data behind a firewall so that only people inside the firewall can see the resource. You apply ACL's (Access Control Lists) that give only the rights needed to the individuals to see the data. Some might need read only access, some might need write only (order entry takers), and some might need read and write access. You employ complex passwords so that people who are not authorized can not easily gain access, and lastly, and most importantly, you apply encryption.

Encryption keeps people who have no other access to the network than a simple connection from eavesdropping on the line and capturing the data. This protection uses complex algorithms to mask the data on the sending side and the same algorithm on the receiving side. There are two categories of encryption. In symmetric key encryption, the key used to encrypt the data is the same one used to decrypt the data. In asymmetric key encryption, a key pair is generated; one key is public and one key is private. If the public key is used to encrypt the data, then only the private key can decrypt the data. If on the other hand the private key is used, then only the public key can decrypt the file. To ensure true protection, a sender would first encrypt the document with his or her private key and the receiver's public key; this would ensure total data protection as the two keys required to open the document would be the receiver's private key (that only he or she would have) and the sender's public key (that many may have). It is the fact that both keys (one held by many and one held by one) make this the best security option. SSH (Secure Shell) uses the dual-key PKI solution for building the encrypted tunnel. This facilitates the security of sending sensitive data of an unsecure LAN or WAN topology.

Integrity of data is another critical part of the C-I-A triad. If you cannot rely on the correctness of your data, what value can you place in the data? If you cannot ensure that the transactions between you and your system are accurate, this will lead to questions that could jeopardize the reputation of your organization. Once reputation is lost, most people will find other places to do their business. To insure the integrity of data, you have to make sure that people cannot capture and modify the data stream. The common attacks used to attack these records are called man-in-the-middle attacks. In such an attack, the hacker hijacks the data stream. Recording the data stream, the hacker will modify something in the data and then allow it to continue on the journey. This attack can work against a server (modifying data before it gets to the server) or against a client (modifying return data coming from the server before it reaches the client). Each part of this triad will utilize many layers of protection. Integrity can be protected by validating the data, checking that nothing in the stream has been compromised, and having routines that normalize the data as it is incorporated into the system. These steps will help protect the integrity; however, encryption will keep most attackers at bay. As you will see in future chapters, there are some weaknesses in SSH that can expose your data to a man-in-the-middle-attack. It is safer to have this layer of protection than not!

Availability, the ability to see the data when and as needed, rounds out this balanced triangle. If you are prevented from accessing the data, no matter how accurate and secure it is, it is useless to the organization. Protecting availability means stopping denial-of-service (DOS) attacks. Connections to the server should be used only by authenticated users to access appropriate data. If these connections are used by attackers to keep people from using them for legitimate business, then availability is compromised. By using PKI encryption methodologies and two-factor authentication, you can prevent some of these issues. Again as we discussed in each section, multiple layers of protection are needed. SSH, while a strong protocol, is not the answer to all of these issues alone. It is a viable part of your solution; however, it is only a part.

Summary

In this chapter we investigated the history of data transmissions and how we went from the centralized data topology to distributed topology. We went from private connections to sending private data over public access links via the Internet. We have seen the times change from where our data was saved internally to a point where data theft is more often than not an inside job. We now have to worry about every aspect of our internal LAN networks just as much as we had to worry about our WAN connections. SSH is an answer to this question: Why don't I use rlogin, rsh, rcp, FTP, and telnet? Because! If you use them you are exposing your sensitive data to prying eyes. Through the growth of the Internet

and the technologies that have been developed around them, data is more vulnerable today than at any point in the past. Laws and legislations have been passed, and more are proposed that require certain types of traffic (legal, financial, and health) to be securely encrypted whenever they cross unsecure networks. SSH, and its suite of utilities, will replace rlogin, rsh, rcp, and ftp and can create tunnels where unsecure data like e-mail and web traffic can be used to protect this unsecure data inside our infrastructure.

You saw the C-I-A triad – Confidentiality, Integrity, and Availability – and how SSH can protect these aspects. We have seen that SSH is not a total answer to your security solution. Layers of defense must be in place, overlapping in some areas to provide a strong security profile. In addition, SSH is not a replacement for VPN or firewalls, as these technologies have functions that apply in other areas of security.

Solutions Fast Track

Why Is There a Need To Use SSH?

☑ Data is no longer centralized in a secure environment.

☑ Communications channels are not point-to-point or private.

☑ Data travels over unsecure public communications channels.

What SSH Does and Does Not Do

☑ SSH encrypts data between a secure client and secure server, thereby replacing rlogin and telnet.

☑ SSH encrypts file transfers using SCP or SFTP in place of rcp or ftp.

☑ SSH does not replace VPN connectivity.

Comparison Between SSH and SSHv2

☑ Hackers have found vulnerabilities in the original SSH that have been addressed in SSHv2.

☑ SSHv2 added stronger encryption technologies, including 3DES and AES

☑ SSHv2, from the OpenSSH foundation, has become the industry leading version due to its open source and open license. Other versions are commercially available and expensive.

What Are SCP and SFTP?

☑ SCP: Secure Copy lets you send files from a client machine to a remote server, replacing rcp and allowing command line (or a scriptable) options for moving files without establishing a session.

☑ SFTP: Secure File Transfer Protocol lets you establish a secure session to move files and execute commands within that session that cannot be eavesdropped on by packet capture protocols.

☑ These protocols help ensure data integrity and confidentiality.

SSH and the C–I–A Triad

☑ Confidentiality: Keeping the data from people who should not see it.

☑ Integrity: Ensuring the data is correct.

☑ Availability: Ensuring that people who need to access it can when they need to.

☑ Ensuring the C-I-A triad is balanced will keep your company from losing the most important asset you have: your reputation.

Frequently Asked Questions

Q: Why shouldn't we use Telnet, Rlogin, RCP and FTP?

A: These protocols send sensitive information in clear text, which is vulnerable to packet capture.

Q: What is the best alternative to these protocols?

A: SSH replaces Telnet and Rlogin, SCP replaces RCP, and SFTP replaces FTP.

Q: Can firewalls block my traffic?

A: Yes, TCP port 22 must be open for these protocols to work.

Q: What are the major differences between SSHv1 and SSHv2?

A: SSH v1 has major vulnerabilities that have been addressed by SSHv2.

Q: Where can I find a good open source version of SSH?

A: OpenSSH is the most popular open source and is available at http://www.openssh.org.

Q: Can I run an SSH client on Windows?

A: Yes, the best GUI/Command line client for Windows is PuTTY.

Q: Can I protect other protocols using SSH?

A: Yes, with port forwarding in SSH, you can create tunnels for SMTP (email), POP3 (email), and HTTP (Web) traffic. Remember that only the traffic in the tunnel is encrypted. After it leaves the other server to the Internet, it will be clear text again.

Chapter 2

OSI Model and Then Some

Solutions in this chapter:

- **50,000 Foot View of the OSI Model**

- **Using the OSI Model to Troubleshoot**

- **Applying the OSI Model to Forensics**

☑ **Summary**

☑ **Solutions Fast Track**

☑ **Frequently Asked Questions**

Introduction

As the title states, this is the OSI model chapter. If you've been in the technical field and read any technical books, you've probably noticed this topic is in many of them. Let me stop you now before you skip over this chapter. This chapter will be different from the typical certification/technical books that are out there. I'll be honest; I personally hate reading the OSI model chapters in the books I have read. It's the first chapter that I want to skip over, so I'm designing this chapter to show you there is an interesting side to the model. I've created this chapter so that it can be applied in the real world. Keep in mind that in order to get to the troubleshooting and forensics section, you still need to understand the basic functionality of the OSI model, so bear with me and I'll show you a side of the OSI model you've never seen before. The OSI portion of this chapter is short in comparison to the other topics. The majority of the chapter is on how to apply the OSI model to real-world scenarios.

50,000 Foot View of the OSI Model

The Open System Interconnection (OSI) model was created by International Standards Organization (ISO) in the late 1970's and early 1980's. This model consists of seven layers that separate the tasks, services, and protocols into various layers of the stack. The word *stack* is used to define the layers that are set upon each other. The higher you go in the stack, the closer you are to the application. The opposite also is true; as you travel down the stack, you're getting closer to the layers that deal with specific network functionality. The layers are usually stated from top down due to how applications communicate: application, presentation, session, transport, network, data link, and physical.

OSI is nothing more than a reference model to help guide the development of new protocols and applications. You will not find it running on the network like TCP/IP or IPX/SPX. Originally it was developed as a protocol stack with the intentions that it would become widely used. It was designed to be vendor neutral and cross-compatible between operating systems. OSI never did take off as a protocol but in time became a model used to help describe what should occur at each layer. The model allows programmers to focus on how their program will talk to the network portion of the stack. This saves the programmer work, and it keeps the industry from having a whole bunch proprietary network protocols that are based strictly on a certain application. As long as vendors base their applications on the OSI model, existing protocol stacks can be used and software integration will be possible with other vendors.

The OSI model is broken down using more layers than other protocols such as TCP/IP or IPX/SPX. It has more layers, which allows for a better definition of what should happen at each level. Each of the protocol stacks has some similarities in each of the layers. Some protocol stacks have layers that are combined differently than others, but overall they can be mapped back to the OSI model. For instance, the upper three layers of the OSI model are equally comparable to the first application layer in the TCP/IP stack. (The use of the words *protocol stack* and *protocol suite* will be used interchangeably throughout the chapter. Both are referring to the alignment of protocols in a vertical manner.) There will be many references to the TCP/IP protocol stack in comparison to the OSI model so that real world examples of how it's used today can be shown. The TCP/IP protocol suite provides the purpose of allowing one networked system to talk to another. Each layer in the stack receives help from the layer below it and provides help to the layer above it. The Internet layer would receive the segment from the transport layer and then place a header onto it to include the source and destination IP address along with source and destination port numbers. Once the header is combined with the existing segment, it sends the combined information off as a packet to the Network Interface Layer, which then adds another header to create a frame. The process of encapsulation is repeated throughout most of the transition from layer 7 to layer 1, as shown in Table 2.1. When the remote side receives the frame, the reverse process is done in order to strip away the layers until only the data is left.

Table 2.1 This Example Shows the Mapping of Layers Between the OSI Model and the TCP/IP Protocol Stack

LAYER	OSI	TCP/IP	
7	Application		DATA
6	Presentation	Application	PDU
5	Session		PDU
4	Transport	Transport	SEGMENT
3	Network	Internet	PACKET
2	Data Link	Network	FRAME
1	Physical	Interface	BITS

NOTE

Each layer in the stack has many protocols that operate at each of the levels. TCP/IP would use different protocols at various levels of the stack than the IPX/SPX protocol would. Don't be confused when you see that each level has many protocols that can operate there. Not all of them operate at the same time nor do they belong to the same protocol stack. It really depends on what protocol stack is being used at the time.

Before we get too far, let's define exactly what a protocol is. A protocol is nothing more a set of rules and guidelines. The word *protocol*, as applied to networking, defines how data should be structured so that it can be sent across the network. When you add the protocols from each of the layers together, you end up with a protocol stack.

This section of the chapter will give you ideas of what processes occur at each layer of the stack. Once the foundation is covered, (Table 2.2), then there will be two scenarios on how to apply the OSI model.

Table 2.2 Flow of Data Through the Protocol Stack from Host A to Host B

LAYER	HOST A	HOST B
7	Application	Application
6	Presentation	Presentation
5	Session	Session
4	Transport	Transport
3	Network	Network
2	Data Link	Data Link
1	Physical	Physical

The word *encapsulation* is a term we need to discuss before walking through the layers of the OSI model. Encapsulation provides the ability to package extra information with the original data in order to tell the network where to send it. For instance, you cannot place data from the application layer onto the network and expect it to get to the destination. You have to tell the operating system to send the data to the computer that contains an IP address of X and a MAC address of Y. Encapsulations (Figure 2.1) allows you to add this additional information in order to guide the data. The computer sending the data will take the data and encapsulate it at each of the layers as it travels down the stack. When the destination host receives the information, it will do the reverse process by stripping away each of encapsulated layers until only the data is left. Each of the layers in the stack knows only how to strip away the encapsulated header and footer that relates to the sending host's protocol stack. An example would be that the network layer on the sending host side encapsulates the information while only the network layer on the receiving host can reverse the process of that same layer.

Figure 2.1 Encapsulation Process at Each Layer of the Protocol Stack

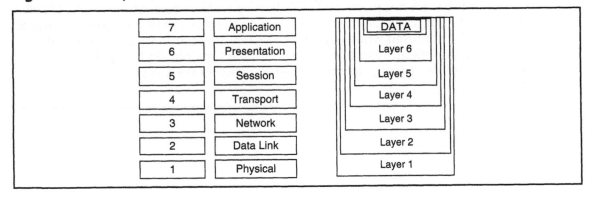

Application Layer (7)

Communication between two networked devices starts at the application layer. This layer is sometimes confused by people who think that the "application layer" refers to the applications with which the user interfaces. This is actually not true. The application layer refers to the protocols that operate at this layer. Thus, if a program needs to send data across the network to another computer, it will pass the data down to the application layer with instructions on what to do with it. A web browser for instance, does not operate at the application layer but the Hypertext Transfer Protocol (HTTP) does. The web browser uses the HTTP protocol in order to communicate. An API (application program interface) (Figure 2.2) is found between the Web browser and the HTTP protocol. The API is responsible for talking to the application layer protocols.

Figure 2.2 How the User Interfaces with the Protocol Stack

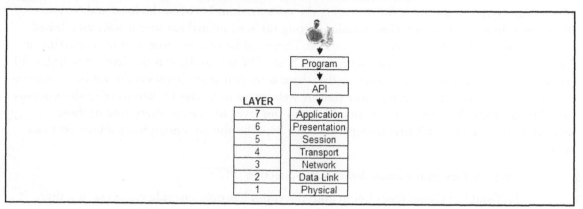

The following is a small list of protocols that operate at the application layer. The easiest way to think of this is to picture what you type into the URL string for your web browser. For instance, if you want to go to Google, you would type "http://www.google.com," which would use the HTTP protocol to access the web server at Google. Whatever URL you choose, it's going to start with HTTP, FTP, or something of that nature. These references are telling the web browser with which protocol to communicate.

- HTTP: Hypertext Transfer Protocol
- SMTP: Simple Mail Transfer Protocol
- POP3: Post Office Protocol version 3
- IMAP: Internet Message Access Protocol
- FTP: File Transfer Protocol
- TFTP: Trivial File Transfer Protocol

Presentation Layer (6)

The presentation layer receives the data from the application layer and translates it into a format and syntax that's readable by other computers. In order for the other systems to recognize this data, it's converted into a generic format that is not application specific. This layer doesn't care what the actual data is. It's merely a translation stage for data formats. Thus, as the application passes the data down the stack, it's translated from what the application understands to a generic format. The system that ends up receiving this data does the reverse process by translating the generic data format into a format understood by that computer. Various operating system and applications may expect the data to be presented a certain way. The presentation layer provides the ability to translate the data to suit the applications needs. Some of the format types found in this layer are as follows: ASCII, EBCDIC, JPEG, MPEG, TIFF, Binary, and so on. This layer is also able to provide encryption and compression if the application layer asks it to do so.

Session Layer (5)

The session layer is responsible for managing the conversations between the local and remote applications from start to end. This includes starting the session, making sure it stays established, and then closing the connection when finished. There can be one or more sessions occurring at the same time between two network-connected hosts. The session layer is the layer responsible for keeping track of each of these sessions so that there is no confusion between the various conversations that may be occurring at the same time. A web server may have thousands of sessions occurring due to people browsing its Web site. It's up to this layer to manage every one of those sessions. This layer may be better understood if we describe the communication modes that can occur here:

1. Simplex: Communications flows in one direction

2. Half-duplex: Communication in both directions but only one side can speak at a time

3. Full-duplex: Communication in both directions and both sides can speak at the same time

Transport Layer (4)

The transport layer takes the data from the session layer and splits it up into smaller pieces of information that are the right size for network transmission. Before sending the data out, this layer makes a checklist of how to ensure that the other side has received all the data and that it is not damaged in any way. It does this by doing a handshaking process prior to sending the data. That handshaking process determines the amount of data to be sent, how to judge if some of the data was lost in the transmission, and how to verify the data was not corrupted. The process that's performed in this layer is often confused with the session layer. The difference between them is that the transport layer is building sessions between the end devices whereas the session layer is building sessions between the applications. There are three protocols that work at this layer: TCP (Transmission Control Protocol), UDP (User Datagram Protocol), and SPX (Sequenced Packet Exchange).

TCP is a connection-oriented protocol, which means it will set up a reliable connection between hosts before sending any data. There are actually three phases used by TCP: connection setup, data transfer, and connection tear-down. In the connection setup phase, transmission parameters are negotiated between the end points. TCP uses the SYN, SYN/ACK, and ACK flags to let both sides participate in the negotiation of how much data should be sent at a time, along with flow control and how to detecting errors while recovering from them. Once the agreement is made between the hosts, the data can be sent. If one of the hosts detects a problem with the received traffic, it will request the segment to be retransmitted. This ensures that the data is error free and completely received by the destination. TCP uses acknowledgements (ACK) in order to tell the sending computer that it has received the expected amount of data and that the integrity of it is good. Any data not acknowledged is re-sent to the destination as it is assumed lost. Finally when the conversation is done, the transport layer closes the conversation between hosts by sending an ACK/FIN (acknowledged finish) packet. The opposite end responds back with an ACK (acknowledgement) that it received the ACK/FIN. Once both sides agree to end the session through the use of acknowledgements, the conversation can close.

A connectionless protocol such as UDP doesn't have the three-phase approach like TCP. It just sends the data as soon as it's ready and assumes the end point receives it all. UDP expects the application to put the data back together instead of the protocol used in this layer.

Network Layer (3)

It is the network layer's responsibility to discover the layout of the network. This layer determines if communication will stay on the same network or will be routed. The network layer does not guarantee that data will get to the destination. It relies on the transport layer for that functionality. The network layer is able to determine if the source and destination hosts are on the same network by inspecting the IP address and subnet mask set to each. If the hosts happen to be on different network, then routing is needed for them to communicate, and this layer can perform that function. Thus, to generalize this statement, the network layer allows one logical address to communicate with another logical address, whether they are on the same or different networks. The term *logical address* is referring to an IP address that you would assign to a computer or network connection device. Each host on the network must have a unique IP address. A few of the more commonly known protocols that operate at this layer are IP (Internet Protocol), ICMP (Internet Control Message Protocol), and IPX (Internetwork Packet Exchange). Protocols in this layer work in conjunction with protocols in the transport layer. For instance, TCP at the transport layer works with IP at the network layer, thereby creating TCP/IP.

Figure 2.3 is an example of communication between two network hosts on different networks. The point of this diagram is to show how the data will travel in order to get from one host to another. On HOST A, the data is encapsulated as it's passed down the protocol stack. At the physical layer, it's converted into voltage, frequency, or light so that it can be sent across the network. It may need to pass through several networks before arriving at a router that contains an interface in the same network as the destination host. Notice that not all network devices will use the entire protocol stack to communicate. A router operates at the network layer and is able to guide the traffic to the correct location based on the IP addresses. It doesn't care about the application itself; it cares only to get the packet to the end host. Once the data gets to the router that has an interface located in the same network as the destination host, it then will cross the IP address to the MAC address and forward it to the switch. From there the switch directs the traffic based on MAC address to the correct network port where the device is connected. HOST B receives the information and performs the opposite procedure of HOST A. It strips each of the encapsulated layers off as it goes up the stack until it has only the data left.

Figure 2.3 Routers Are Network Devices
that Do Not Use the Entire Protocol Stack

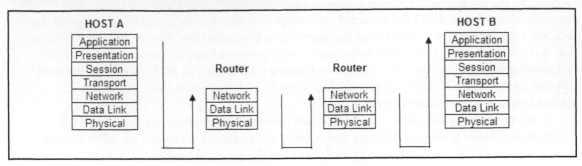

Data Link Layer (2)

The data link layer takes the packet from the network layer and breaks it into frames. The header in this layer provides the source and destination MAC addresses. It is the data link layer that will convert the data into binary digits such as 1 and 0 and then prepare them for the physical layer. This layer has to be aware of what type of network interface card (NIC) is being used in order to prepare the packet in a certain way. A frame prepared for Ethernet format would not be understood by a network set up with Token Ring. Thus, this layer takes the network interface into consideration before converting the packet. Cyclic redundancy Checking (CRC) is another feature found in the data link layer that provides the ability to detect if a received frame was damaged. This checking feature is normally done by the LAN switch or WAN frame relay switch.

Layer 2 devices that operate at this level are switches and bridges. They work by guiding the traffic to a destination based on the MAC address. The MAC address is a unique series of numbers and letter used to identify a certain network card. They are sometimes referred to as the physical address because this address is hard coded into the network card. A switch can direct traffic to the correct computer only if it's aware of what port the computer's network card is attached. This is done by the computer presenting the MAC address from its network card to the switch when it first comes online.

There are a variety of protocols that work at this layer. Some are used by hosts and others by network devices such as switches. STP (Spanning tree protocol) and RSTP (Rapid spanning tree protocol) are examples of protocols used by switches in this layer. They provide the ability to make sure there is only one layer 2 path to get to a destination. PPP (Point-to-point protocol) and L2TP (Layer 2 Tunneling protocol) are used by hosts. PPP provides the ability for a host to make a connection with a remote side using a modem. L2TP allows a host to connect to a remote side using a secure connection.

Physical Layer (1)

The last layer in the protocol stack is the physical layer, which converts the binary information presented from the data link into electrical signaling. This layer also takes into consideration the network interface card for the reason that it needs to know what kind of signaling to send through the media. An example would be the difference between a network card using a fiber interface and one using an unshielded twisted pair (UTP) interface. Each presents the information differently to the media. Network cards with fiber interfaces require the binary information to be converted to light patterns, whereas UTP cabling uses voltage and frequency variations to communicate. The physical layer also provides physical layer features to determine the speed (i.e., 10, 100, or 1000 MBs at which to transmit the data, along with what to do in case line noise or cross-talk occurs.

Using the OSI Model to Troubleshoot

For the purpose of this section, the TCP/IP protocol stack will be the primary focus as it is what the Internet is based off of. It then will be compared to the OSI model to give you an idea of where sections of this chapter fit. The following few paragraphs are based on an actual problem, but applied to a fake company. The method used to troubleshoot this scenario can be used to fix many connectivity problems. They are based off of testing devices and services that operate at each layer of the TCP/IP Stack.

Scenario: E-tronix Inc., is a company that uses its Web site to sell electronics over the Internet. Recently the internal Web site that is used to fulfill the orders is not accessible by the company's staff. The goal of this section will be to troubleshoot why the Web site cannot be accessed. A chart will follow at the end of the story that shows the troubleshooting steps and how they relate to the various levels of the OSI model versus the TCP/IP protocol stack.

Your name is John Smith, and you work as an IT professional for E-tronix. Your responsibility is to provide technical support and troubleshooting whenever the business needs it. The date is currently June 17, 2008, and it's the early morning. You've just fallen asleep when your cell phone rings. The phone has caught you off guard and startled you. The first thing that that goes through your mind is to make the phone pay for disturbing your rest, but instead you decide to look at the phone number that's on the display. You're quite familiar with the number displayed as it's the E-tronix support desk.

The following conversation occurs on the phone call:

Ring...

John: Hello this is John.

Helpdesk: Hi John, this is Brian from the help desk. We currently are not able to access the internal Web site in order to satisfy the orders placed from the Internet. Please look into the situation right away.

John: Alright Brian, I'll look into it.

Helpdesk: Thanks John, bye.

You yank the covers off in the bed and hobble down the hallway to the home office where your laptop is located. For times like these, you've purposely left the laptop running and remotely connected into the company's network. The first step you perform is testing access to the Web site by opening the web browsers and typing the URL into the address bar. As expected, nothing occurs. The browser indicates that the page cannot be displayed. Just to cover all areas, you decide to start from square one and walk through everything that needs to occur in order for you to access the Web site. The following is a walkthrough of the commands you performed in order to review the problem.

Step 1. Make sure DNS resolves the Web site name properly. You're looking for the name orders. etronixinc.com to resolve to an IP address. Figure 2.4 is the output of the nslookup command that you ran from the command prompt on your laptop.

Figure 2.4 Nslookup Is Used as a DNS Verification Test

```
C:\Documents and Settings\jsmith>nslookup orders.etronixinc.com
Server:  ns1.etronicinc.com
Address:  192.168.1.200

Name:   Orders.etronixinc.com
Address:  192.168.1.10
```

DNS seems to be working properly as it responded with the IP-address related orders. You decide to move on to checking the network connectivity.

Step 2. Check to see if the HTTP service is running on the server by telneting to the server on port 80, as shown in Figure 2.5. This test allows you to verify if the problem is related to the service or the actual web content.

Figure 2.5 Telnet Can Be Used to Test TCP-Based Ports for Connectivity

```
C:\Documents and Settings\jsmith>telnet 192.168.1.10 80
Connecting To 192.168.1.10...
Could not open connection to the host, on port 80: Connect failed
```

The connection to the HTTP service on TCP port 80 failed. This tells us two things: either the web service is down or the server has a network connectivity problem.

NOTE

In testing scenarios like these, you need to be aware if there is a firewall that may be blocking traffic. The firewall has configurations that either allow or deny traffic based on source address, destination address, and port. Pay attention to the response messages from the telnet command. They give you hints to whether the problem is firewall or service-related. Messages will vary between Linux and Windows Operating systems. A couple of examples are shown below:

telnet: Unable to connect to remote host: Connection timed out
telnet: Unable to connect to remote host: Connection refused

Next we need to test if the server will respond to pings, which will prove if there is network connectivity.

Step 3. Make sure that the server responds to basic network-testing commands like ping. The ping command is able to test connectivity by sending a series of ICMP echo packets to the destination host. If the destination host receives them, it will respond back with an ICMP echo-reply. The results of the ping test will tell you if packets were received or lost, as shown in Figure 2.6.

Figure 2.6 Ping Will Respond Even if the Application is Down

```
C:\Documents and Settings\jsmith>ping 192.168.1.10

Pinging 192.168.1.10 with 32 bytes of data:

Request timed out.
Request timed out.
Request timed out.
Request timed out.

Ping statistics for 192.168.1.10:
    Packets: Sent = 4, Received = 0, Lost = 4 (100% loss),
```

This test proved that the IP communication found in layer 3 of the TCP/IP stack is not working because our pings failed. In order for layer 3 to work, layers 2 and 1 need to be working also. Thus, the next test will be on layer 2.

Step 4. Prove that the switch can see the MAC address of the server. This will tell us that layer 2 is functioning. Traffic cannot make it to the server if the switch cannot find the server's MAC address. E-tronix happens to use managed Cisco switches that give the support technicians the ability to log in to them and do troubleshooting. We start by locating the port to which the server is connected. It shows us that that the server is connected on Fast Ethernet Port 0/9 using a speed of 100 and a duplex setting of full. That doesn't fully tell us that the connection is working, so we need to go one step further by seeing if the switch has seen a MAC from the server on Fast Ethernet port 0/9. In this case, it has not, as there was no response to the second command. See Figure 2.7 for to see what a non working MAC reply would be and Figure 2.8 for a working MAC on the port.

Figure 2.7 Data Cannot Get to Its Destination if the Mac Is Not Visible on the Network

```
Switch#Sho int status | include orders
Fa0/9 orders webserver connected    7    A-Full    A-100 100BaseTX/FX

Switch#Sho mac-address-table int fa0/9
<no mac displayed>
```

No MAC address was seen by the switch on the port, so layer 2 connectivity is not working correctly.

Figure 2.8 Sample of How a Working Connection Would Show Up on a Switch

```
Switch#Sho mac-address-table int fa0/2
Non-static Address Table:
Destination Address   Address type   VLAN   Destination Port
------------------    ------------   ----   -------------------
00e0.8105.2682        Dynamic           7   FastEthernet0/2
```

In Step 4, we proved that layer 2 is not working because the switch is not able to see the MAC address of the server. We have only layer 1 left to check, and that deals with the physical connectivity. This leaves only a few possibilities: the server's network card, the patch panels, the cable or switch port. Unfortunately, to check each of these, this will take time.

Step 5. We arrive at work and walk into the server room where the web server is located. While looking at the network card in the server, we see that it does not have a link, which is odd because the switch showed a link. We remember seeing an issue just like this. The problem was due to a cable issue where the receive (rx) strand was damaged. Because it's now 2 a.m., the last thing we feel like doing is changing out the cable. It occurs to you that the physical layer problem may be as simple as a loose cable. You go to the server, patch panel and switch and reseat the cable ends. You find that at the patch panel there was a loose Ethernet connection and that reseating it solved the problem.

Validation and summary: Two steps are needed to validate that the server is online and functioning. We need to prove that the server has network connectivity and that the web service is running. False indications might occur if you test the web service only at the application level. You might think that the server is down if you cannot connect to the service, but in reality, it might only be the web service that's not started. Thus, by using ping, you test the lower and mid layers of the stack; while using telnet to test the service, you check the mid and upper layers. The following tests were performed to validate that the server was back online. The second line of each command was added to include DNS in the test.

Ping 192.168.1.10

Ping orders.etronixinc.com

telnet 192.168.1.10 80

telnet orders.etronixinc.com 80

The ping showed us replies back from the destination, and the telnet showed HTTP information. Thus, the test of the web server passed. Let's review what steps occurred and where they fall in the protocol stack. Table 2.3 shows the mapping of steps to the TCP/IP stack and the OSI model.

Table 2.3 Troubleshooting Steps and How They Map Back to the OSI Model

Layer #	OSI Model Description	TCP/IP Stack	Troubleshooting Steps
7	Application	Application	Test connectivity using telnet to the TCP service.
6	Presentation	Application	Is the data being presented correctly to the server?
5	Session	Application	Use sniffer to see if sessions start, stay connected and end properly.
4	Transport	Transport	Use a sniffer to inspect the TCP 3 way handshake?
3	Network	Internet	Is the IP address of the network device pingable by the router, firewall or others? Use traceroute to see if you can reach the destination device?
2	Data Link	Network Interface	Does the switch see the MAC address of the connected device? Use "**arp –a**" to see if the computer sees any other MAC addresses?
1	Physical	Network Interface	Check cables, network cards and lights.

There's one last test worth mentioning, and it works well in situations where there is a host firewall that's blocking ICMP packets. This particular test works only with hosts found in the same network. The test will tell you if a device is online even if host firewall is blocking ICMP. This test uses a combination of ping and checking the arp table on the tester's computer. For the purpose of this test, we have two IP addresses: the IP (192.168.1.10) is on a server with a local firewall turned on and the other IP (192.168.1.9) is not associated to any connected device. Essentially 192.168.1.9 is used to simulate a device that has a network connectivity problem. Open three DOS windows by clicking START | RUN | type cmd. In one window, ping 192.168.1.9; in the second window, ping 192.168.1.10; and in the third window, type "arp –a". Let the ping attempts fail twice before running arp –a in the last window. You'll need to perform the arp –a before the pings end. Output for the pings are shown in Figures 2.9 and 2.10 respectively.

Figure 2.9 Sample Ping to a Non-Existent Device

```
C:\Documents and Settings\jsmith>ping 192.168.1.9

Pinging 192.168.1.9 with 32 bytes of data:

Request timed out.
Request timed out.
Request timed out.
Request timed out.

Ping statistics for 192.168.1.9:
    Packets: Sent = 4, Received = 0, Lost = 4 (100% loss),
```

Figure 2.10 Ping Command Run Against the Server with the Firewall Activated

```
C:\Documents and Settings\jsmith>ping 192.168.1.10

Pinging 192.168.1.10 with 32 bytes of data:

Request timed out.
Request timed out.
Request timed out.
Request timed out.

Ping statistics for 192.168.1.10:
    Packets: Sent = 4, Received = 0, Lost = 4 (100% loss),
```

Notice in the output that there is a valid entry for the server and an invalid entry for the non-existent device. These commands were run from John's laptop within the same network. As I mentioned, this test works only with hosts in the same network. If you had a scenario where the hosts were on different networks, you could do a similar test but you would need to do the ping and arp test from the router or firewall that had an interface in the same zone as the end devices, as shown in Figure 2.11.

Figure 2.11 arp Command Used to Show the Difference Between an Invalid and Valid arp Response

```
C:\Documents and Settings\jsmith>arp -a

Interface: 192.168.1.200 --- 0x3
  Internet Address      Physical Address      Type
  192.168.1.1           00-02-b3-9d-d9=1a     dynamic
  192.168.1.9           00-00-00-00-00-00     invalid
  192.168.1.10          00-0c-29-00-6a-fc     dynamic
```

Q: So why does this work if ping is failing?

A: The reason this is working is because John's laptop does an arp broadcast asking who has the IP prior to pinging it. The server is able to respond back but the non-existent device cannot. Therefore, John's laptop fills in the non-existent entry with all 0's. The firewall on the server is filtering layer 3 but not layer 2.

Applying the OSI Model to Forensics

The following pages contain a real scenario captured from an infected Windows XP computer that was running IIS with web services enabled. The scenario has been slightly changed to fit into story form. I will run through the scenario and then tell you how it applies to TCP/IP stack, which will be mapped back to the OSI model.

> Ring, Ring.....
>
> Bill: Hello, this is Bill from Security.
>
> Helpdesk: Hi Bill. This is Nancy from the Helpdesk. I need your assistance in figuring out a problem that many users are having. Just shortly after 9 a.m., the helpdesk started receiving calls from several users, which were complaining of slow responses back from the web server. Along the same time, we started receiving alert notices from the intrusion detection system of possible virus activity from the same server. Prior to calling you, we worked with an administrator from the server team to confirm that the server's antivirus and Microsoft patches were up to date. Can you go check out the web server and see what's going on? If you find a virus, please gather a sample of the executable so that we can send it off to the antivirus vendor. This will allow them to create a new definition to detect and correct this strain of virus.
>
> Bill: No problem Nancy, I'll gather my tool kit and go over there right now.

Bill walks over to the server room and heads back to where the server is located. He starts to log in and notices that even the login process is really slow. He has two suspicions: the first is that there is a connectivity problem with the domain controller that provides the authentication and the second is that some process is using up all the process power on the server. The server eventually logs him in, so he disregards his first thought. He starts by opening a command prompt window on the web server and types "netstat –ano". The results he sees are kind of disturbing. The output of netstat normally is contained within a few screens, but now it is showing 20+ screens worth of information. The screen shot on the next page is what he saw. Based on this output he was able to make the following determinations, as shown in Figure 2.12:

- TCP 6667 is used for IRC
- The web server was scanning for other web servers on TCP 80. This is typical behavior of a virus trying to spread.
- There was an unknown process connecting to another server on TCP 65520.
- Each of the sessions using tcp ports 80, 6667, and 65520 had an associated PID (Process ID). This allowed him to relate the network traffic with a service running on the web server.

NOTE

The following Web sites can be used to find out the uses of different TCP and UDP ports. The first Web site shows ports for normal services; the second shows ports for malicious services.

- http://www.iana.org/assignments/port-numbers
- http://www.neohapsis.com/neolabs/neo-ports/

Figure 2.12 Output of the netstat –ano Command Done on the Web Server

```
Active Connections

  Proto   Local Address          Foreign Address          State          PID
  TCP     0.0.0.0:7              0.0.0.0:0                LISTENING      1648
  TCP     0.0.0.0:9              0.0.0.0:0                LISTENING      1648
  TCP     0.0.0.0:13             0.0.0.0:0                LISTENING      1648
  TCP     0.0.0.0:17             0.0.0.0:0                LISTENING      1648
  TCP     0.0.0.0:19             0.0.0.0:0                LISTENING      1648
  TCP     0.0.0.0:80             0.0.0.0:0                LISTENING      1572
  TCP     0.0.0.0:135            0.0.0.0:0                LISTENING      784
  TCP     0.0.0.0:443            0.0.0.0:0                LISTENING      1572
  TCP     0.0.0.0:1027           0.0.0.0:0                LISTENING      832
  TCP     0.0.0.0:1028           0.0.0.0:0                LISTENING      1400
  TCP     0.0.0.0:1029           0.0.0.0:0                LISTENING      1572
  TCP     0.0.0.0:1033           0.0.0.0:0                LISTENING      1764
  TCP     0.0.0.0:1043           0.0.0.0:0                LISTENING      4
  TCP     0.0.0.0:1129           0.0.0.0:0                LISTENING      552
  TCP     0.0.0.0:1130           0.0.0.0:0                LISTENING      2120
  TCP     0.0.0.0:1131           0.0.0.0:0                LISTENING      1196
  TCP     0.0.0.0:1801           0.0.0.0:0                LISTENING      1764
  TCP     0.0.0.0:2103           0.0.0.0:0                LISTENING      1764
  TCP     0.0.0.0:2105           0.0.0.0:0                LISTENING      1764
  TCP     0.0.0.0:2107           0.0.0.0:0                LISTENING      1764
  TCP     0.0.0.0:5000           0.0.0.0:0                LISTENING      1048
  TCP     68.60.175.83:1129      63.138.101.136.6667      ESTABLISHED    552
  TCP     68.60.175.83:1130      210.202.247.102:65520    ESTABLISHED    1148
  TCP     68.60.175.83:2201      68.60.3.150:80           SYN_SENT       2120
  TCP     68.60.175.83:2202      68.60.179.215:80         SYN_SENT       2120
  TCP     68.60.175.83:2203      68.60.197.53:80          SYN_SENT       2120
  TCP     68.60.175.83:2204      68.60.235.215:80         SYN_SENT       2120
  TCP     68.60.175.83:2205      68.60.110.73:80          SYN_SENT       2120
  TCP     68.60.175.83:2206      68.60.254.143:80         SYN_SENT       2120

  <edited... the above syn scan for tcp 80 occurs for many pages>

  UDP     0.0.0.0:7              *:*                                     1648
  UDP     0.0.0.0:9              *:*                                     1648
  UDP     0.0.0.0:13             *:*                                     1648
  UDP     0.0.0.0:17             *:*                                     1648
  UDP     0.0.0.0:19             *:*                                     1648
  UDP     0.0.0.0:500            *:*                                     616
  UDP     0.0.0.0:1030           *:*                                     1016
  UDP     0.0.0.0:1032           *:*                                     1764
  UDP     0.0.0.0:1034           *:*                                     1016
  UDP     0.0.0.0:3456           *:*                                     1572
  UDP     0.0.0.0:3527           *:*                                     1764
  UDP     68.60.175.83:123       *:*                                     832
  UDP     68.60.175.83:1900      *:*                                     1048
  UDP     127.0.0.1:123          *:*                                     832
  UDP     127.0.0.1:1900         *:*                                     1048
```

Bill is running through the situation in his head and determines that he needs to relate network traffic back to files and services running on the web server. He decides on the following tools and procedure to observe network traffic, memory, and hard drive content:

1. Wireshark™ Sniffer to capture the network traffic.

2. Netstat for relating network traffic to Process ID's (PID).

3. Process Explorer to relate PID to service names and executables. This also shows if there are any sub-processes being spawned under a root service.

4. Windows search tool with advanced options set to search system folders, hidden files and folders, and to search subfolders.

5. Winhex to inspect what's running in memory.

Figure 2.13 shows a sample sniffer capture that was taken on the web server. This capture allows us to verify that the traffic we saw occurring within the output of the netstat command is really occurring on the network. We need to run the sniffer because netstat takes only one-second snapshots of network traffic. That will not provide you with enough data to determine all the connections that may have occurred. The sniffer allows us to continue capturing all traffic until we decide to stop it. We want to know we've captured enough information to tell us what were dealing with. So far, we're able to determine that the IRC session on TCP 6667 is not an encrypted session because the contents shown on line 141 are readable in the hex decode window. The content in this case happens to be the nickname used on the IRC channel. We also see that the web server that contains 68.60.175.83 is looking for other web servers running on port 80 to exploit. The [SYN] packet is the first packet used in a TCP three-way handshake. If we saw a [SYN, ACK] response back, we would know that the remote IP had the web service running on it. If it was not running a web service, we would most likely see a reset [RST] back. Once the infected server has identified another destination IP running a web service, it would then do a banner check to identify the version of the web service. If it matched the vulnerable version for which this virus was looking, it would then be exploited and then the process would be repeated from the newly infected computer. The last suspicious packet we see on this screen is evidence that another computer is trying to see if TCP 3389 is open on the web server. This port is used for the remote desktop service, which allows someone to log in to the server and take control. This is bad news because from the appearance of this capture, it doesn't look like we have an Internet firewall that's blocking any traffic.

Figure 2.13 Sample Sniffer Capture Using
Wireshark™ to Show Evidence of Network Traffic

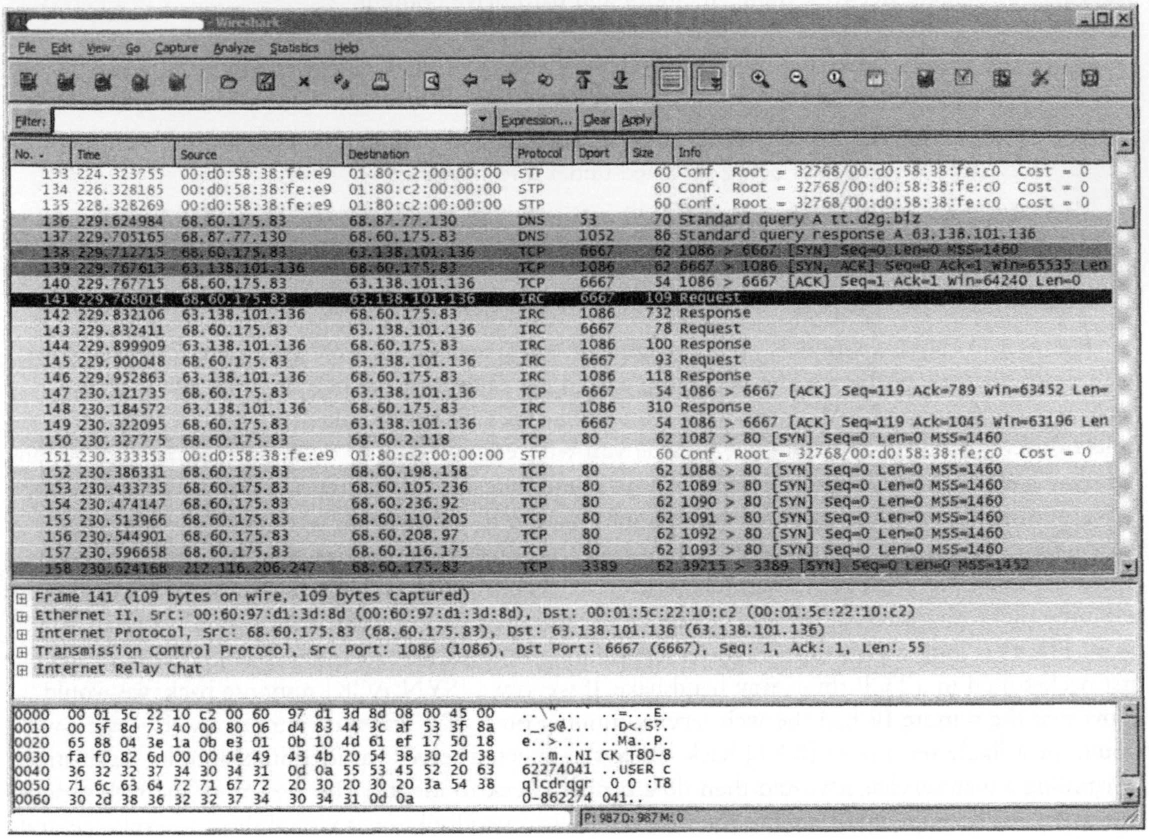

We can move on to analyzing processes with Process Explorer (Figure 2.14) because we have a sample of netstat taken already. We're going to use the PID columns in the Netstat capture to relate to the PID column in Process Explorer. We will be able to identify the process using that PID. There were three suspicious PIDs with values of 552, 1148, and 2120; shown in Figure 2.12 in the netstat capture that we want to look at. By analyzing the screen shot in Figure 2.14 we're able to cross PID 552 to process winlogin.exe, 1148 to maxd641.exe, and 2120 to qwlgkyd.exe. Any root process or sub-process to a suspicious PID should be considered not trustable and be investigated. It's obvious that the last few lines in this screen shot have something going on, but what about 552? Winlogon. exe is a valid Microsoft service and should not be trying to use IRC as shown in the netstat capture. This service must have been replaced with a trojaned process. In a normal investigation, you would look into each of the suspicious processes, but for the purpose of this demonstration, we are going to follow only a portion of it.

Figure 2.14 Process Explorer Gives You the Ability to See a Malicious Sub-Process Running Under a Parent Process

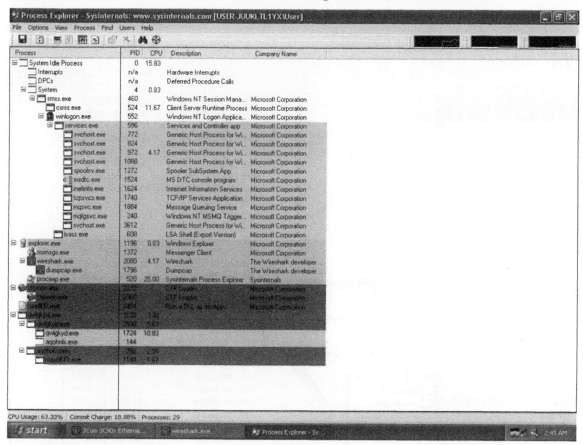

At this point, we have a pretty good idea of the files we need to look for based on the processes we saw in Process Explorer. The Windows search tool works decently if you have it set to search in system folders and also look for hidden files. If for some reason your search does not find the files your looking for, try using a tool that finds alternate data streams. We configured the search tool and let it loose looking for maxd641.exe. It found the file in c:\windows\system32 with a modified date of 1/24/2007 11:03 PM. Oddly enough, there are several other files with the same exact time and date that also showed up in the Process Explorer window. Based on seeing the similar times between the files, we decide also to search for other files that were modified around the same time. This turns up another handful of files. One of those files was explorer.exe, which was not identified as being an issue, as shown in Figure 2.15. Now it's a suspect that needs to be checked.

Figure 2.15 Visual Observation of Files Should
Not Be Overlooked as It Might Uncover More Evidence

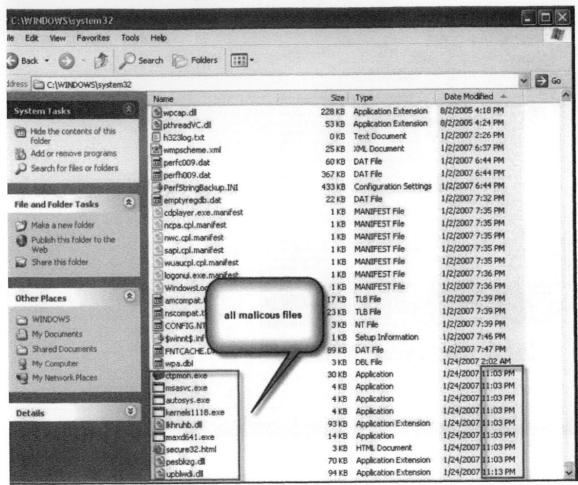

The system32 folder was sorted by date and time in order to see all the files modified around 11:03 p.m. All the files with the common date and timestamps, along with the ones identified in Processes Explorer, are zipped to be shipped to the antivirus vendor. For curiosity's sake, we'll look in memory for Explorer to see if anything odd is happening, as shown in Figure 2.16. Sometimes it's helpful to dump the contents of memory to gain further insight on the problem. As suspected, Explorer has been tampered with. Based on what is seen in Figure 2.16, Explorer was probably injected with a keylogger to watch for people logging into any of the banks listed. The keylogger would record any information typed while on the bank's Web site.

Figure 2.16 Winhex Is Showing the Section
of Memory Utilized by the Explorer Process

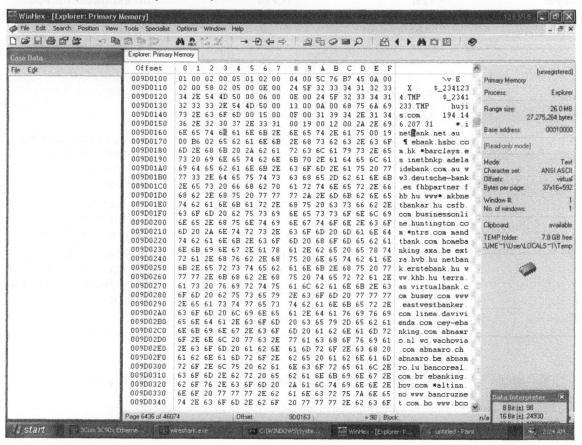

There's much more we could look into, but we're going to stop here and review how this
applies to the OSI model and TCP/IP stack, as shown in Table 2.4. There were some steps performed
that don't fit into the comparison chart. They were shown only to demonstrate the full process. Keep
in mind that the TCP/IP stack and OSI model deal only with how to get the data to the application.
Once we get past the protocol stack, were dealing with the actual applications, memory, and disk
space.

Table 2.4 Investigation Steps Mapped Back to OSI Model

Layer	OSI	TCP/IP	Investigation Steps
7	Application	Application	Identify what protocols are being used for communication
6	Presentation		
5	Session		
4	Transport	Transport	3-way handshake for connection to TCP services on remote devices
3	Network	Internet	Look at netstat and sniffer output for virus propagation
2	Data Link	Network	Look at arp table on infected server for large list of contacted devices
1	Physical	Interface	

You might be wondering how this story can relate to you. Ask yourself these questions:

1. Has your computer ever run slowly, and you couldn't figure out why?
2. Do I trust that my antivirus checker will catch all viruses?
3. Am I sure there is nothing malicious on my computer right now?
4. Do you know who your computer is talking to and what it is sharing with others?

If any of these questions make you feel uneasy; use the steps in this story to find what is occurring on your computer. Antivirus checkers will not find everything out there. Be proactive and check for yourself what is occurring. A good practice I tell my friends is to take a couple of baseline screen shots of how their computers are running from a clean build when they are not exposed to the Internet. Those screen shots should consist of Task Manager (Application, Processes, and Performance tabs), netstat –ano, and Process Explorer. Also the baseline should include a sniffer capture of the network traffic to see what normal traffic from that computer looks like. Then when a situation arises, compare the current status with baselines results to see what is different.

Summary

If you're in the IT field it is essential to know the OSI model. It provides you with the guidelines about what to look for at each layer. Many people consider the model as information that was only intended for a test, but fail to realize that it can be applied to real-world scenarios. It's impossible for an administrator to troubleshoot if he or she does not understand the fundamentals of the network stack. The data doesn't just magically get from one computer to another. There is a process that occurs between both sides that allows them to talk. That process is determined by the protocol stack. Understand the protocol stack and you'll be able to grasp concept of network connectivity.

Solutions Fast Track

50,000 Foot View of the OSI Model

☑ The OSI model is not a protocol. It is only a reference model.

☑ The higher you go in the stack, the closer you are to the application. Conversely, as you travel down the stack, you're getting closer to the layers that deal with specific network functionality.

☑ The application layer is handed the data with instructions of what to do with it.

☑ The presentation layer converts the format and syntax of the data. It also encrypts and compresses it.

☑ The session layer manages conversations between applications.

☑ The transport layer builds session between end devices and ensures that data is received.

☑ The network layer provides a path between end devices.

☑ The data link layer converts packets from the network layer into frames.

☑ The physical layer converts bits to voltage, frequency, or light before sending these bits across the media.

Using the OSI Model to Troubleshoot

☑ Understand what hardware and protocols work at each layer of the model. This will help you determine if you have a network issue or application issue.

☑ Have a set of tools that make it possible for you to test each of the layers.

☑ When troubleshooting, start at the top of the stack and work down until you come across the problem. Sometimes you can cheat and start in the middle if you have an idea of what might be occurring.

☑ Verify that the information being supplied to you is accurate. Test the scenario yourself and see if you get the same results as listed in the problem call.

Applying the OSI Model to Forensics

☑ In order to investigate a security issue such as a virus, you'll need to use tools that can inspect the network traffic, hard drive contents, and memory.

☑ Train the IT staff on how to use the chosen security tools prior to day of incident.

☑ It's likely that someone else has seen the same problem before you. Use search engines to look for information related to the problem. You'll need to have a starting point such as a service or file name before being able to search.

☑ Be aware of how your network is set up. Don't assume your firewall rules are perfect.

☑ Know the difference between malicious and safe TCP/UDP ports. These ports reference services running on the computer. If you see extra ports that you don't recognize, consult the IANA or neohapsis Web sites to find out what might be using them.

Frequently Asked Questions

Q: Telnet operates at the Application layer, so why doesn't SSH?

A: SSH operates at the top three levels of the OSI model due to the extra features it has.
Application layer: Terminal access and file transfer abilities
Presentation layer: Encryption
Session layer: Connection and synchronization

Q: Why would someone choose to use UDP over TCP if it doesn't check to make sure the packet made it to the destination?

A: The need to use UDP is based on the application requirements and speed. UDP is a faster protocol than TCP. It relies on the application to make sure that the data is received.

Q: What is the difference between the session layer and the transport layer?

A: The difference between them is that the transport layer is building a session between the end devices, whereas the session layer is building sessions between the applications.

Q: Into what layer in the OSI model does a network card from a computer fall?

A: The network card actually falls into the data link and physical layers.

Q: What happens if the MAC address of the computer's network card is not seen by the switch?

A: The switch will not know to where to direct the data.

Q: A network switch operates at layer 2. At what layer does a hub operate?

A: A hub is considered a repeater and operates at layer one.

Q: What kind of information can you determine by looking at a MAC address?

A: The first six characters of the MAC address represent the manufacturer of the network card. The last six characters represent a unique number/letter combination specific to that network card. This site will tell you the manufacturer that the first six characters represent: http://standards. ieee.org/regauth/oui/index.shtml.

Q: What does a MAC address of FF-FF-FF-FF-FF-FF mean?

A: This represents a broadcast address. This is used when all hosts on a network should process the frame.

Q: If you cannot ping a host's IP address, does it mean it's offline?

A: Generally the answer is yes, but you need to be aware if there is a firewall that may be filtering the ping.

Q: How would you verify if a service like SMTP is running on a host without using an email client?

A: You can use a command like the following: telnet *<host>* 25. Just replace *<host>* with the DNS name or IP address. If you make a successful connection, it will show a banner with information related to the mail service and version.

## Chapter 3

An Introduction To Cryptography

Solutions in this chapter:

- Cryptography and Information Security
- Cryptographic Protocols and Applications
- Cryptographic Systems
- Introducing Cryptographic Algorithms and Ciphers
- Cryptographic Key Management
- Cryptographic Functions
- Digital Signatures
- Attacks on Cryptosystems
- Cryptography and SSH

☑ Summary

☑ Solutions Fast Track

☑ Frequently Asked Questions

What is Cryptography?

Cryptography is a sub-discipline of cryptology, whose meaning is derived from the Greek words "kryptos" and "logos," meaning "hidden word." Cryptography is the science of securing the content of messages and communications. Cryptanalysis, the other sub-discipline, seeks to compromise or defeat the security achieved by cryptography. The foundation for both cryptography and cryptanalysis is mathematics.

Cryptography is commonly associated with encryption, the transformation of data and information into a form that is unusable by a person not authorized to access that information. Historically, cryptography was used to protect the confidentiality of sensitive messages used for military and diplomatic communication. Based on this traditional definition, cryptography can be seen as the science of encryption and decryption of messages, where the primary concern was to protect a message in the event it was disclosed to someone other than the intended recipient.

With the expansion of the information economy where transmission of sensitive information across untrusted media has become a common practice, the use of cryptography has become a common practice not only with organizations, but also with individuals.

Today, cryptography has come to mean much more than the acts of encryption and decryption. While encryption and decryption techniques are used to secure sensitive information where confidentiality is important, (e.g., to protect the privacy of a message or to maintain the confidentiality of an online transaction), there are other aspects of information security implemented through encryption. These include authentication of the message, sender, and recipient, the integrity of the message, and non-repudiation of the message transfer. The term cryptography as used today refers collectively to techniques and applications used in protecting both stored and transmitted information.

Cryptography and Information Security

Cryptography strives to achieve the following four key objectives of information security, both in the storage and communication of information and data:

- Confidentiality
- Integrity
- Authentication
- Non-repudiation.

Confidentiality

Sometimes also known as "privacy" or "secrecy," confidentiality is ensuring that data and information are usable by only persons authorized to access and use that information. Encryption is used to protect the unauthorized disclosure of the message by rendering the information unintelligible to unauthorized persons. Authorized users of information will be able to decrypt and interpret the information contained in the message. If the secrecy of the encryption and decryption keys has been maintained, unauthorized persons intercepting this message will not be able to read and understand the message.

Figure 3.1 A Simple Message Rendered Unreadable Through PGP Encryption

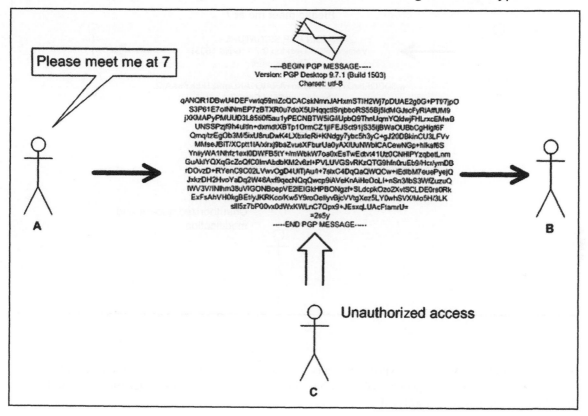

For example, if A sends an encrypted message to B, the confidentiality of the message is retained even if C intercepts it in transit.

Integrity

Maintaining the integrity of information and data is ensuring that it is modified only through authorized processes in an authorized manner. Unauthorized modifications include insertion, deletion, and substitution of data elements. Cryptography provides the ability to both prevent and detect unauthorized modifications. Typically, this is achieved by attaching a cryptographic signature to the data being protected.

Figure 3.2 An Example of a Message Signed Using PGP

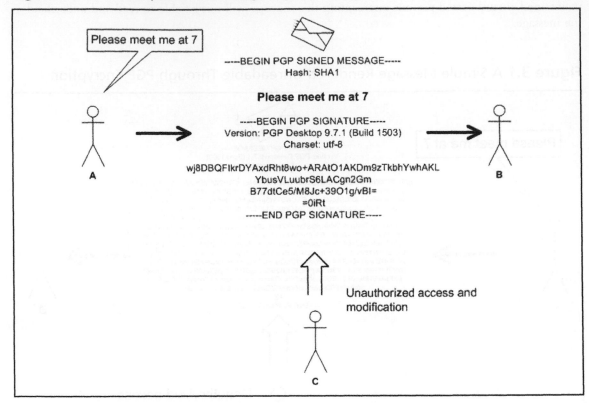

In this example, A sends a cryptographically signed message to B. If the message is modified in transit, the cryptographic signature will no longer be valid, thus immediately alerting B to the fact that the message has been modified.

Authentication

The process of identifying, and verifying the identity of parties in data access or communication processes is known as authentication. Authentication provides assurance to the confidentiality and integrity of data transactions by providing a mechanism to verify the identity of the authorized parties or entities. Authentication can be applied to entities participating in a data transaction, the data accessed or communicated in the transaction, or to both entities and data. Aspects of authenticity typically verified are the sender and the recipient of the data, the point of origin, date and time of origin, and the actual data itself.

Non-Repudiation

Non-repudiation prevents an entity taking part in a data transaction from denying their participation in that transaction. In the previous examples in Figures 3.1 and 3.2, A will not be able to deny that he or she did not send the message when non-repudiation is incorporated into the cryptographic processes.

Cryptographic Protocols and Applications

Cryptography is used to secure data and information security, both when stored and in transit. This is achieved by using cryptographic applications and protocols. Cryptographic protocols are built on cryptographic algorithms and describe how an algorithm works. Cryptographic protocols are used in user applications or in developing other protocols.

A cryptographic application or a protocol is a collection of cryptographic protocols, techniques, and methods combined with a user-friendly interface. While cryptographic algorithms and techniques are complex, these applications and protocols enable end users to achieve the benefits of cryptography without having to become proficient in the algorithms or the mathematics behind these algorithms.

Following are some commonly used cryptographic protocols and applications.

Domain Name Server Security Extensions

Domain Name Server Security Extensions (DNSSEC) is a protocol designed to secure distributed name services. As the name implies, it adds a layer of security to otherwise unsecured DNS communication traffic. As DNS information is meant to be publicly accessible, DNSSEC is not aimed at making the traffic confidential. Rather, it is aimed at the integrity of the data and the authenticity of the data origin, and the availability of the service through specifying alternate authenticated DNS servers.

Secure Sockets Layer/Transport Layer Security

Secure Sockets Layer (SSL) is a protocol used to secure Internet traffic carrying sensitive information. Currently in version 3.0, SSL was extended and renamed Transport Layer Security (TLS) by the Internet Engineering Task Force (IETF).

SSL was initially developed to provide confidentiality of messages. However, SSL and TLS can be extended to provide authentication and message integrity. These protocols are currently used in applications such as Web browsing, e-mail, Internet faxing, Internet messaging, and Virtual Private Networks (VPNs). Typically, SSL and TLS are used to secure the communication channel, not the message itself.

Using cryptographic methods, TLS provides two types of authentication: end point and mutual authentication. Endpoint authentication provides a user with a means to verify the identity of the server with whom the communication is being made. Mutual authentication uses public key infra-structure, another cryptographic methodology, where the two end points of the communication mutually authenticate and verify the other parties' identity.

Secure Hypertext Transfer Protocol

Secure Hypertext Transfer Protocol (S-HTTP) is another protocol that uses encryption to provide confidentiality, authentication, and integrity of Web traffic. While S-HTTP uses encryption as a technique for security, it does not limit itself to a particular type of cryptographic system or format. It can actually apply many security transformations such as encryption, signing, and message authentication code (MAC).

S-HTTP encrypts and secures individual messages. It cannot be used to secure the communication channel. Therefore, unlike SSL and TLS, S-HTTP cannot be used to create VPNs.

Secure Shell Protocol

Secure Shell Protocol (SSH) is a cryptographic protocol that allows mutual authentication and secure communications. Most common applications of SSH are the provision of secure terminal sessions and data transfer. However, SSH can be used to "tunnel" or forward arbitrary Transmission Control Protocol (TCP) connections while providing security to the communication channel.

A typical SSH session has two levels of authentication: the client server authentication, where the two communicating nodes authenticate against each other, and the user session authentication. User authentication can be either symmetric or public key-based as version 2 of SSH supports the storage of private keys.

Internet Protocol Security

Internet Protocol Security (IPSec) is a suite of protocols that provides encryption and security services at the network layer. IT supports peer authentication, data origin authentication, data integrity, and encryption services.

IPSec operates in two modes: tunnel and transport. Tunnel mode provides encryption at a packet level and is known as a VPN. Transport mode creates a secure connection between two end points, typically two gateways, and encrypts the Internet Protocol (IP) payload within the packet.

Cryptographic Systems

Cryptographic systems, or cryptosystems as they are commonly called, convert a plaintext message to a ciphertext message using a cryptographic key. The mechanism that applies the key to the message is called a cryptographic algorithm or a cipher.

Figure 3.3 The Encryption Process

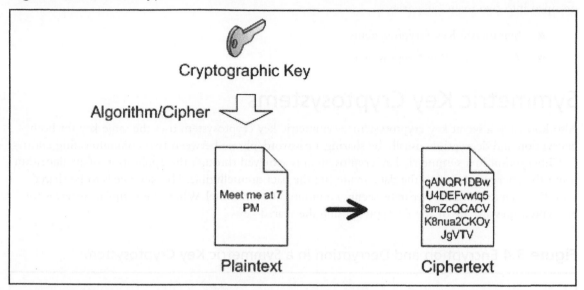

In the example given in Figure 3.3:

- Plaintext, also known as cleartext, is data in its original, readable format before being encrypted.

- Ciphertext is the encrypted output resulting from the application of a cryptographic method on plaintext.

- Cryptographic key is the password or other cryptographic mechanism used in the transformation of the plaintext to ciphertext.

- Algorithm or cipher is a series of well-defined computational steps that is used to transform/encrypt a message.

- A cryptosystem applies the cipher in such a way that it is extremely difficult to apply the reverse procedures on the ciphertext to retrieve the original plaintext.

A cryptographic algorithm ensures that it is extremely difficult to apply the reverse procedures on the ciphertext to retrieve the original plaintext. Since the working of the algorithms is generally known and accessible, many modern cryptosystems rely on the cryptographic key to provide the required security. The secrecy of the algorithm is no longer required to maintain security; a ciphertext can only be decrypted if the decrypting key corresponds with the encrypting key.

Based on the type of key used for encrypting and decrypting data, most cryptosystems can be grouped into two main categories:

- Symmetric Key Cryptosystems
- Asymmetric Key Cryptosystems

Symmetric Key Cryptosystems

Also known as a secret key cryptosystem, a symmetric key cryptosystem uses the same key for both encryption and decryption, usually by sharing a password/phrase between two communicating entities.

Encryption in a symmetric key cryptosystem is achieved through the application of an algorithm using the encryption key to the data, rendering the data unintelligible. The key needs to be shared with the recipient, using a separate, secure communication channel. When the recipient receives the encrypted message, he or she decrypts it using the shared key.

Figure 3.4 Encryption and Decryption in a Symmetric Key Cryptosystem

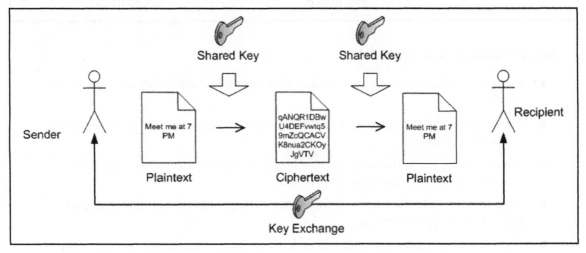

In the above example (Figure 3.4), the sender and the recipient share the same encryption key. The sender encrypts the message using the shared key and sends the resulting ciphertext to the recipient. The recipient decrypts the ciphertext using the shared key. The security of the message is reliant on the strengths of the key as well as the security of the key exchange.

Asymmetric key cryptosystem can be applied on data streams, which operate faster than a symmetric key cryptosystem. Therefore, symmetric key cryptosystems are used when large amounts of data require encryption.

Symmetric key algorithms can be divided into block ciphers and stream ciphers based on how they are applied to the plaintext message. Block and stream ciphers are discussed in the next section of this chapter.

Data Encryption Standard (DES) and Advanced Encryption Standard (AES) are examples of symmetric key crypto systems.

Asymmetric Key Cryptosystems

Asymmetric key cryptosystems, also known as public key cryptosystems, is more modern practice than the symmetric key cryptosystems. In asymmetric key cryptography, the decryption key is different than the key that was used to encrypt the message.

Each party taking part in the communication stream in an asymmetric key cryptosystem has a pair of keys, known as the public key and the private key. The private key is highly protected and is only known to the owner of that key. The public key is distributed to other entities that take part in the communication. When the goal is to achieve confidentiality, a recipient's public key is used to encrypt messages. On receiving the message, the recipient is able to decrypt the message using his or her pri-vate key. In an asymmetric key cryptosystem, a public key cannot be used to derive the private key.

In addition to confidentiality, asymmetric key cryptosystems can also be used to achieve user authentication and non-repudiation aspects of information security. A message encrypted using a private key can be decrypted using the corresponding public key. As the public key may be common-ly known, this would not provide confidentiality. However, since the private key is only known to the sender, it authenticates the sender, and the sender cannot deny that he or she sent the message.

Figure 3.5 Encryption and Decryption in an Asymmetric Key Cryptosystem

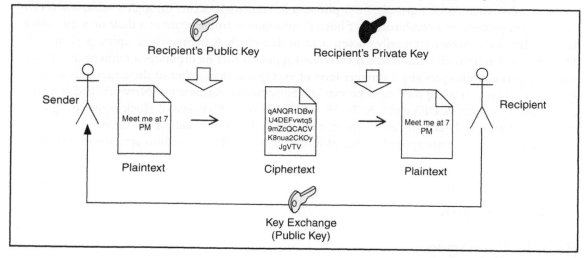

Figure 3.5 shows an example of how an asymmetric key cryptosystem works. The recipient distributes his or her public key to entities wishing to secure their communications with the recipient. Unlike in the symmetric key cryptosystem, the secrecy of the key is not a requirement as it can only be used to encrypt messages. In fact, many asymmetric key cryptosystems have public key servers where users can publish their public keys.

Using the recipient's pubic key, the sender now encrypts the message. When the recipient receives the message, he or she can decrypt and access the message using his or her private key, which has never been released to any other party.

Compared to symmetric key systems that are used to encrypt large amounts of data, asymmetric key cryptosystems are typically used to encrypt shorter messages. A combination of the two systems can be used for efficiency. A common scenario is to use symmetric key encryption to encrypt large databases and exchange the shared key using asymmetric encryption.

The security of an asymmetric key cryptosystem relies on the security of the private key.

The Diffie-Hellman (D-H) key exchange protocol, the Digital Signature Standard (DSS), and the Rivest, Shamir, & Adleman (RSA) algorithm are some examples of asymmetric key cryptosystems. These systems have been implemented in commonly used cryptographic applications such as SSH and SSL.

Introducing Cryptographic Algorithms and Ciphers

A cryptographic algorithm, or cipher, is a set of well-defined but complex mathematical instructions used to encrypt or decrypt data. The encryption and decryption processes depend on a cryptographic key selected by the entities participating in the encryption and decryption process. Typically, details of the algorithm are public knowledge. However, operation of the algorithm and the security of the encrypted message is dependent on the cryptographic key used in the encryption and decryption process.

The transformation of a message from plaintext to ciphertext occurs through a substitution or a transposition process, or a combination of both. A substitution cipher replaces a digit or a data block in a message with another arbitrarily chosen digit or data block. A transposition cipher generates different permutations of a data block. A combined approach that incorporates a number of substitutions and permutations provides a stronger level of encryption than either of these methods used individually. This combined method is known as a Substitution-Permutation Network, and is used in cryptosystems such as DES and CAST-128. CAST-128 is another type of block cipher designed by Carlisle Adams and Stafford Tavares, the name is taken from the initials of the creators.

Based on how they are applied on the plaintext, cryptographic algorithms are categorized into two types:

- Block ciphers
- Stream ciphers

Block Ciphers

As the name implies, block ciphers work on a fixed-length segment of plaintext data, typically a 64- or 128-bit block as input, and outputs a fixed length ciphertext. The message is broken into blocks, and each block is encrypted through a substitution process. Where there is insufficient data to fill a block, the blank space will be padded prior to encryption. The resulting ciphertext block is usually the same size as the input plaintext block.

Block ciphers are mostly used in symmetric key encryption. Typically, a block cipher uses a simple substitution-permutation or a substitution transposition process where the block of plaintext is substituted with and arbitrary bit of ciphertext. DES, Triple DES, RC2 (Rivest Cipher 2 named for Ron Rivest one the creators of RSA), and AES are based on the block ciphers.

Based on the mode of operation, block ciphers can be further categorized.

Electronic Code Book Mode

The Electronic Code Book (ECB) mode uses simple substitution, making it one of the easiest and fastest algorithms to implement. The input plaintext is broken into a number of blocks, and encrypted individually using the key. This allows each encrypted block to be decrypted individually. Encrypting the same block twice will result in the same ciphertext being returned twice.

Cipher Block Chaining Mode

In Cipher Block Chaining (CBC) mode, the first block of the plaintext is exclusive-OR'd (XOR'd), which is a binary function or operation that compares two bits and alters the output with a third bit, with an initialization vector (IV) prior to the application of the encryption key. The IV is a block of random bits of plaintext. The resultant block is the first block of the ciphertext. Each subsequent block of plaintext is then XOR'd with the previous block of ciphertext prior to encryption, hence the term "chaining." Due to this XOR process, the same block of plaintext will no longer result in identical ciphertext being produced.

Decryption in the CBC mode works in the reverse order. After decrypting the last block of ciphertext, the resultant data is XOR'd with the previous block of ciphertext to recover the original plaintext.

The CBC mode is used in hash algorithms. Discarding all previous blocks, the last resulting block is retained as the output hash when used for this purpose.

Output Feedback Mode

In Output Feedback (OFB) Mode, an IV is placed in the least significant bits of the input block. Any unused bits within the block are set to 0s to create the input plaintext block for enciphering. This input is then divided into data units of 1 to 64 bits, inclusive. The encryption process is then applied to each data unit of "modified" plaintext. The output ciphertext from this process is then XOR'd with the most significant bits in the input block to produce the final ciphertext. The size of the resultant ciphertext block size is the same as the size of the input plaintext block.

The resulting ciphertext can be varied based on the key, the IV, and the number of bits fed back into the process during each step.

In the decryption process, plaintext is produced by XORing ciphertext with the most significant bits of the output block.

Cipher Feedback Mode

The Cipher Feedback Mode (CFB) mode uses a similar approach the OFB mode. It can operate on data units of 1 to 64 bits. The main difference between OFB and CFB modes is that the actual ciphertext is fed back into the block cipher, rather than the resultant text from the initial application of the cipher block.

Stream Ciphers

In contrast to the block ciphers, a stream cipher is applied to single bits of data. While stream ciphers still use substitution to encrypt, a cryptographic key is used to generate a pseudo-random stream of digits that are combined with the plaintext digits to create the ciphertext. Sometimes, one-time pads are used to generate a completely random stream of digits for use in the encryption stage.

The sequence of (pseudo) random digits used in enciphering plaintext is called a "keystream," and needs to be of the same length as the plaintext message. The keystream is typically XOR'd with the plaintext using a bitwise operation on individual bits.

Stream ciphers provide faster encryption and decryption capability than block ciphers, and can be used in both symmetric and asymmetric key cryptosystems.

There are two types of stream ciphers:

- Synchronous stream ciphers
- Asynchronous stream ciphers

Synchronous Stream Ciphers

In a synchronous stream cipher, the keystream is generated independently of the plaintext and ciphertext messages. The keystream is then applied to the plaintext for encryption (or ciphertext for decryption). Typically, the operation applied in this process is the XOR. For encryption and decryption to work, both the sender and the recipient must use the same key, and at the same position within the keystream. If the keystream is altered, the decryption process will fail. Re-synchronization can be achieved through a re-initialization process. To avoid having to re-initialize the entire transmission process, special markers or tags are placed within the ciphertext.

Synchronous stream ciphers are useful when the transmission error rate is high, as single-digit corruption of alteration of the message only affects a single digit of the decrypted plaintext.

Asynchronous Stream Ciphers

Asynchronous stream ciphers, otherwise known as self-synchronizing stream ciphers (SSSC), can self-correct the output stream when there are limited errors in the transmission. When a recipient detects an error in the transmission, an automatic re-synchronizing process with the keystream generator occurs.

Self-synchronizing stream ciphers are commonly used in low bit error rate contexts. Even if the ciphertext is modified in transition, it is possible to decrypt the message with minimal loss of plaintext, because it is only reliant on a fixed number of previous digits in the ciphertext.

Cryptographic Key Management

It was mentioned earlier that many of the modern algorithms are publicly known and that the security of a cryptosystem is reliant on the secrecy of the cryptographic key.

Typically, keys need to be distributed or exchanged between two or more parties taking part in the cryptographic process. This can be between persons taking part in a communication or two automated applications. Keys need to be generated, stored, transmitted, authenticated, and used without compromise, and there has to be a method to revoke and replace a key in the event that it becomes compromised.

The above applies to both types of key-based cryptosystems. In a symmetric key system, the shared key needs to be protected. In an asymmetric key system, while the public key can be distributed freely, the secrecy of the private key needs to be maintained at all times. It is also very important in the case of a private/public key pair, that the public key cannot be used to derive the private key.

Cryptographic key management is a set of provisions to ensure that the confidentiality and the integrity of the key are maintained through out the life of the process.

Examples of key management protocols include:

- Internet Security Association and Key Management Protocol (ISAKMP)
- Diffie-Hellman key exchange protocol

Internet Security Association and Key Management Protocol

Used in IPSec-based applications, ISAKMP provides a framework for establishing, negotiating, modifying, and deleting security associations. It provides authentication and key management capabilities to IPSec by using a consistent framework for transferring key and authentication data independent of the key generation technique, encryption algorithm, and the authentication mechanism.

ISAKMP uses digital signatures based on a public key cryptography to provide strong authentications and to prevent Man-in-the-middle (MITM) attacks against the encrypted communication channels.

Diffie–Hellman Key Exchange Protocol

Based on public key cryptography, the D-H algorithm is a method for securely exchanging a shared key between two parties over an untrusted network. It is an asymmetric cipher used by several protocols including SSL, SSH, and IPSec. It allows two communicating parties to agree upon a shared secret, which can then be used to secure a communication channel.

The D-H algorithm requires each of the communicating parties to have public/private key pairs. By the sender using a private key and the receiver using a public key, the sender and the receiver compute a shared secret number. If the same public/private key pairs of the same sender and recipient are used, both parties will arrive at the same number.

This number is then used as a shared symmetric cryptographic key and can be used as a key-encryption key (KEK) or to generate a content-encryption key (CEK). The CEK is commonly known as a session key. To prevent the same key from being generated in subsequent communication sessions, a random value is incorporated into the initial KEK generation process. This ensures that the resulting KEK is unique for each communication session.

In IPSec implementations, this uniqueness of keys from one key exchange to another is used to provide perfect forward secrecy. D-H is also used by the Internet Key Exchange (IKE) Protocol during session setup, where the identities of the communicating parties established and preferred encryption methods and shared secrets need to be agreed upon between the two entities.

D-H is used in SSL for authentication of the communicating parties and the negotiation of session keys and encryption methods.

When establishing a communication session, the SSH client and server compute a shared secret using the D-H algorithm. A hash of this shared secret is then generated and used as the session key to encrypt the communication channel.

Cryptographic Functions

Cryptographic functions are mathematical computations carried out on messages or data. The resulting values from these calculations are used as building blocks in cryptographic applications. Some common applications that use cryptographic functions include:

- Cryptographic key generation and exchange

- Data encryption and decryption

- Digital signature creation and verification

Basic cryptographic functions include cryptographic hashes and message authentication codes, and are generally classified as one-way functions.

Basic Cryptographic Functions

Some basic cryptographic functions are:

- One-way functions

- Cryptographic hashes

- Message authentication codes

One-way Functions

A one-way function cryptography is a mathematical function that is significantly easy to compute in one direction, but is difficult to inverse the results to compute the original data, even when some of the data is known. In other words, it is hard to compute the inputs based on the outputs of a one-way function.

The difficulty in the inversion limits a one-way function's usability for encryption and decryption. To overcome this problem, public key cryptosystems use one-way functions with a built-in "trap door." Secret information built into the private key is the trap door, which allows the inverse process to be carried out using the secret information. In this scenario, the one-way function based on the public key is used to encrypt messages and verify digital signatures, while the inverse function based on the private key is used to decrypt messages and sign documents.

Cryptographic Hash Functions

Cryptographic hash functions are used to compute a fixed-size string based on any arbitrarily sized plaintext. The resulting hash value is called a "message digest," or a "digital fingerprint." Hash functions and the resulting values are used in various contexts (e.g., to compute the message digest for use in a digital signature or to check the integrity of a file). They are also used in the verification of passwords.

Cryptographic hash functions typically compute 160-bit hash values. However, computing 128-bit hash values or values larger than 160 bits is not an uncommon practice.

The most common hash functions used currently are:

- Message Digest Algorithm 5
- Secure Hash Algorithm (SHA-1)
- RACE Integrity Primitives Evaluation Message Digest (RIPEMD-160)

Message Digest Algorithm 5

Message Digest Algorithm 5 (MD5) is a cryptographic hash algorithm that can be used to create a 128-bit string value from an arbitrary length string. Although there has been insecurities identified with MD5, it is still widely used. MD5 is most commonly used to verify the integrity of files. However, it is also used in other security protocols and applications such as SSH, SSL, and IPSec. Some applications strengthen the MD5 algorithm by adding a salt value to the plaintext or by applying the hash function multiple times.

Secure Hash Algorithm

Secure Hash Algorithm (SHA-1) produces a 160-bit hash value from an arbitrary length string. Like MD5, it is also used widely in applications such as SSH, SSL, S-MIME (**Secure / Multipurpose Internet Mail Extensions)**, and IPSec.

The main premise behind the security of SHA-1 is that it is computationally infeasible to find a message that corresponds to a given message digest, or to find two messages that produce the same message digest. However, there has been research that indicates that this premise is no longer valid. While there have been no successful attacks on SHA-1, more secure variations of SHA-1 are currently being tested to replace the current 160-bit version. These include SHA-256, SHA-384, and SHA-512, with the numbers reflecting the strength of the message digest created on application of the algorithm.

RACE Integrity Primitives Evaluation Message Digest

RACE Integrity Primitives Evaluation Message Digest (RIPEMD-160) is a 160-bit cryptographic hash function designed to replace MD4 and MD5. The developers expect it to be secure for the next ten years. However, there is already research underway to develop stronger versions with 256- and 320-bit message digests for hash functions that require a longer hash result.

Message Authentication Codes

A Message Authentication Code (MAC) is a tag attached to a message to ensure the integrity and authenticity of the message. It is derived by applying a MAC algorithm to a message in combination with a secret key.

MAC functions share similarities with cryptographic hash functions, however, they address different security requirements. The purpose of a MAC is to authenticate the source of a message and its integrity. Unlike a cryptographic hash, the MAC can be generated only by the intended recipient who has access to the secret key. Provided that the algorithm used to generate the MAC and the secret key are the same, a given message will always produce the same MAC.

The algorithm used to generate and verify the MAC is based on the DES.

A keyed Hash Message Authentication Code (HMAC) is an extension to the MAC function to include cryptographic hash function and a secret key in deriving the message authentication code. Typically, MD5 and SHA-1 cryptographic hash functions are used to calculate the HMAC value. The type of cryptographic hash used in creating the HMAC is appended to indicate the algorithm (e.g., HMAC-MD5 and HMAC-SHA1).

Digital Signatures

A digital signature is a means of verifying the authenticity and integrity of a message. This is achieved by using public key cryptography techniques combined with cryptographic hash functions. Combined with trusted time-stamping mechanisms, the digital signature can also be used to provide non-repudiation functions.

The digital signature process begins with creating a cryptographic hash of the message. This hash value is also known as a "digital fingerprint" and is a unique value. The digital fingerprint is then encrypted with the sender's private key, and the resulting value is appended to the message. This message is then sent to the recipient.

When the message arrives, the recipient decrypts the digital fingerprint appended to the message, creates a digital fingerprint of the message itself, and compares the two. If they match, the integrity of the message has been intact and the authentication of the sender is established. Please see Figure 3.6.

Figure 3.6 Digital Signing and Verification Process

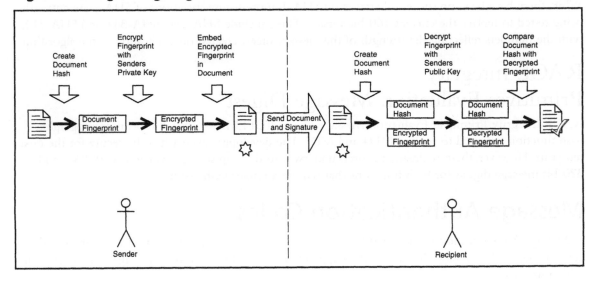

Attacks on Cryptosystems

While cryptography is aimed at protecting data by providing confidentiality, integrity, authenticity, and non-repudiation, there are many attacks targeting cryptosystems. It is important to have an understanding of these attempts to subvert or circumvent cryptographic controls designing or implementing a cryptosystem.

It was mentioned earlier that cryptographic algorithms are public knowledge, and that the security of most cryptographic solutions are dependent on the security of the cryptographic key. Protecting the cryptographic key, whether it is a shared key in a symmetric cryptosystem or the private key in an asymmetric cryptosystem, is the most important security requirement to protect any implementation of cryptography. Many attackers target users using social engineering and various technological attacks, because getting access to a key is much easier than using cryptanalysis to break encryption.

Attacks on cryptosystems also target weak implementations. Too often, cryptographic implementations are not planned properly. A system does not become secure simply because a cryptographic technology was implemented. Sometimes security is weakened to increase usability. Attackers target these systems, as once again, it is easier to gain access to these systems than trying to break encryption.

Sometimes MITM attacks target the cryptographic communication and the key exchange process. An attacker intercepts the communication channel, typically by pretending to be one of the communicators, and exchanges his or her own key with each of the communicators. The attacker can then decrypt and re-encrypt the message before passing it on to the intended person. In this scenario, the communicators are not aware that they have involuntarily disclosed the contents of the communication to a third party.

The above shows that it is easier to target the users and the systems on which cryptographic controls are implemented, than to attack the cryptography itself.

However, we know that cryptanalysis is a branch of cryptology that is concerned with the inversion of cryptography. There are several cryptanalysis techniques that are used to subvert cryptography and carry out attacks on the cryptosystems themselves. These attacks aim at the inversion of the cryptographic process to recover the plaintext or the cryptographic keys. Many of these attacks are based on knowing one part of the message: the plaintext or the ciphertext.

Plaintext-Based Attacks

With a known plaintext attack, the attacker has knowledge of the plaintext and the corresponding ciphertext. This information is used to decrypt the rest of the ciphertext.

With a chosen plaintext attack, the attacker can get a plaintext message of his or her choice encrypted, with the target's key, and has access to the resulting ciphertext. This information is used to derive the encryption key. This type of attack is against public key cryptosystems where the attacker has access to the public key.

With an adaptive chosen plaintext attack, which is similar to a chosen plaintext attack, the attacker can get several plaintext messages of choice encrypted with the target's key.

Ciphertext-Based Attacks

With a ciphertext-only attack, the attacker has access to the ciphertext, but not the contents of the plaintext. The patterns and context of the message is used to derive the contents of the message. Frequency analysis has been used to break traditional ciphers using this method.

With a chosen ciphertext attack, the attacker has access to ciphertext he or she knows about. This information is supplemented with publicly available information and other knowledge he or she has about the message to find the corresponding plaintext.

With adaptive chosen ciphertext, which is similar to chosen ciphertext, the attacker has access to several chosen ciphertexts.

These attack methods provide the basis for most of the other cryptanalysis attacks such as linear and differential cryptanalysis.

Understanding that cryptography, like any other security system, is susceptible to attack, helps in designing, implementing, and maintaining better cryptographic systems.

Cryptography and SSH

SSH is used both as a communication protocol as well as a suite of remote access applications. It is designed to provide both confidentiality and integrity of the transmitted data. Both symmetric and asymmetric key technologies can be used in an SSH implementation, making it suitable for a range of applications from remote administration to tunneling of other, more vulnerable protocols and data.

SSH is aimed at protecting data from network threats such as password exposure, traffic sniffing, and MITM attacks and impersonation of hosts. The current version of SSH is mostly resilient against cryptanalysis-based attacks.

The SSH architecture comprises the following three layered components.

Transport Layer

The transport layer establishes the initial connection and provides algorithm negotiation, key exchange, and a cryptographically secured communication channel. This layer provides server authentication, confidentiality, and integrity. Currently, the D-H algorithm is used by default as the key exchange protocol. Integrity is provided by using HMAC-based message authentication codes.

User Authentication Layer

The user authentication layer runs over the transport protocol and provides client authentication to the server. Authentication options include shared key (password), public key, or host-based authentication.

Connection Layer

The connection layer multiplexes the encrypted communication channel into several logical channels. The connection layer runs over the user authentication protocol. The multiplexed communication channels allow the setting up of secure interactive shell sessions, tunneling of arbitrary TCP connections, and forwarding X11 sessions.

SSH Key Exchange

SSH version 2 by default uses the D-H key exchange method to set up a shared secret or a session key, which is signed by the host key to provide host authentication. Currently, the default protocol for key exchange is diffie-hellman-group-exchange-sha1. Using D-H as the key exchange provides perfect forward secrecy (PFS) for the SSH session.

Figure 3.7 Packet Capture from an SSH Session

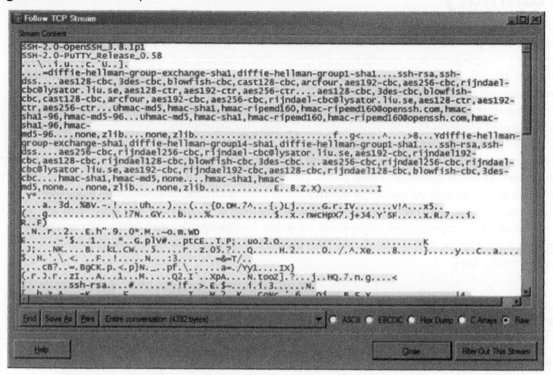

Figure 3.7 shows a packet capture from a SSH session. Note how the supported communication protocols are presented between the client and the server. Also note how the communication has been encrypted after the initial key exchange.

Encryption Algorithms Supported by SSH

By default, SSH uses the 128-bit AES (aes-128-ctr) with a 16-byte block size. 198- and 256-bit AES as well as 3DES are currently supported by SSH.

Summary

Cryptography is the science of encrypting and decrypting data. Based on complex mathematics, cryptography provides several important information security services such as authentication, confidentiality, integrity, and non-repudiation. Cryptographic protocols and applications make cryptography user-friendly and enable users to secure their data without having to carry out the complex mathematics themselves.

Modern cryptography relies on cryptographic keys, usually a short string of text, for encoding and decoding messages in combination with cryptographic algorithms.

Based on the type of keys used, cryptography is classified as either symmetric or asymmetric key cryptography. Both symmetric and asymmetric key cryptography provide data confidentiality. Asymmetric key encryption is sometimes called public key encryption. Digital signatures, one of the by-products of public key cryptography, enable the verification of authenticity, integrity, and non-repudiation.

While cryptography enables security, there are attempts to circumvent and subvert its use. Since most of the cryptographic algorithms are public knowledge, security of the data is reliant on the security of the cryptographic key. This makes it very important to safeguard the cryptographic keys.

Solutions Fast Track

Cryptography and Information Security

☑ Cryptography provides confidentiality, integrity, authentication, and non-repudiation aspects of information and data security.

☑ Encryption is used to preserve confidentiality.

☑ Cryptographic signatures are used to provide authentication, integrity, and non-repudiation.

Cryptographic Protocols and Applications

☑ Cryptographic protocols and applications give users the ability to use cryptography without having to concern themselves with the complex mathematical problems used in cryptography.

☑ Cryptographic protocols describe how cryptographic algorithms are used in cryptosystems and cryptographic applications.

☑ Cryptographic applications are collections of protocols, functions, and methods combined with user-friendly interfaces. Cryptographic applications are collections of protocols, functions, and methods combined with user-friendly interfaces

☑ DNSSEC, SSL, TLS, S-HTTP and SSH are some examples of cryptographic protocols and applications.

Cryptographic Systems

- ☑ Based on the types of keys used, cryptosystems are categorized into two main groups: symmetric key and asymmetric key cryptosystems.

- ☑ Symmetric key cryptosystems use the same key for encryption and decryption. This key is known to both the sender and recipient of a message.

- ☑ Asymmetric key cryptosystems use public/private key pairs. The public key is used for encryption and the private key is known only to the key owner and is used for decryption of the message.

- ☑ Cryptographic protocols used in both types of cryptosystems are public knowledge. Security of these systems is dependent on the protection of the cryptographic keys.

Introducing Cryptographic Algorithms and Ciphers

- ☑ Cryptographic algorithms (ciphers) are complex mathematical instructions applied to data to perform cryptographic functions on the data.

- ☑ Based on how the algorithm is applied on the data, they are classified as block or stream ciphers.

- ☑ Block ciphers are applied to fixed-length blocks of plaintext data.

- ☑ Stream ciphers are applied to individual bits of data.

Cryptographic Key Management

- ☑ Cryptographic key management protocols ensure that cryptographic keys are securely generated, exchanged, authenticated, stored, and used.

- ☑ Key management protocols also provide a mechanism to revoke a key if it has been compromised.

- ☑ D-H key management protocol is one of the most commonly used key management protocols in modern cryptographic applications.

Cryptographic Functions

- ☑ Cryptographic functions are mathematical computations carried out on messages or data. Resulting values are used in cryptographic applications.

- ☑ Cryptographic functions are typically carried out in one direction. It is near impossible to reverse the process to obtain the original values.

- ☑ Message authentication codes and cryptographic hashes are examples of cryptographic functions.

Digital Signatures

☑ Digital signatures provide the means to verify the integrity and authentication and non-repudiation aspects of information security.

☑ A combination of public key cryptography methods and cryptographic hash functions are used in digital signatures.

☑ A digital signature is a cryptographic hash of the messages encrypted with the sender's private key appended to the message.

Attacks on Cryptosystems

☑ Cryptography is based on complex mathematical problems. These mathematical problems are difficult to inverse, but not impossible

☑ Attackers typically target users and weak implementations of cryptosystems, before attempting to break the cryptosystems.

☑ Cryptanalysis is the study of inversion of cryptography and forms the basis of attacks against cryptosystems.

☑ Cryptanalysis is typically reliant on knowing either the plaintext or the ciphertext. Typically, the objective of a cryptanalysis-based attack is to derive the encryption key.

Cryptography and SSH

☑ SSH is both a protocol and a suite of applications based on cryptography and used to provide authentication, confidentiality, and integrity of data.

☑ SSH is used to protect data from network-based attacks.

☑ Both symmetric and asymmetric key techniques can be used in SSH to provide data security.

☑ SSH uses D-H key exchange method by default. 128-bit AES is used in the encryption.

Frequently Asked Questions

Q: What is cryptology?

A: Cryptology is the combined study of cryptography and cryptanalysis. Cryptology is concerned with coding and decoding of messages.

Q: What is cryptography?

A: Cryptography is the science of designing cryptosystems for encryption and decryption.

Q: What is plaintext?

A: The term plaintext refers to the original message prior to encryption.

Q: What is ciphertext?

A: Ciphertext is the name used in cryptography for an encrypted message.

Q: What is an encryption key?

A: An encryption key is a piece of information.

Q: What is a symmetric key cryptosystem?

A: A symmetric key encryption system is one where the same key is used for both encrypting and decrypting a message.

Q: What is an asymmetric key cryptosystem?

A: An asymmetric key cryptosystem is one where two separate keys are used for encryption and decryption. These keys are called a public and private key pair.

Q: What is a one-way cryptographic hash?

A: A one-way hash is a mathematical function that generates a fixed size output from an arbitrarily sized string. It is called a one-way hash because deriving the input string from the fixed length is considered to be impossible.

Q: What is a digital signature?

A: A digital signature is a message digest encrypted with the sender's private key. A digital signature is used to verity the authenticity and integrity of the message.

Q: What is cryptographic key management?

A: Cryptographic key management refers to processes related to the secure generation, distribution, storage, and revocation of keys.

Q: What is cryptanalysis?

A: Cryptanalysis is the study of how to inverse cryptography. It is concerned with deciphering messages without knowledge of the cryptosystem.

Chapter 4

SSH Features

Solutions in this chapter:

- Introduction to SSH
- SSH Standards
- SSH vs. Telnet/Rlogin
- SSH Client/Server overview
- Packet Capture Detection

☑ Summary

☑ Solutions Fast Track

☑ Frequently Asked Questions

Introduction to SSH

The SSH (Secure SHell) protocol was designed as a secure alternative to Telnet and Rlogin. Telnet and Rlogin send all data in a clear text format over the network, allowing packet capture programs like Sniffer™ and Wireshark™ to read the interactive session and display the session in clear text. SSH uses encryption to protect the session from view if captured. Encryption is a process that converts clear text into cipher text through an algorithm (such as 3DES, AES, etc.). The client and the server have to agree on the algorithm and the key. There are two types of keys, symmetric and asymmetric. With symmetric keys both sides use the same key to encrypt and decrypt the file. Asymmetric keys use a public/private key pair to handle encryption. Whatever is encrypted by the private key can only be decrypted by the public key. This is also known as PKI (Public Key Infrastructure). This gives a higher level of protection when connecting to remote devices across unsecure network connections.

Notes from the Underground...

Packet Capture Programs

You can get Wireshark™ from http://www.wireshark.org/ and Network General from http://www.netscout.com/products/infinistream.asp. These packet capture programs will work across a switched network with the correct network adapter. There are a few known issues using Wireshark™ that can cause Denial of Service attacks against the machine running the packet capture. See http://www.wireshark.org/security/wnpa-sec-2007-01.html.

According to RFC 4253, SSH utilizes symmetric encryption, asymmetric (Public Key) encryption, hashing, and message authentication encryption algorithms.

There are three major protocols:

- **SSH-TRANS** A Transport Layer Protocol that services authentication, confidentiality, and integrity of the session. It also can provide for data compression to speed up the transmission session.

- **SSH-USERAUTH** This protocol negotiates the client side authentication with the server.

- **SSH-CONNECT** This handles the breaking down of the encrypted data session into multiple logical channels across the IP session.

The IANA (or Internet Assigned Numbers Association)-assigned standard TCP Port for SSH is TCP Port 22.

NOTE

The RFCs for SSH can be found at http://www.ietf.org/rfc.html. These RFCs will give you more details on this and other protocols. For protocol assignment information go to www.iana.org/protocols.

SSH Standards

When a SSH Client negotiates a SSH session with the server they must both send an 8 bit "SSH-protoversion-softwareversion SP comments CR LF" message to verify version information, where protoversion-softwareversion is the protocol version number and the comments are optional. The SP is a Space character (ASCII Code 32). The CR and LF are ASCII codes 10 (HEX a) and 13(HEX d) respectively. If the client or server is using an older version of SSH the CR LF may not be sent. Figure 4.1 depicts Wireshark™ capturing the initial packet of an SSH Session. In the figure below you can see that the first part of the display is in clear text and the arrow shows that this version sent the CR and LF characters (HEX a and d).

Figure 4.1 Wireshark™ Capture Showing the HEX Control Codes CR and LF (HEX a d)

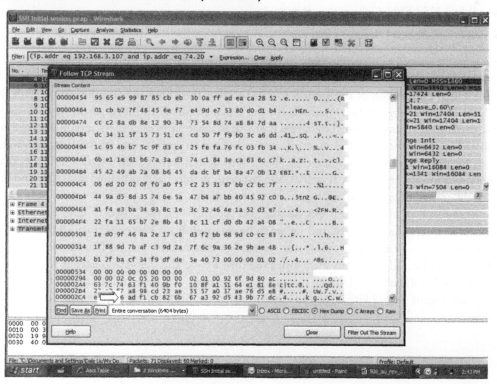

NOTE

The ASCII character set can be found at http://www.asciitable.com/

The current version of SSH is 2.0 but some devices are not using the current protocols. Other versions are 1.5 or 1.3. If the client or server is not using 2.0 the proto-version field will read 1.99 to show pre-version 2.0 protocol standards. If the proto-version flag is 1.99 the CR character (ASCII 13) should not be sent.

The IETF (Internet Engineering Task Force) is the repository of all the standards that define the Internet. Below is a brief listing of some of the RFCs (Request For Comments) that define the SSH Standard. These documents will supplement your review of the SSH Standard.

- RFC 4250 SSH
- RFC 4251 SSH Architecture
- RFC 4252 SSH Authentication Protocol
- RFC 4253 SSH Transportation Layer Protocol
- RFC 4254 SSH Connection Protocol
- RFC 4335 SSH Session Channel

This is not a complete or exhaustive list but a good starting point for further review.

In order to initiate the SSH session, the client must already know the server's public host key. This is used in the initiation of the session to validate that the client is communicating with the correct SSH server. There are two methods for the client to know the server host key association. The first method is to have a local database that stores these keys and their server association. The second is to have a central CA (Certificate Authority) to store them. In the first situation, the database is locally stored and maintained so each client would have its own database that is managed and maintained locally. In the CA scenario, one database would be maintained centrally and all clients would access it for the public key to host associations.

Due to the lack of a centralized CA database on the Internet, the protocol does allow for the first communication between client and server to be done without key checking. This should only be allowed on the first session as it is vulnerable to man-in-the-middle attacks. The first session without the host key would be allowed only to transfer the host key to the client and accept it into the host key table on the local machine. During the initial session you will be asked if you want to save the server key (see Figure 4.2). This allows the client to then establish future connections with the server public key.

Be aware that the use of a session without the host key leaves you open to three different man-in-the-middle attacks: The attacker may place a device in between host and client and accept the client session and open a separate session with the host. The second is when the keys are unknown and false keys are accepted by the client during initial connection. The third is the attacker attempts to manipulate packets after the encrypted session is established. This last attack is highly unlikely due to the strength of the protocols used to encrypt the sessions.

Figure 4.2 Public Key Exchange Between
SSH Client (PuTTY) and SSH Server (Cisco PIX Firewall)

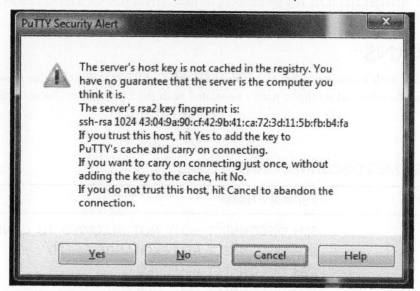

SSH Message Types

SSH uses an 8 bit message number to tell what type of traffic is contained in the packet. These message numbers correspond to the three major protocol types in SSH, referenced above.

The message numbers are:

- SSH-TRANS

  - **1 to 19** Generic Transport layer packets (for example, ignore, disconnect, debug, etc)

  - **20 to 29** Negotiation of the algorithm

  - **30 to 49** Key exchange method specific information (these number can be reused for different method types)

- SSH-AUTH
  - **50 to 59** Generic user authentication types
  - **60 to 79** Specific user authentication types (Again number my be reused)
- SSH-CONNECT
  - **80 to 89** Generic connection protocol messages
  - **90 to 127** Messages related to channel information
- Reserved types for client protocol
  - 128 to 191 Reserved
- Local Extensions
  - 192 to 225 Local Extensions

The initial messages and their IDs by protocol include SSH-TRANS, SSH-USERAUTH, and SSH-CONNECT.

SSH-TRANS

The first message with a message value of 1 is the SSH_MSG_DISCONNECT; this message can contain the reason codes and symbolic names associated with the SSH session disconnecting shown in Table 4.1.

Table 4.1 SSH MSG DISCONNECT Reason Codes

Reason Code	Symbolic Name
1	SSH_DISCONNECT_HOST_NOT_ALLOWED_TO_CONNECT
2	SSH_DISCONNECT_KEY_EXCHANGE_FAILED
3	SSH_DISCONNECT_RESERVED
4	SSH_DISCONNECT_MAC_ERROR
5	SSH_DISCONNECT_COMPRESSION_ERROR
6	SSH_DISCONNECT_SERVICE_NOT_AVAILABLE
7	SSH_DISCONNECT_PROTOCOL_VERSION_NOT_SUPPORTED
8	SSH_DISCONNECT_HOST_KEY_NOT_VERIFIABLE
9	SSH_DISCONNECT_CONNECTION_LOST
10	SSH_DISCONNECT_BY_APPLICATION
11	SSH_DISCONNECT_TOO_MANY_CONNECTIONS
12	SSH_DISCONNECT_AUTH_CANCELLED_BY_USER
13	SSH_DISCONNECT_NO_MORE_AUTH_METHODS_AVAILABLE
14	SSH_DISCONNECT_ILLEGAL_USER_NAME

The next message with a message value of 2 is the SSH_MSG_IGNORE. This message type has been used in the protocol to work around some of the key exchange problems in various methods. It has been combined with other messages to send parts of the password. It has also been used to pass information from server to client that established some of the client information but did not need to be processed by the client session.

Message type 4 SSH_MSG_DEBUG is used to send session debugging information for diagnostics with SSH sessions that do not successfully connect. Type 5 and 6 SSH_MSG_SERVICE_REQUEST and SSH_MSG_SERVICE_ACCEPT are part of the protocol that is used to start service sessions. As described above, you can start the session with an unknown client and server keys. These are the messages used to establish that initial connections and start the process to exchange the SSH keys.

Finishing up the SSH-TRANS message types are 20 and 21, which are SSH_MSG_KEXINIT and SSH_MSG_NEWKEYS. The SSH_MSG_KEXINIT starts the protocol negotiation and the SSH_MSG_NEWKEYS begins the use of the new key pair. Once the KEXINT is sent no other packets can be accepted until the NEWKEYS has been received. The KEXINT Packet contains the key exchange algorithm, server key algorithm, client to server encryption algorithm, the server to client encryption algorithm and other fields to negotiate the new key exchange. Remember the SSH_MSG_KEXINIT is sent clear text to initiate the encryption negotiation. This can be read in a packet capture session using Wireshark™.

SSH-USERAUTH

The four message types defined here in the SSH_USERAUTH are messages 50 to 53 in this section of RFC 4250. The SSH client initiates the session with a SSH-MSG-USERAUTH_REQUEST, type 50. This starts the authentication session and contains the following three fields: the user name, service name, and method names. If the information can be validated by the SSH Server, it will respond with message 52, SSH_MSG_USERAUTH_SUCCESS, granting the SSH Session. If the SSH server determines the information is invalid or incorrect, message 51 will be returned SSH_MSG_USERAUTH_FAILURE by the SSH server to the failed client. The last message type 53 is the SSH_MSG_USERAUTH_BANNER message, which sends the sign-on banner to the client. This banner would normally contain the legal disclaimer against unauthorized use and legal recourse against said unauthorized use. As displayed below in Figure 4.3 you can see the steps that lead to the authentication. After the below steps the SSH_MSG_USERAUTH_BANNER would then be displayed. See Figure 4.4 below showing banner.

Figure 4.3 Establishing the Initial SSH Session

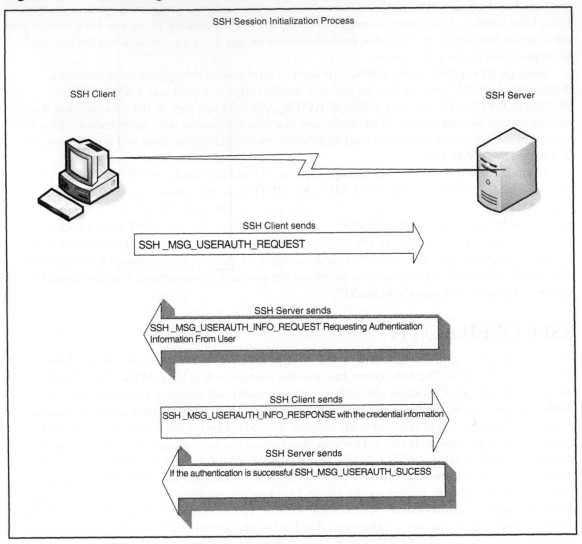

Figure 4.4 After SSH Session is Established Banner is Displayed

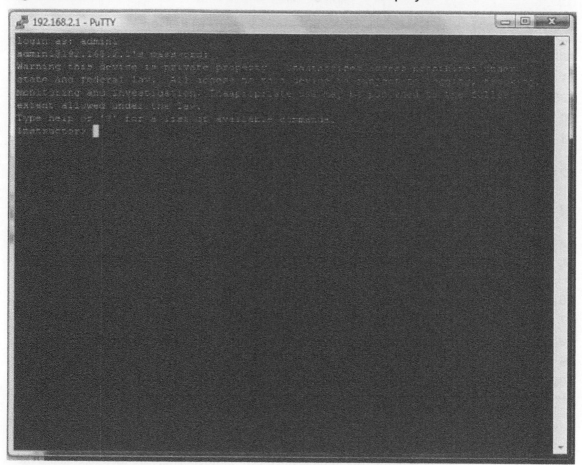

SSH-CONNECT

The messages here are for the control of the session channels built and torn down during the SSH session itself (see Table 4.2). As pointed out above, during an SSH session many separate encrypted channels will be used as needed to facilitate moving the information from the client to the server and the information returning to the client from the server.

Table 4.2 SSH CONNECT Protocol Message Types and Descriptions

Message Number	Name	Reason
80	SSH_MSG_GLOBAL_REQUEST	Global message request
81	SSH_MSG_REQUEST_SUCCESS	Message successful
82	SSH_MSG_REQUEST_FAILURE	Message failed
90	SSH_MSG_CHANNEL_OPEN	Open a new channel
91	SSH_MSG_CHANNEL_OPEN_ CONFIRM	Channel open successful
92	SSH_MSG_CHANNEL_OPEN_ FAILURE	Chanel open failed
93	SSH_MSG_CHANNEL_WINDOW_ ADJUST	Flow control open
94	SSH_MSG_CHANNEL_DATA	Data packet
95	SSH_MSG_CHANNEL_EXTENDED_ DATA	Extended character data
96	SSH_MSG_CHANNEL_EOF	End of file packet
97	SSH_MSG_CHANNEL_CLOSE	Close specific channel
98	SSH_MSG_CHANNEL_REQUEST	Channel specific request
99	SSH_MSG_CHANNEL_SUCCESS	Channel request successful
100	SSH_MSG_CHANNEL_FAILURE	Channel request failure

The above messages are included in the current standard SSHv2 and may be revised as the standard is updated. The flow of the data in these three TCP protocol layers are used to establish the connectivity between the SSH server and the SSH Client.

Having looked at the messages sent in the three different protocols we can now look at a diagram of how SSH establishes its primary connectivity.

You can use a program like Wireshark™ to view the negotiation of the SSH session. The first and second steps are the clear text negotiation of the encryption protocols available from the client and server. Once the negotiation is complete the next steps are to create the diffie-hellman key exchange from client and server. Once these steps have occurred the rest of the data is encrypted.

The next figure (Figure 4.5) is the packet stream establishing the session (the SYN ACK flags) and the final figure (Figure 4.6) is the ending of the session (the FIN ACK flags). In these you will also see the diffie-hellman key exchange requests and replies. In between the initial exchanges and the final exchanges you will see the SSH traffic package.

Figure 4.5 Capture Illustrating Initial Connections (SYN ACK and Key Exchange)

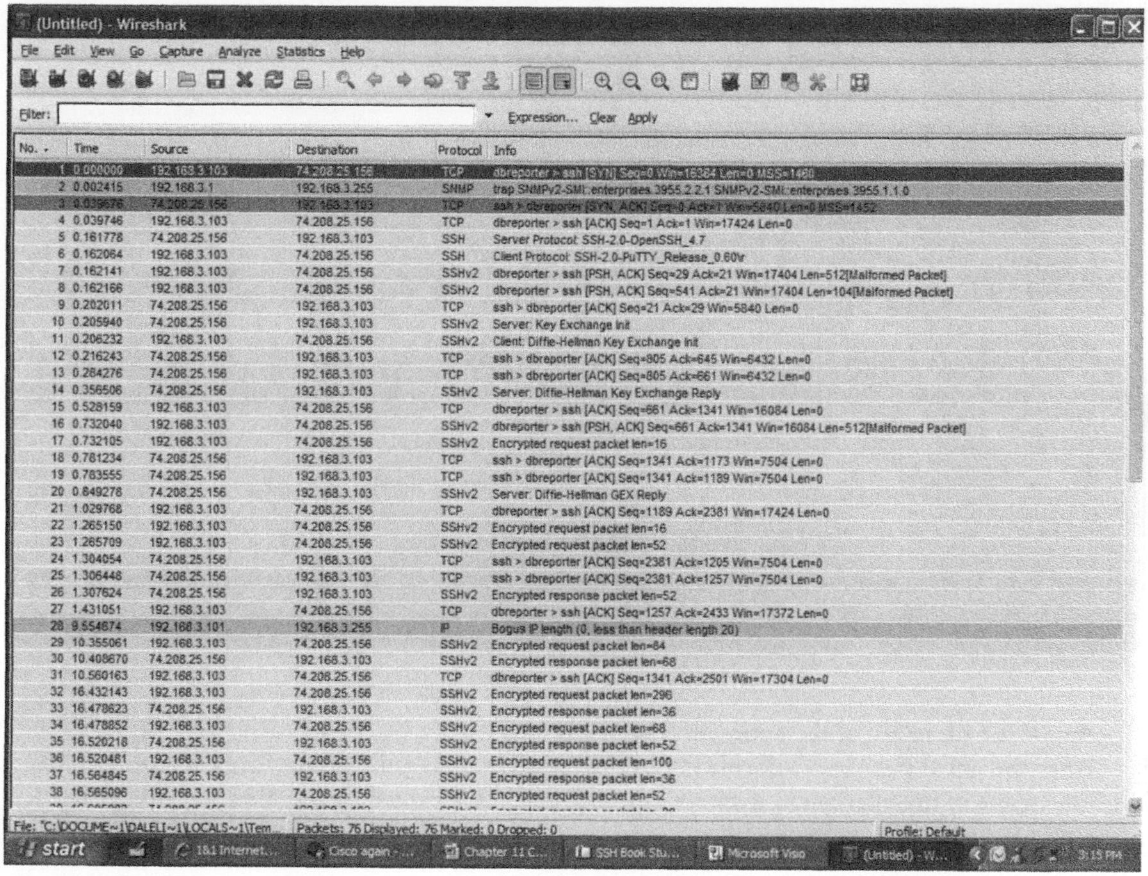

Figure 4.6 Capture Illustrating End of SSH Session (FIN ACK)

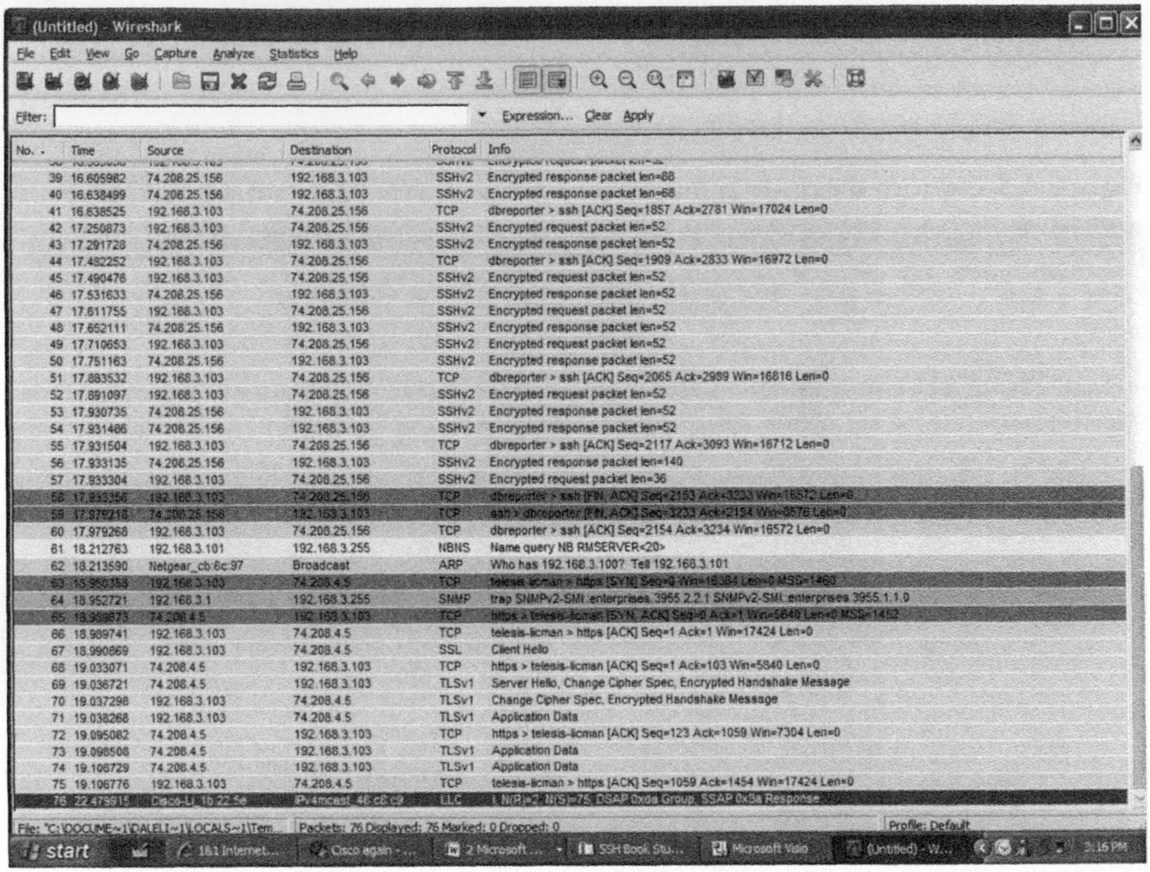

Below is a summary of the entire process.

After the initial passing of information in clear text the rest of the sessions are encrypted. Below are listed some of the encryption methods currently used, as accepted by the SSH working group:

- **3DES (Triple Data Encryption Standard)** Designed by IBM in 1978 using a 64 bit block size.

- **ARCFOUR (Alleged RC4)** An accepted standard allegedly based on Ron Rivest's private, unreleased, algorithm.

- **twofish symmetric key block cipher** 128 bit block size and key space up to 256 bits.

- **serpent** A cipher that was considered in the AES (Advanced Encryption Standard Contest) using a 128 bit block size and keyspace of either 128, 192, or 256 bits.

- **blowfish** A public domain protocol using symmetric key block cipher mechanisms.

- **AES (Advanced Encryption Standard)** A NIST Standard encryption accepted as the standard encryption for the US Government (FIPS 197).

As other standards become accepted by the industry at large they may be used with SSH.

During key exchanges a hashing algorithm is used to send secure key information from the two systems. The hashing algorithms currently supported in SSH in the SSH-TRANS packets are: *diffie-hellman-group1-sha1* and *diffie-hellman-group14-sha1*.

The diffie-hellman portion of the above algorithms are named for the two people who developed the algorithm: Whitfield Diffie and Martin Hellman. The group number 1 or 14 is the SSH accepted group space numbers and sha1 is the Secure Hashing Algorithm version 1. These two methods of key hashing are the current standards; legacy standards like MD5 (Message Digest v5) and MD4 (Message Digest v4) have been breached with increasing frequency and are not currently recommended.

Between the encryption standards and hashing algorithms we have an effective and secure way to send and receive data from client and server.

SSH vs. Telnet/Rlogin

Both rlogin and telnet were developed when the internet was still a private government network (ARPAnet) and was only used by government and university researchers in a closed environment. During those days security was not as much an issue as the number of users was controlled and personal computers had not become the standard. In the mainframe world, packet capture and accessing other people's data was not unheard of, but much less common.

Telnet was initially developed in the late 1960s to allow sessions to be established between a user on one mainframe to a different mainframe. Rlogin was introduced in BSD (Berkley Software Distribution) release 4.2 of their open source UNIX in 1983. Again, BSD was released at a time where ARPAnet was still the major network used by universities and research facilities and security was less of a critical issue.

In 1990 the ARPAnet was given to the National Science Foundation and became the NSFnet. While this network was still a privately controlled network, it was opened up to high tech development companies. The National Science Foundation established a backbone of T1s and added six supercomputers to facilitate the sharing of information. In 1995 the National Science Foundation sold off the backbone to private carriers (such as AT&T, UUNet, GTE, etc.) and the Internet as we know it today was established.

In December 1995, the Internet became a service of interconnected networks open to users across the world with approximately 16 million users connected. In 2008 there are approximately 1.4 billion users sharing this network space. We are doing more on this network, making more of our business and personal resources accessible across this ever-expanding global network of networks. As entire segments of businesses, government agencies, medical and financial institutions, and voice and data companies place more and more of our personal data on the Internet, our need for encryption and security grows as well. SSH is one of the tools developed to allow us to use the open network in a more secure and encrypted fashion.

In the late 1980s Gerald Combs, a University of Missouri Kansas City graduate, developed Ethereal (now called Wireshark™) out of the need to be able to capture network traffic to analyze traffic for diagnostic and troubleshooting reasons. This tool also gave people the ability to look at other people's data communications. This shareware utility is one of the most popular packet capture programs in use today.

NOTE

The change of the name from Ethereal to WireShark™ was due to trademark issues after Combs left the company.

With tools like WireShark™, formerly Ethereal, you can capture and display entire telnet and rlogin sessions (see Figure 4.7 below).

Figure 4.7 Capture of a Telnet Session with Ethereal™ Between a Telnet Client and a Cisco Router

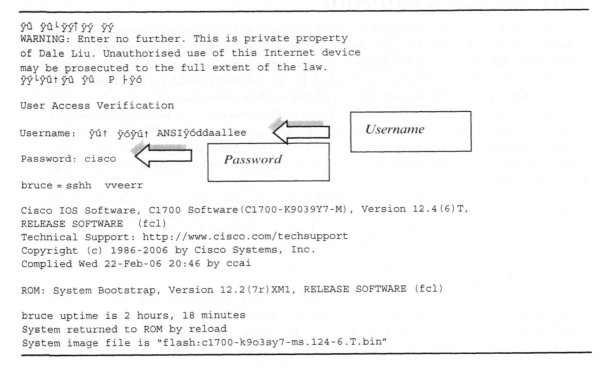

```
ÿû ÿûᴸÿÿ↑ÿÿ ÿý
WARNING: Enter no further. This is private property
of Dale Liu. Unauthorised use of this Internet device
may be prosecuted to the full extent of the law.
ÿýᴸÿûↄ ÿü ÿü  P ╞ÿó

User Access Verification

Username:  ÿû↑  ÿóÿû↑ ANSIÿóddaallee

Password: cisco

bruce = sshh  vveerr

Cisco IOS Software, C1700 Software(C1700-K9039Y7-M), Version 12.4(6)T,
RELEASE SOFTWARE  (fcl)
Technical Support: http://www.cisco.com/techsupport
Copyright (c) 1986-2006 by Cisco Systems, Inc.
Complied Wed 22-Feb-06 20:46 by ccai

ROM: System Bootstrap, Version 12.2(7r)XM1, RELEASE SOFTWARE (fcl)

bruce uptime is 2 hours, 18 minutes
System returned to ROM by reload
System image file is "flash:c1700-k9o3sy7-ms.124-6.T.bin"
```

Username

Password

As you can see above, the username *dale* and the password *Cisco* are clearly displayed in this capture. Any person who viewed this telnet session would then be able to take over this network router. As more and more people learn how to use these tools the need for encryption becomes more and more important. For example, books like *Wireshark & Ethereal Network Protocol Analyzer Toolkit*, published by Syngress, show how to use these tools and analyze traffic. SSH (Secure SHell) gives us that protection. In the SSH session all data is securely encrypted so people capturing the packets see only gibberish (see Figure 4.8).

Figure 4.8 Capture of SSH Session from PuTTY Client and a Cisco Router

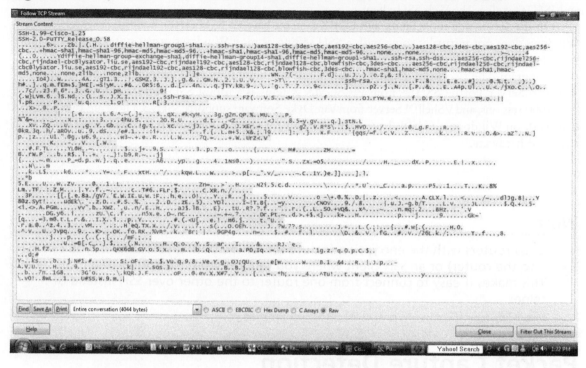

Here, the two captures reflect the strength of SSH versus the clear text weakness of telnet. In today's open and exposed networks, when sending data over unsecured networks it is imperative to use protocols that help protect our confidential data. The only things viewable in the SSH capture in clear text are the version numbers of the SSH client and the SSH Server.

SSH Client/Server Overview

While this book will focus primarily on PuTTY, there are a variety of SSH clients that can be used to establish SSH sessions. This chapter will spend a little time on a few of the SSH clients and servers available for different platforms.

On the client side there are applications that run on Windows, MAC OS, various flavors of Linux, and UNIX. Some clients are built into the operating systems, some are add-ons. The most popular add-on clients for Windows are PuTTY and Secure SSH (now known as Reflection for Secure IT).

On the MAC OS X side the following clients will run SSH as a client application: Browser Shell and ISH, as well as the Web SSH client.

On the server side most Linux and UNIX systems have an SSH server built in; however, Windows does not normally come with a SSH session as most Windows server systems don't support the Telnet command line connectivity. To use SSH on a Windows server you have to buy a third party program. The two most popular in the Windows community are FortressSSH™ Server and VShell™ Server. FortressSSH™, from PRAGMA systems, is a robust SSH service that will handle over 1000 sessions, and VShell™ Server from Van Dyke Software supports SSHv2. These are two packages that work on Windows and both have 64Bit versions for compatibility with today's sophisticated and advanced hardware.

NOTE

Cisco routers with the encryption feature set can be both an SSH server (you can SSH into the router) or an SSH client where you can SSH from the router to an SSH server. This makes it easy to connect from one router to the other over SSH instead of telnet.

Packet Capture Detection

This chapter has discussed the topic of packet capture and the need for encrypted sessions with SSH instead of telnet or rlogin. How can you tell if someone on your network is running a packet capture program on your network? There are two types of people that you need to focus on. First is the employee. The people on your network that have usernames and passwords have some rights on your network. These people have established connections and are on your network on a regular basis. The other is the "outside" person. This person, who is maybe giving a presentation to your company and has a laptop in the building that does not have permissions on your network, if this person gains wire level access to the network they can run packet capture programs as well.

In the first scenario, you need to make sure that users do not have the rights and permissions to install software. Using things like Group Policy in Windows and permissions in Linux and UNIX you can control how systems are utilized by your users. If users do find a way to bypass these restrictions you will still need to deploy a tool that will look for these programs.

In the second scenario you have to be a lot more vigilant; if your company has wired jacks or a wireless network established, any machine that connects to the network can automatically obtain a network address through protocols like DHCP (Dynamic Host Configuration Protocol) or BOOTP. These people now have "wire level" access to your network and can sweep the network looking for devices and then establish one of the three types of packet capture.

TIP

Choosing a Packet Capture Detection Program
When selecting a packet capture detection program make sure it can identify all three types of packet capture techniques: IP-based sniffing, MAC-based sniffing, and ARP-based sniffing.

The three methods of packet capture are IP (Internet Protocol address)-based sniffing, MAC (Media Access Control address)-based sniffing and ARP (Address Resolution Protocol)-based sniffing.

In IP-based sniffing the network adapter is put into a special mode called promiscuous mode. Once in promiscuous mode the network adapter accepts all network traffic that it receives even if the traffic is not to that destination. Network switches help make this type of sniffing more difficult. In IP-based, promiscuous sniffing the adapter and the capture program just gather every packet that comes from the network cable, and the network switch learns all of the MAC addresses that are on each port and only forwards frames to the port that the appropriate MAC address is located on. This reduces the amount of traffic that goes out to each port.

In MAC-based sniffing the network card is again placed in promiscuous mode and traffic is captured based on a MAC address filter. Switches do help minimize this as well but even in a switch-based network there are tools like dsniff created by Dug Song that will capture over a switched network.

The third method of sniffing, ARP-based sniffing, does not put the card into promiscuous mode. It uses the fact that all ARP packets are sent using the universal broadcast address of 255.255.255.255, and it must go to every device on every port of each switch. This means that every device receives every ARP packet and can then poison the ARP table to send all traffic to a specific gateway (not the true gateway) and this device will capture each packet and then forward to the appropriate gateway. This is very effective on a switched network as all traffic at layer 2 of the OSI network model, Data Link Layer, is broken into Frames for flow control and error correction. Switches operate at this layer and all Frames passed through the switch use the MAC address to determine where to forward the traffic. So if someone poisons the ARP table to say that the IP address associated with the MAC address of the destination is changed to the attacker's MAC, then the traffic will go to the attacker first and then either be cleanly captured and forwarded or captured then modified and forwarded. The initiating host would not be aware of this diversion of traffic.

The answer to the question of how to prevent that is to find tools that will monitor for the use of packet capture programs. There are many programs that can detect the use of promiscuous mode enabled network adapters. But to really identify network sniffing programs you need to be able to monitor for all three types. In the 2003 SANS/FBI top 20 tools for network security they recommended a tool called PromiScan. This tool was developed and made available by a company called Security Friday Ltd. Co, and the Web site is www.securityfriday.com. Tools like this scan the network for devices attempting to capture network traffic. Monitoring your network is one step in preventing capture programs. The other is to layer your network defenses. SSH is a good protocol for keeping terminal sessions secure; however, if something can be attacked by a man–in–the–middle attack you may need a second layer of encryption to eliminate these risks. A firewall can be deployed on the LAN between the users and the secured server.

This firewall could be used to establish VPN access to the segment that contains the secure sever, then after the VPN is established, a SSH terminal session could be established. This would give you two layers of encryption as well as preventing a man-in-the-middle attack as you have established a point-to-point encrypted connection first with the VPN access device, then the firewall, so no traffic is routed to the man-in-the-middle attacker.

The flat switched network is the most common type of network. Every device on the network can see, at wire level, every other device on the network. Even if the device is not authenticated to the domain it can still run tools like nmap™ and superscan™; these tools will do ping sweeps and port scans and discover each device on the flat network.

To better protect the network you can deploy physical firewalls between the flat network and sensitive resources in what is becoming known as a "Zoned Trust" network. In this layout each sensitive device is protected by a firewall, so when an internal computer or outside user attempts to run a ping sweep the firewall will block it from seeing the server. When a user needs to access the secure server it must first make the VPN connection to the firewall and then they can establish the second secure connection with SSH. The firewall can then log the VPN connections and can also notify the Systems Administrator of any attempts to do the ping sweep and port scan.

Summary

We have seen that SSH is a good alternative to telnet and rlogin. SSH is a valuable tool for remote terminal sessions. However, SSH is not a replacement for other encryption tools. Digital signatures are still the best method for secure e-mail, and VPNs (Virtual Private Networks) are still the best method for remote connectivity over insecure Internet connections to remote office networks.

SSH, as we have shown above, has many features that help ensure secure connectivity and robust encryption standards; however, be mindful that the first packets sent to establish the key exchange are still clear text and are susceptible to capture. Also be mindful that there are man-in-the-middle attacks possibilities—if you are not sure of the server don't connect!

Tools like WireShark™ and Sniffer™ are still able to capture the packets; in an SSH session the data will be encrypted using one of the many encryption protocols that are in the accepted standards list, but still, anything that can be encrypted can at some point be decrypted. If you are in a high security environment you may wish to establish layers of security by placing a firewall before the SSH server and establishing a VPN connection first then a SSH session thus combining two levels of encryption of the data.

While PuTTY is the most common third party SSH Client, it is by no means the only one. For every platform available there are many clients, each with their benefits and draw backs. Consider your needs and requirements before selecting one client over another.

If you are using a Windows server, note that there is no SSH server native to the OS, you will need a third party application to use SSH with Windows. In this chapter we mentioned two available products that can resolve this problem.

Remember there are some network devices, like Cisco routers, that can be an SSH client and an SSH server. This makes administration of the WAN (Wide Area Network) easier as you can establish an SSH session from your desktop client into the Cisco router and from there SSH from router to router to manage other devices, using only the one SSH session from the desktop. The figure below illustrates Putty being used to log onto a Cisco™ Voice Router then the SSH command line being executed to connect to another Cisco™ Router called instructor. This ability to SSH from device to device enables us to configure devices throughout the WAN (Wide Area Network), when our desktop may not be able to directly see them on the IP Protocol. Please see Figure 4.9.

Figure 4.9 SSH from One Cisco™ Device to Another Cisco™ Device

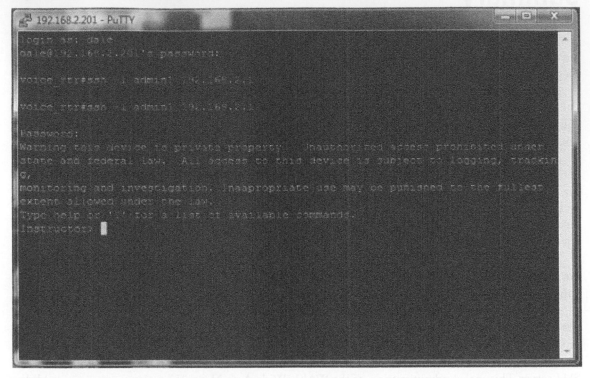

Solutions Fast Track

Introduction to SSH

- ☑ SSH is an IETF standard protocol that uses TCP port 22.

- ☑ It sends industry recognized encrypted traffic from a client to a server.

- ☑ It is an encrypted telnet session for terminal emulation.

SSH Standards

- ☑ There are three major protocols used with SSH: they are SSH-TRANS, SSH-USERAUTH, and SSH-CONNECT. These are TCP Protocols.

- ☑ The initial transmissions may be clear text to allow for key exchange if no central Certificate Authority is available.

- ☑ Messages are grouped by message number.

SSH vs. Telnet/Rlogin

- ☑ Telnet is a clear text protocol for terminal emulation that uses TCP port 23.

- ☑ Rlogin is a clear text protocol for terminal emulation that uses TCP 513.

- ☑ SSH is an encrypted terminal session that uses TCP 22.

- ☑ Packet capture programs can display usernames and passwords of clear text terminal emulation sessions like telnet and rlogin but cannot easily display SSH information, due to encryption.

SSH Client/Server Overview

- ☑ Most UNIX/Linux devices have SSH Servers and Clients native.

- ☑ Windows does not have a native SSH Client.

- ☑ Windows does not have a native SSH Server.

- ☑ PuTTY is the most common SSH client for Windows.

- ☑ Some devices like Cisco Routers can be both SSH clients and servers at the same time.

- ☑ Third party SSH servers are available for Windows.

Packet Capture Detection

- ☑ There are three types of packet capture: IP-based sniffing, MAC-based sniffing, and ARP-based sniffing.

- ☑ Multiple layers of security and encryption, including internal firewalls, can help to reduce the vulnerability of packet capture.

- ☑ Internal firewalls, known as "zoned trust" networking, provides not only extra security through encryption, it also gives you better accountability.

- ☑ Packet capture detection programs need to be able to detect all three types of packet capture methods.

Frequently Asked Questions

Q: What are the most popular packet capture programs?

A: WireShark™, Sniffer, and dsnif

Q: What port is used for SSH?

A: TCP Port 22

Q: What port is used for rlogin?

A: TCP Port 513

Q: What port is used for telnet?

A: The telnet protocol runs on TCP port 23.

Q: What is the difference between telnet the protocol and telnet the application?

A: Telnet the protocol is a terminal session protocol for connecting to remote systems. Telnet the application will let you connect to many different remote services that are clear text, including SMTP, HTTP, POP3, etc. In a Windows-based system from the command line you could type telnet mail.domain.com 25 to attach to that mail server on the SMTP protocol port.

Q: Why is SSH a more preferred protocol than telnet?

A: Telnet sends all data in clear text and can be viewed using commonly available shareware packet capture programs. SSH only sends, in some instances, the initial packets in clear text. Everything else sent by SSH is encrypted using industry standard protocols like 3DES, AES, etc.

Q: Is one client for SSH better than the others?

A: While PuTTY is the most common client in use today, all clients have their strong points and weak points. The benefit of PuTTY is that there is both a GUI (Graphical User Interface) based startup and command line options (see chapter 11) that give it some ability to be used in different ways. Some clients are either all GUI or all command line interface.

## Chapter 5

SSH Shortcomings

Solutions in this chapter:

- Attacking SSL: Hacking the User

- Recognizing an SE Attack

- Responding to an SE Event

- Defending Against Social Engineering Attacks

- Social Engineering Scenarios for Awareness Training

☑ Summary

☑ Solutions Fast Track

☑ Frequently Asked Questions

Introduction

SSL has become the de facto standard for security transactions on the Internet. History proves it's a secure protocol and continued development provides real security improvements. Unfortunately, this protocol has provided a false sense of safety for the security and financial fields. SSL protocol can be breached based on the shortcomings of the user. This chapter will provide you with the information to protect SSL from compromise and help you develop a security strategy for handling one of the few proven methods of successfully attacking SSL.

Attacking SSL: Hacking the User

One of the few ways you can breach SSL is by using social engineering (SE). Many people will argue that SSL can't be compromised. They are correct that the socket layer is secure but nothing exists by itself in the computer world. While the tunnel may be safe, both ends are open and that's where the problem exits. Securing the users from the users is priority number one if you want the protocol to be safe.

SSL is compromised by utilizing social engineering on the end users. These types of attacks are not protected against or recorded by many IT companies. Also lacking is the belief that SE works on their users and the belief that SSL is a safe system for exchanging information.

Concepts of Attacking the User with Social Engineering

The SE attack has 3 aspects: the *Physical attack*, the *Psychological attack,* and the *Request.*

Physical attack refers to how the attacker contacts the victim. Does the attacker call, write, e-mail, or contact the victim in-person, at a workplace, or in a non-work situation? This is the delivery method for the request.

Psychological attack refers to the feelings and emotions used during the attack. Is the attacker yelling, crying, or offering to give them something "free"?

Request is what the attacker wants. This is more than just passwords or placing key loggers. Companies have been socially engineered out of keys for offices and trucks, company credit cards, and trade secrets, so please be aware of the larger area the request can cover.

Getting the Request to the Target: Physical Attack

Two common physical attack vectors in social engineering are *Human based* and *Technology based.* Both have been used successfully for many years. The newer blended attack where technology and in-person are both used against a company has become a major threat to most organizations. Sadly, most organizations, while they can successfully deploy SSL, they fail to adequately protect the end point. Compromise the user and you've compromised SSL.

Attacking with Technology

Using technology to deliver the request is expanding rapidly. Think of how much we use technology now and this threat vector becomes massive. Cell phones, IM, e-mails, and cross site scripted Web sites are all ways of attacking the user with technology.

Sending e-mail with a key logger as the request is using technology to deliver another technology attack. The victims never see the person who has compromised them. Using technology allows more victims to be reached in a shorter amount of time, giving attacks a higher chance of success. Yes, some people still believe they are the 10,000th visitor to the Web site or they just won the British lottery without even buying a ticket. These are the people who will compromise your SSL.

Cross site scripting (XSS) attacks now allow redirection of the victim to another site where they are infected with Trojans and loggers. XSS continues to be a major problem with no end in sight.

An attacker may impersonate an important end user on the phone and bully company personnel to reveal information. The intimidation phone attack is a common social engineering attack today. The older tech support call where the attacker acts as a tech support person is not as effective as it used to be.

Instant Messages (IM) offering to show pictures of a nude star or a star's new baby are already in use. Once these sites are visited Trojans or loggers are loaded.

As technology advances you will see more attacks where the attacker never meets the victim. These technology-driven mass attacks can already be seen in our current security threat matrix. When you evaluate technology please evaluate how it might be used for social engineering attacks.

Attacking in person

In person social engineering attacks are the stuff of legends. Attackers dressed as service professionals have removed servers, stolen workstations, and even stolen backup tapes while pretending to be tech support. In person attacks take the most ability but can yield the greatest results.

Dumpster diving is listed by many as a social engineering attack, but to me it is more physical security, as a social engineering attack requires someone to engineer. This smelly method of attack yields interesting results. Old credit card forms, all the internal forms and memos and posted notes, all contain valuable information helping the social engineering attacks. Organizational structure, staff names, and departmental names are available to the dumpster diver.

WARNING

While dumpster diving usually gives great results it does have its dangers. You'll need several items to keep this a polite process. Always take along extra clothes to wear just for this as sometimes dumpsters have real garbage in them. Take several pairs of latex gloves and leather work gloves. I usually wear the latex gloves as liners to the work gloves because icky stuff soaks through the work gloves but not the latex liner. A long stick with a hook of some type always helps and keeps you from having to reach so far in the dumpster. New dumpsters are tall so take some form of step stool to get in and out easily. I like to dive mid evening when it's quiet. Lastly, always call to see what the cafeteria has for lunch because it may end up in the dumpster you're diving in. Never dive when spaghetti is on the menu.

Shoulder surfing is the lowest tech attack but does supply login credentials and pin numbers. The attacker stands behind the victim and looks over their shoulder to see their pin number or password. This type of attack works great with administrators who log on to computers locally. The attacker is usually an insider as most employee screens are faced away from public view (We hope). Watch people at the ATM machine: some use their bodies to shield the keypad while they punch in their PINs, while other don't really care who is watching.

The human based attack has great advantages over computer based in that the attacker has the ability to adjust the attack based on real-time feedback. Monitoring the victim for physical signs of stress allows the attacker to have full control of the situation and the victim.

Blending attacks

The accuracy and success rate of SE attacks have increased with the use of blended attacks. The victim gets a phone call, an e-mail, a written letter, and a personal visit just to deliver the request. This complex undertaking is a sign of a highly organized attack and the business is targeted by a specific person or group.

Attacking the Psyche

The psychology attack refers to the emotions used during the attack. Several standard methods exist for the psychological attack.

Aggression We all know this one; it's the typical yelling boss attack. The victim is threatened with their job, the destruction of their business and loss of everything they hold dear.

Depression "I'll lose my job if I don't _____" works well on many working people who don't want to be responsible for this poor person looking their job.

Confusion Fast requests, rapid in nature, or facts that make sense but the request doesn't follow. Lots of stress induced in the victim. Used commonly with aggression.

Misdirection Ask for one thing then change the request to more sensitive information.

Ingratiation Doing something nice for others helps people feel they should do something nice for you.

Ignorance Asking for help with forms or simple items. The questions or help needed then escalates to the desired request or the small separate bits of information can be combined into a complete SE attack.

Friendliness Few people are friendly to low level office people, making them the perfect target for this attack. Politeness and smiles over a period of time do make a successful attack.

The first question to ask when performing forensics analysis on the psychological attack is "What technique did they use in making themselves so powerful that staff gives them the requested information?" The ability of the attacker to control the situation is the key to the psychology attack and the key to breaking the psychological attack.

WARNING

Social Engineering is not "snake oil" or just pathological lying. It took great strides with the development of Neuro-Linguistic Programming. Researchers studied successful therapists and taught others the methods. Attackers are now using NLP techniques in e-mails, Web sites, and in-person attacks. Lots of information on this topic is available, so just search NLP. Here are some of my favorite sites for NLP:

- **www.saladltd.co.uk/** Be sure and check out the Tips archive.
- **www.nlpinfo.com/** Downloads, exercises, and articles.
- http://en.wikipedia.org/wiki/Neurolinguistic_programming Good for basic understanding.

Giving Away the Farm

The Request is what you want from the victim. Most people incorrectly assume it's only computer related items that are the desired result (such as passwords, PINs, e-mail addresses, etc.). The first request might be for some small item but the request can escalate to more forbidden information. This technique is used by politicians when placing yard signs. If they ask you to put a large sign in your yard, most say no. If they ask about a small sign most would say yes. Once you say yes, the politician returns and ask for a little bigger sign. In the end, you have a huge sign in your yard.

Methods of Attacking

Every year we see more ways of attacking the end user. Here are the current forms of attack that have proved successful in compromising SSL.

E-mail

E-mail has become ubiquitous. With more people receiving e-mail there are more chances of compromising SSL. More e-mail with tax rebates information, disaster relief giving, an award, or unbelievable free stuff arrives daily. While these may seem more like a bother than an attack, all these e-mails can lead to compromising SSL.

Phishing

Phishing is one of the most useful techniques for delivery of Trojans and key loggers when breaking SSL. Standard phishing techniques attempt to acquire sensitive information from the user by having them respond to a message, visit a Web site, or download a Trojan or key logger to the victims' machine.

Spear Phishing

Targeting one particular person or business is spear phishing. When you blast an entire company with loggers and Trojans, somebody is going to take the bait. E-mail addresses for all employees can easily be found with programs such as *goog-mail.py* which searches Google for any mail address with the specified domain name. Tracking your SE attacks will give you the information needed to assess if you're a Spear Phising target.

Site Redirection

The user enters a Web site that is not the original intended site. It has all the graphics linked to the real site so any change in the real site is reflected to the fake site. This "chroming" of the fake site with the real site's information improves the belief that this is indeed a correct site. Once a victim visits the site they "logon" to the system where their information is captured or it simply downloads a key logger onto the victim's machine. This logger then gathers information needed to compromise the SSL.

Key Loggers

Another method of social engineering that we can use to break SSL is by using key loggers. While key loggers are not in themselves a SE attack, it's the SE attack that gets the logger to the victims. These loggers come in several forms and are easy to use. That's why they have become very popular hardware or software. The loggers record all the keystrokes anyone types on the computer. This gives the person who placed the logger all the information needed to compromise SSL.

Software key loggers are gaining in popularity. These key loggers can be added in several ways that make them a greater threat than the hardware type. They can be put on by an outside consultant, via e-mail, or through spyware or XSS. I am seeing more and more software key loggers appearing on business machines. Many of these can be tracked directly back to e-mails that should not have been opened but were.

Hardware

Hardware loggers have been around awhile, and they are easily placed on the keyboard cable. Being the same color, size and shape of the end of the keyboard makes detection difficult. The social engineering attack is to convince the person to leave the room for a minute making it possible to install the logger. Many computers will accept the keyboard being unplugged and plugged back in without giving an error message.

At a future date the person who placed the logger goes back and retrieves it and the data. This can allow several accounts to be compromised.

Trojans

With the entrance of organized crime into the hacker realm we have seen a growth of Trojans that target banking and SSL. These Trojans can be delivered via multiple attack vectors giving them access to more victims.

Trojan-Phisher-Rebery was designed to attack the banking industry. It was uncovered by Webroot Inc. and was active in 125 countries. This Trojan took it all: username, Social Security numbers, passwords, phone numbers, and log-ins. The interesting feature about it is that it only "wakes" when an online financial site is visited.

A newer banking Trojan is *Silentbanker*. Discovered in early 2008 it is a wonder to watch work. Its ability to bypass two factor authentication by inserting itself into the traffic before it's encrypted makes it a sophisticated threat. This early insertion allows it to authenticate certificates and cookies and offer a username and password when asked. Because it enters before SSL protocol starts, it completely compromises SSL, making this protocol now totally worthless.

Once inserted it can change the transaction destination without the user's knowledge, letting money be sent to a totally different account. To keep track of the financial sites it downloads a database of 400 different institutions to monitor for connections.

An even more dangerous threat this Trojan presents is its ability to ask for missing information. If the attacker has incomplete data on you, it can modify the Trojan to present a field requesting the missing data. This is done on an HTML authorization page so most users have no idea they have been compromised.

NOTE

Try Social Engineering for yourself! Listen to people when they speak, I mean really listen. Everybody speaks at a different rate (fast or slow), everybody uses specific words (couch, divan, davenport, sofa, or settee) and everybody has a dominant sense: "He never *hears* me" or "She never *sees* my side." Men tend to be visual while women are often aural.

Try to adapt your natural style to others in the group, become the fast visual or the slow aural speaker. Listen and decide what sense people you like are and what people you don't like are. You may not like someone because they are exactly opposite of you. Notice your family. What are you?

Recognizing an SE Attack

One of the most difficult things for staff to recognize is when they are under a social engineering attack. Even harder is for the IT staff to believe that SE is a real threat to their security. Most security professionals can list information about SE, but no real action to track or contain this type of attack.

How Do You Know if You're Under an SE Attack?

Several common signs of attack are:

- **Name dropping** This is common to put the victim under threat of losing their job.

- **Intimidation** This is one of the most common types of SE attacks; yelling and threatening the victim has been successful for many years.

- **Pretexting** Pretending to be someone else is also common and frequently used to spy on the HP Board.

- **Rushing the conversation** Attackers rush the conversation in hopes of flustering the victim into giving them the requested information.

- **Small mistakes (spelling, grammar, name pronunciation)** Many attackers don't know the inner workings of the organization, how names are pronounced, or nicknames for staff.

- **Odd questions** Questions that any employee should know or not in line with the original request.

- **Requesting forbidden information** Social Security numbers, passwords, anything not usually given out.

- **"Doesn't feel right"** Victims sometimes get the feeling they're being "played," especially after SE training.

- **Refusal to give name or call back number** Most people want to be contacted in important matters.

- **Overly nice** You always catch more with sugar than vinegar.

The collection of attack information is often overlooked by corporate security. These types of events can be done over several weeks or months from various physical attack media. Without a centralized logging system of SE attacks, the attack would be completely missed.

SE Tripwires

An inexpensive method of increasing security related to SE is to have question or codes for staff who call in. Many help desks give you their number and ask employees for some form of identification. When a caller asks for a vacation person, respond with a misdirected question. Ask new employees some common question that insiders would know but is not generally known outside the organization, such as "What about that new color in the cafeteria?" which hasn't been painted in 20 years.

These tripwires act as an early warning system to alert front line staff of a possible SE attack. Training on these can be included in the front line outfacing border staff event.

Are You Owned?

Attacking SSL from the Inside

This is one of the oldest attacks to a network. It started with floppies and now uses 8 GB USB drives. Get a nice USB drive and load it with software that automatically starts when the drive is plugged in (search pod slurping). Add NetCat to start when the device boots, and you'll be able to track it to the exact machine. Now throw the drive down in the staff parking lot. We do several locations just to ensure a great hit rate. It usually takes about half a day but we find that someone will eventually pick up the drive and plug it into their work computer. Success! You now own their network!

Responding to an SE Event

Response to any security event should be in an organized way with written policies and procedures driving the process. Trained front line staff who can sound the alarm when an event happens and a timely, correct response by IT staff is of critical importance. Without the front line staff's awareness that they are under a social engineering attack, the tracking and response never starts.

Having Front Line Staff Respond

When front line staff is under attack they are purposefully confused or disoriented. To stop this type of attack, the victim must remove themselves from the attacker. Yes, this does sound like some old horror film where you must flee the villain but it is true today in defending against an SE attack. Please treat all staff who report an attack with seriousness and professionalism. If you make fun of this, the front line staff will stop reporting and you lose to the attacker.

One phone technique is to have front line staff place any person who is suspected of SE on hold while they "get the data." This breaks the direct contact with the attacker stopping the influence of intimidation, confusion, and misdirection. During this break the staff should be able to inform IT about the current attack. Resuming the call with excuses for lack of data provides time for the security staff to analyze the physical aspects of the attack.

If the attack is in person, have the staff call for someone to assist them in person, the quicker the better. Never leave the workstation unattended while help is sought. This could be the request of the entire attack, to get the front line staff to leave their desk. Always consider that not everyone comes in the front door so make sure you have proper physical security and assistance at all doors. This is just good access control.

Staff needs to know how they can report a SE event currently in progress and how they should document the event. The best method is to send an alert during the call so IT staff can monitor the event in real-time. Time is important here as the attacker might become suspicious and break off the attack. Worst case is the attacker now targets a staff member for SE attack.

Being able to say no to requests and not worrying about job repercussions is important in preventing SE attacks. Staff should feel like the organization's policies and procedures back them up when dealing with aggressive, abusive, or inquisitive people. They should know the IT department and Human Resources supports them in reporting this type of event and good will and rewards could come from this process.

IT Responses

Every organization should have a designated Incident Response Team. These are called by many names and all that's important is that they know what they're doing. This concept is similar to a Code or Trauma Team that responds to medical emergencies. The team has trained responding to different types of security breaches and understands what the current policies and procedures specify for a response.

When a front line staff member notifies IT that a possible SE attack is taking place the organization's policies and procedures for handling this type of event should kick in. The IT staff should record in the security database the pertinent information, including the following:

- **Date, Time** When did the event take place? Note the shift if it's a shift work schedule.
- **Media** Phone, email, walk in, package, postage?
- **Who reported** Name of the person who was the victim?
- **Department** Where does the victim work?
- **Request** Password, phone number, e-mail, access to server room, company car keys?

- **Information Given** Okay, everybody leaks some information before they notice it's an attack. Encourage front line staff to note what they said before they got suspicious.

- **Caller ID/E-mail address** What technology-based information do you have on the attacker?

- **Resolution** How was the problem solved? Caller hung up, e-mail not responded to, attacker left building.

Not sure how much information your phone system can give you on the caller? Check with your phone system provider and they'll tell you what capabilities you have for tracking calls to the point of origin. These vary by system and provider. While descriptions and recordings of the caller's voice can be done, software that hides gender and location is plentiful and inexpensive.

E-mails that contain Trojans or loggers should be viewed by IT staff and verified they were not loaded. Constant updating of the AV software should keep this vector to a minimum. Spam will be increasing in the future so working to decrease this will help decrease phishing attacks.

All of this makes no sense if you don't have a Unified Security Database that is updated and reviewed. Most companies can tell me how many port scans they had last month, or how many spam e-mails with attachments were stopped, but few can tell me how many requests for passwords were granted or what information front line staff is not allowed to give out.

IT staff and security personnel should meet regularly and discuss all threat surfaces. Trends in threats should be noted and marked for enhanced protection. Any interesting items, such as Bob losing his password three times last week, should be considered for closer examination. Resolutions of recent threats should be analyzed for effectiveness and timeliness.

Try this in your organization. Ask front line people what information they shouldn't give out. Use any official list of protected information and you'll be surprised how much they do give away.

TIP

When you start protecting your business from SE attacks, some of your staff will just want to buy more firewalls. As a group, IT is not known for its mastery of the social ways. We usually work in basements with others who would rather work with things than directly with customers. Don't let your staff dissuade front line staff from reporting SE events. Remember that SE is the best way to crack SSL. You can go to the bank on that!

Management Response

Senior management has a part in the response process also. Without their agreement and sanctions no security program could exist. Management helps decide policy and procedure, where money for protection is spent, how often training occurs, who gets trained, and even if you have security personnel or not. Management makes the security world go round.

Management needs to be aware of the threat of SE attack and that SSL is vulnerable to attack. I have unfortunately found that reminding them they may go to jail if they fail to have security only makes them mad, making your contract null and void. What does work is to give brief reports to upper management on trends and totals. This keeps security at the top of their mind, helping you move your needed projects ahead.

Legal Response

This is a large variable subject for SE attacks. Someone trying to get a password usually won't get reported. Someone getting the password and stealing protected customer information would be reported. Which laws are you affected by? FISMA? HIPAA? SoX? The surprise is that most organizations fall under several Federal guidelines, not just one.

These items should all be addressed by your legal staff and management (hopefully) before you have an incident. Not just SE events, but all forms of breaches should be considered when addressing who should be notified and when. During active security breaches these can change as the event moves forward.

The matter of due diligence and due care enters the conversation here so you should be aware of them while you're planning. Finding where your risk lies through proper risk assessment is due diligence. Now that the problems are found, you need to actively fix them (due care). Not knowing about a problem or not fixing problems you know you have are both bad security practices and bad legal maneuvering.

Defending Against Social Engineering Attacks

The "*defense in depth*" approach should be taken similar to the defense in depth used to protect networks. Training staff in awareness of SE attacks and policy and procedures is the first line of defense. You make staff aware that your organization takes security serious and you have the legal means to punish those who cause security breaches. While many organizations currently have ample policy and procedures many do not cover social engineering. Most also have training but few cover this growing threat.

Technology-driven defenses also exist and should be considered when evaluating controls for SE attacks. These are now used in the financial and housing software market.

What's Currently Working?

Businesses are now becoming aware of the SE attack and are spending money defending against them. Let's look at current methods and see how they apply directly to your business and how they help protect SSL.

Fraud detection tools These help financial institutions become aware of social engineering threats. The software packages monitor a number of parameters, for example, where you spend your money, how much you normally spend, or credit cards having multiple entries simultaneously. I'm sure many of you've been on vacations when someone from the credit card industry calls and asks if you were out of the country. This fraud detection software is becoming more accurate as development goes on.

Screening high risk payments These payments are from people who have other outstanding payments. Most software now prints out these customers for tracing and decision making. This type of control is also common in the multi-family management software and as a fee for service.

Customer Awareness and Education The most powerful, cost-effective, and useful tool for defeating SSL and social engineering is making the victim aware of the behaviors that can make them a victim. Simply breaking the connection to the attacker is all that's needed.

- Education can take the shape of an awareness campaign that makes customers aware that your organization takes security seriously. A great marketing point nowadays is to show how proactive your business is.

- Financial institutions are doing a good job of educating users of personal computers about security. These awareness campaigns can be seen on television, flyers, brochures, posters in banks, and even the tellers make you aware of this.

- Several facilities offer their end users a discount or free anti-virus software to reduce the chances of them logging on with an infected computer. This is a growing trend because taking care of your customers reduces your attack surface from customers.

Staff Awareness and Education Your staff has two different groups who need awareness and training. Most will get the standard security training with extra emphasis on the SE threat, policy and procedures, and methods of response. The second group includes the staff who deal mainly with the public. Think of this as your border routers and perimeter security. Both should be hardened to reduce the likelihood of a successful attack.

- When you're hardening your personnel against social engineering attacks, awareness and training sessions should include anyone who regularly answers the outside phone line or who regularly meets the public.

- All employees should be aware of the policies and procedures on social engineering attacks, especially what data cannot be given out and how to notify IT of an SE event. Practice sessions for all employees should include role playing of various SE attacks. At least one demonstration of an aggressive confrontation needs to be shown, helping people understand how to handle this attack. Nobody likes to be yelled at and this role playing helps them to just say "no."

- Awareness sessions should include the signs of SE attack and role playing of common situations. Without this awareness many staff will offer up the information asked for by the intruder and the businesses totally misses the fact it has just been compromised.

WARNING

Out of office messages can attract an attack! This signifies that it's not business as usual. Call up the vacation person and demand information from whoever answers. "Bob promised to send that before he left! What type of company are you! Send it now!" You'll be surprised that this actually works. If you do use Out of Office messages, please make sure you can't be tracked to your home address. It's like telling the entire Internet you won't be at home so stop by for a free gift!

■ Practice sessions for the external facing people and new employees should be held regularly and the importance of the data they are releasing should be made clear.

Are You Owned?

H@x Me!

Ok, try to social engineer your own business. Go ahead, it's part of your job. Pretend you're new and lost your password; see how much information you can get. Try both intimidation and friendliness on different staff. Consider this your SE perimeter control verification test and document it, good or bad.

Covering More in Awareness

All the firewalls in the world and all the certificates are not going to keep attackers out if your staff has just given them permission to enter your network. By using a key logger the attacker gains access into the network and also gains password which help the attacker move through the network. Here are more areas that you can incorporate into your awareness and training sessions.

Actually Looking at the Browser Training

Most people never look at their browser except to type in an address. Browser awareness is a new awareness area so users can prevent problems based on browser information. Most browsers have an alert that changes color based on authenticity and the issuing of the certificate. From making sure SSL is engaged when buying or donating online to proper verification of certificates, the new browser are helping with security awareness.

Two Factor Methods

Expanded validation by using two factor authentication can protect SSL from SE attacks and cause only minor pain to end users. Two factors of identification are becoming more popular with businesses because they do provide better authentication. I hate passwords and would rather use biometrics and tokens to validate to the network. When a surgeon who just finished performing a bilateral-salpingo- oophorectomy tells me they can't remember a seven-letter word of their choice, I know we have a problem. Think how you might use alternate factors to verify.

Using a key logger to capture your passwords is easy; it's hard to capture something you have unless it's physically taken from you. An important question to ask when assessing your validation is: can all the information needed to break your SSL be captured from a key logger?

Policy and Procedures for SE Attack

Every institution should develop a policy on what information is allowed to be given out and the policy should state that people who are asking for more information need to be referred to a manager or be put on a callback list. I especially see the problem of social engineering in the medical field because many hospital employees are trained to help. They are in the helping field.

The policies and procedures designed for social engineering should be specific enough to be understood and general enough to be enforceable. This is a fine line and should be approached together with staff, management, and legal counsel.

Please check your policies and procedures and verify that you can answer the following questions in Table 5.1.

Table 5.1 Areas to address in Policies and Procedures R/T Social Engineering

Access controls	What types of access control mechanisms are currently in place?
	Who is responsible to monitor these activities?
	How is remote access handled?
	Is call-back in place?
Access control Physical	Is hardware monitored and signed for as it leaves the building?
	Who audits off site equipment?
	How is this done?
	Who is responsible?
Setting up accounts	Who does the actual job of creating the accounts?
	Do they give out passwords to end users?
Access approval	What process do you have for the approval of new employees?

Continued

Table 5.1 Continued. Areas to address in Policies and Procedures R/T Social Engineering

Access modification	How and why is access changed for users?
	How is this carried out?
	Who is responsible for this?
Password changes	How often and how many letters / numbers?
	How are passwords distributed?
	Who can change passwords?
	Who can employees get help with on passwords?
	How is the policy enforced?
IDs	Are IDs required for everybody?
	Who checks IDs?
	How is a lost ID replaced?
	What procedures do you have to remove access from the lost ID?
	Are IDs legible from a distance?
	Do they contain employees' full name and department?
Shredding	Are these cross cut?
	Can you re-assemble the document?
	Does your commercial shredder have a NDA?
	Have you watched your commercial shredding service for violations?
Data classification	Employee should be able to identify confidential information before they give it out.
	Do you have a specific list of things never to discuss on the phone?
Record keeping	Are attempted SE attacks reported to the appropriate person?
	Do you have a running total of attacks and how they were targeted?
Analyzing SE attack	Does staff know when they are under SE attack?
	How does staff report and to whom is it reported?
	Are SE attacks analyzed for patterns?
SE Breach	How do you know you've been breached by SE?
	What procedures do you have for an Incident Response Team for SE?

As you can see your policy and procedures need to address many areas. Without adequate policy and procedures you have no way of punishing those who break the rules.

Social Engineering Scenarios for Awareness Training

During your security awareness sessions, those people who are facing toward the public should be thoroughly trained on how to deal with a social engineering attack

I'll Have You Fired!

This is one of the classics of social engineering someone out of information. I'm always amazed this still works. To roleplay, select two people: one for the caller and the other for the receptionist. Please be careful when selecting the people as sensitive people can become depressed when a co-worker yells at them. Best approach is to pick someone who doesn't look like a yeller to be the yeller. Note this scenario does get loud!

Caller: Where is Bob the CEO, he owes us now!

Staff: Sorry Mr. Green is away, how may I help you?

Caller: Send the %*&## designs now or we'll pull all the financing. This was supposed to be done before he left! What's wrong with your company?! Fax them now to this number! What's your name? The board will hear about this!

This tempering by fire of the staff is something people remember. Staff will laugh during this session but they do get the message. This scenario should be done with staff and executives.

The best execution of this I have ever seen was done by a diminutive female as the caller and a massive male for the staff. She brow beat him beyond belief and smiled the whole time. Co-workers report she was more authoritative after this session.

You're So Wonderful!

The old adage that you catch more with sugar than vinegar is very true when trying to get information from staff members. Most staff feels underpaid, underappreciated, and over worked. This attack is popular with younger attackers who can't really appear or sound dominant.

This scenario is from an actual event at the ABN Amro Bank in Antwerp. A "business man" frequented the bank to make deposits to his safe deposit box. He was a regular and treated all the staff well, even bringing the staff chocolates. While visiting his deposit box he was robbing the other boxes which belonged to diamond merchants. Total stolen: 120,000 carats of diamonds. This attack worked very well and the only weapon was charm.

Pick two people, better if they are friends.

Caller: Hi Friend, I'm stuck, can you leave your company car keys at the desk for me? I'll be careful!

Staff: Well, it's against policy

Caller: Hey, it's okay, we're friends!

Ask the participants how easy it would be for someone they know to "borrow" something for a few hours. Help them realize that the resources are for company usage and that your policies and procedures reflect that.

We'd Like to Check Your Connections

"Hi, I'm with the phone company and we're testing your lines for the next few hours so don't pick up the phone if it rings because the lineman will get electrocuted. Thank you now!" Now ring the phone non-stop for three hours!

This high school prank is profitable if you add this twist: ask the staff to provide passwords so that the service person from phone/network/electrical can check the line.

Caller: Hi, I'm the phone guy and we need to check your VOIP line.

Staff: VOIP?

Caller: Sure, VOIP. Okay, just give me your logon password and I'll take it from there.

Staff: Sure, thanks for helping

Please Help Me Save My Job!

This scenario is from a situation that occurred in 2007. People's natural tendency to help those in distress is what makes this work. An attacker pretended to be a new medical intern who was doing badly in school. He told the staff that he had lost his password and couldn't get in. If he didn't finish his patient note he could lose his job. He also used ingratiation by giving the victim a nicely wrapped box of chocolates said to be for his fiancé but he had to make that note first. The victim gave over the terminal and the attacker stole the entire patient billing database.

Caller: Hi, this is Bob the new IT guy and I have a big problem.

Staff: How can we help you today?

Caller: I'll give you five hundred dollars for your password because without getting my work done, I'll lose my job. So, five hundred is cheap to keep my job. How about it?

Summary

SSL is gaining favor as a secure method of communication. A realization that the protocol might be secure but no protocol exists by itself gives IT professionals a false sense of security while using SSL. Using social engineering attacks against the ends of the protocol has been shown to compromise SSL.

Failure by most companies to understand or protect their staff and customers from SE compromise exacerbates the problem, making social engineering attacks more successful. Most companies have no method of tracking attacks, no polices or procedures covering SE, and little staff or customer training.

Compromising SSL by use of key loggers or Trojans placed by social engineering is getting easier. New computer Trojans that load before the SSL and capture all information should cause concern for anyone who uses SSL and wants to keep it secure.

Two main defenses exist against the SE attack on SSL. The first is training for anyone using the protocol. This includes customers, staff, management, and IT personnel. They should be able to recognize the sign of an SE attack. Secondly, policies and procedures that include specifics on how to deal with requests for information.

As external-facing computers should be hardened before connecting them to the Internet, so should your exterior-facing staff be hardened against SE attacks. When you make it harder to attack the hardware and software, the only threat vector left is you and the staff.

Solutions Fast Track

Attacking SSL: Hacking the User

☑ There is and unfounded belief that SSL can't be compromised.

☑ Many IT professionals don't believe Social Engineering (SE) really works so they're not prepared for any type of SE attack.

☑ Social engineering, Trojans, and key loggers all have already compromised SSL.

Recognizing an SE Attack

☑ Companies are unprepared for SE attacks because their staff isn't trained to identify an attack.

☑ Without tracking SE events, businesses have no idea if they're a target or not.

☑ Placing SE tripwires is a cost-effective method of early warning.

Responding to an SE Event

☑ Front line staff should be trained to recognize and respond to an SE event.

☑ IT departments should have a trained Incident Response Team to help manage, analyze, and report on all types of security events, including SE. Documentation is important.

☑ A Unified Security Database where attacks of all types are tracked and analyzed is essential in today's complex security world.

☑ Management needs to support IT in their security efforts or they will be at fault.

Defending against Social Engineering Attacks

☑ Businesses should provide awareness training and discounted or free AV software to their customers.

☑ Policies and procedures should be updated to include social engineering aspects.

☑ Defense in Depth analysis for SE attacks should be considered and controls put in place.

Frequently Asked Questions

Q: Does social engineering really work?

A: Sure does, just ask Kevin Mitnick and others. It relies on gaining the power over staff so they comply with your requests. I suggest reading Johnny Long's excellent book: "No Tech Hacking: A Guide to Social Engineering, Dumpster Diving, and Shoulder Surfing."

Q: How do I track SE attacks?

A: Your training sessions should make staff aware of what the signs and symptoms of an SE attack are. They should then refer to the policy and procedures on SE attacks and respond appropriately. Logging of this information into a central security database is a must because it allows for monitoring and analysis of SE events.

Q: We're a poor organization, how can we protect ourselves and customers from SSL compromise?

A: Organizational and customer awareness training give great ROI. Keeping your customers' computers clean of Trojans and key loggers reduces the chance of attack on your SSL. Free or discounted AV software, tips in monthly bills, or customer events which create awareness of SE threats can be done within your existing structure since most businesses already do mailers and events.

Q: How do I know what information staff shouldn't give out?

A: The Federal Government has helped here. To start, check HIPAA and GLB for what they consider protected information. Look at your business and decide what information you wouldn't want someone to have. NIST provides great resources so look at 800-66 (An Introductory Resource Guide for Implementing the Health Insurance Portability and Accountability Act (HIPAA) Security Rule) and 800-50 (Building an Information Technology Security Awareness and Training Program).

Q: Why bother with the role playing scenarios during training?

A: Your staff will be better able to defend against SE attacks; this will give them the awareness they need to alert IT about this problem.

Q: Why so much on Policy and Procedure?

A: Every organization uses Policy and Procedures to help their staff understand what is expected from the company. Having written documentation that staff can refer to when questions arise helps a company maintain security. Front line staff under attack can use the policy and procedures to ensure the process is done correctly.

Q: What's a central security database?

A: Many companies track their attacks in a central database where IT can enter the security problems they find. This gives you an easy way to spot trends. This becomes especially important when tracking SE attacks because of their varied nature.

Q: I've heard of Defense in Depth (DiD) for my network, but how does that work with the staff and customers?

A: Just as DiD works on several layers of the OSI model, your staff works at those same layers. People put in the Cat5 wire, people set the router paths, people setup users, people send and receive everything. Make a list of jobs that work at each level, think how SE at each level could affect your business. What controls will you have at each level to monitor or deflect the attacks?

Chapter 6

SSH Client Basics

Solutions in this chapter:

- **Understanding Network Encryption**
- **Using OpenSSH to Encrypt Network Traffic Between Two Hosts**
- **Installing OpenSSH**
- **Configuring SSH**
- **Implementing SSH to Secure Data**
- **Distributing the Public Key**
- **The SSH Client**

Introduction

In this chapter, you will learn about solutions to deploy strong encryption to enhance network security. Encryption ensures data confidentiality by using algorithms to encrypt data before it is sent over a network. The receiving host then decrypts the data to a readable format. The solutions in this chapter combine both authentication and encryption, and they include a step-by-step guide to implementing encryption over an insecure network by utilizing the SSH client software.

Understanding Network Encryption

Network encryption ensures that data sent across a network from one host to another is unreadable to a third party. If a sniffer intercepts the data, it finds the data unusable because the data is encrypted. Therefore, a hacker cannot view any usernames or passwords, and any information sent across the network is safe. The requirement is that all communicating systems support the same network encryption technique. One such technique is Secure SHell (SSH).

Network encryption is used for any data transfer that requires confidentiality. Because the Internet is a public network, network encryption is essential. E-commerce transactions must ensure confidentiality to protect credit card and personal information. Personal banking Web sites and investment companies often require extremely sensitive information to be sent, such as bank account numbers and tax identification numbers. If these usernames, passwords, and personal information fall into the wrong hands, the information could be used for a front-door attack because the hacker could pose as a legitimate user. Rlogin, remote shell (rsh), and Telnet are three notoriously unsafe protocols. They do not use encryption for remote logins or any type of data transmission. For example, if you are an administrator and you want to log in to a system via Telnet, your username and login are sent in clear text. Rsh and rlogin send all data between two hosts in clear text as well (but a password is not required).

If a packet sniffer captured the packets destined for the administrator's system, it would eventually capture the packets containing the username and password, and the attacker could then enter the system as a legitimate user.

Using OpenSSH to Encrypt Network Traffic Between Two Hosts

OpenSSH (www.openssh.org) is an open source program that encrypts all traffic between hosts using Secure SHell (SSH). It is a secure replacement for common Internet programs used for remote connectivity. These programs include Telnet, rlogin, and rsh. Because it encrypts all traffic, it always hides usernames and passwords used for remote logins. After the login occurs, it continues to encrypt all data traffic between the hosts. Open SSH is a free version of the SSH Communications Security Corporation's SSH suite (www.ssh.org). As with most open source software, the tradeoff is that vendor support is not available. Do not confuse OpenSSH with the fee-based SSH suite. The OpenSSH home page is shown in Figure 6.1.

The OpenBSD Project (www.openbsd.org) developed OpenSSH and the Unix operating system, which is OpenBSD. OpenBSD is a free 4.4BSD-based OS that is designed with security in mind. It uses strong encryption techniques to ward off hackers.

Figure 6.1 OpenSSH Home Page

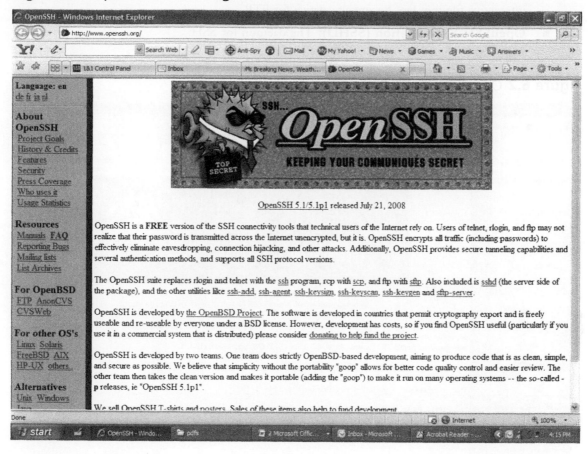

OpenBSD claims that the default installation has not experienced a remote hole in over three years. The OpenBSD Project has ported OpenSSH to other operating systems, including Linux, HP-UX, AIX, Irix, SCO, MacOS X, Cygwin, Digital Unix/Tru64/OSF, SNI/Reliant Unix, NeXT, and Solaris. The OpenBSD home page is shown in Figure 6.2.

The OpenSSH Suite

OpenSSH is a suite of secure networking connectivity programs. The OpenSSH suite includes the following programs:

- **OpenSSH SSH client (SSH)**: Remote login program that is used for secure remote logins and session encryption. It is a secure alternative for rlogin and Telnet.

- **Secure copy program (SCP)**: Remote file copy program that is used to securely copy files between network hosts. It supports usernames and passwords.

- **Secure file transfer program (SFTP)**: Remote login program that is used for secure interactive file transfers. Secure alternative for FTP.

- **OpenSSH SSH daemon (SSHD)**: The daemon for SSH.

Figure 6.2 OpenBSD Home Page

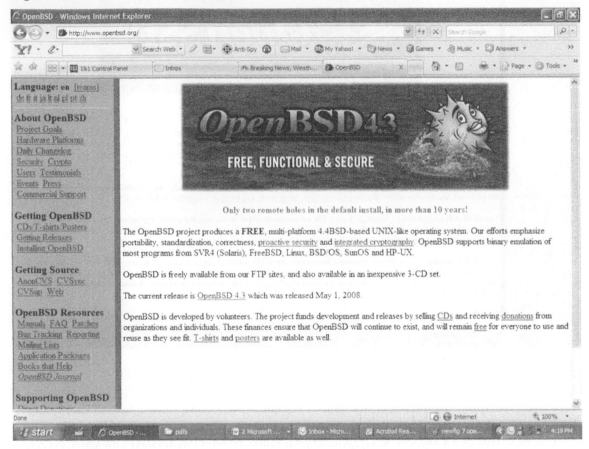

Many features are included in the OpenSSH suite that ensure secure transmissions across a network, and they extend the usefulness of the program. Table 6.1 lists several of the OpenSSH features.

Table 6.1 OpenSSH Features

Feature	Description
Strong encryption using Triple Data Encryption (3DES) and Blowfish	The 3DES and Blowfish encryption algorithms are patent free in all countries. 3DES is time proven, and Blowfish provides faster encryption by using fast block cipher. Either encryption algorithm can be used. They are applied before authentication to ensure that all usernames, passwords, and session data are encrypted
Strong Authentication using public keys, One-Time Passwords (OTP's) and Kerberos authentication	Protects against authentication vulnerabilities such as IP and Domain Name System (DNS) spoofing and fake routes. There are four types of authentication methods used with OpenSSH: ■ Public key authentication only ■ Public key-based host authentication along with .rhosts ■ One-time passwords with s/key ■ Kerberos authentication
X11 forwarding for encrypting X-Windows traffic	Encrypts X-Windows traffic between remote systems. Protects against remote external snooping and hijacking.
Encrypted port forwarding	Allows TCP/IP ports to be forwarded to another system over an encrypted channel. This is ideal for internet protocols that do not inherently support encryption. These protocols include POP and SMTP.
Agent forwarding for single network logon	A user's authentication keys can be stored on the user's local machine, which becomes the authentication agent. When a user accesses the network from another system, the connection is forwarded to this authentication agent. This prevents the authentication keys from being installed on any network system, and it allows the user to securely access the network from any system.
Interoperability	Complies with multiple SSH protocol versions (SSH 1.3, 1.5, and 2.0).
Data compression	Allows data compression to occur before data encryption. This is important for networks with slow connections.
Passes Kerberos and Andrew File System (AFS) Tickets to remote systems	Allows users to access AFS and Kerberos services by entering their passwords only one time.

Installing OpenSSH

OpenSSH implementations are significantly different between operating systems because of authentication. In fact, the developers split development into two categories:

- **OpenBSD-based development**: Produces secure, clean, and simple OpenSSH code for the OpenBSD operating system.

- **OpenSSH Portability Team**: Uses the OpenBSD OpenSSH code to develop portable versions for other operating systems. Each portable version is indicated with a "p" to differentiate it from the OpenBSD version. Portable versions are not released at the same time as the OpenBSD versions. They usually take longer to release, because more time is required for the additional code.

Make sure that you are downloading the specific version for your operating system. To determine if your operating system is supported, visit the Portable OpenSSH Web page at www.openssh.org/portable.html The download links for each version are located at the bottom of the Web page. Simply scroll down to locate the download site nearest you, and then identify your particular operating system.

OpenSSH is becoming very popular, and operating systems are now released with OpenSSH installed by default. For example, Red Hat Linux installs OpenSSH during the installation process. The following operating systems also include OpenSSH into the base system: Red Hat, SuSE, Mandrake Linux, FreeBSD, and others. From the preceding information, you can now determine whether you need to download and install OpenSSH. The examples in this chapter use Red Hat Linux. A portable version of OpenSSH has already been created. It is a Red Hat Package Manager (RPM) that is included into the base system of Red Hat Linux. We are ready to begin configuring OpenSSH after we confirm that OpenSSH is installed.

TIP

If your distribution of Linux does not have RPM Package manager, you can download the source from http://wiki.rpm.org/Download.

1. To ensure that OpenSSH RPM is installed on your system, enter the following:

   ```
   rpm -qa | grep ssh
   ```

2. You should receive the following response if SSH is installed:

   ```
   openssh-askpass-gnome-3.9p11-8.RHEL4.17
   openssh-clients-3.9p1-8.RHEL4.17
   openssh-3.9p1-8.RHEL4.17
   openssh-server-3.9p1-8.RHEL4.17
   openssh-askpass-3.9p1-8.RHEL4.17
   ```

If you receive this response, you are ready to configure OpenSSH.

3. If you receive no response, access www.openssh.org/portable.html to locate the download site nearest you, and download the portable version that matches your operating system. (For example, because I am located in Los Angeles, I would locate the Santa Barbara, CA, USA section, and select the "Linux RPMs" link.) Then, choose the *RH70*/directory (or equivalent), and download the corresponding RPMs from Step #2.

4. Multiple versions will exist for each RPM. Download the latest version of each.

5. Install the RPMs by using the rpm –i command. Once installed, you are ready to configure OpenSSH.

Configuring SSH

SSH is the OpenSSH SSH client, and it works with the SSHD (SSH daemon). They work together to replace rlogin and rsh. SSH is also a replacement for Telnet. SSH is used to log in to a remote system and execute commands on the remote system. The difference between SSH and Telnet, rlogin, and rsh is that SSH is secure.

At the beginning of this chapter, you used a Telnet connection to log in to a remote host. The entire session was unsecure because all data was sent in clear text, including the username and password. Using the packet sniffer Wireshark, you were able to capture the Telnet session packets and follow the Transmission Control Protocol (TCP) stream. You discovered the username and password used to establish the connection. Because you now have the username, password, and remote host Internet Protocol (IP) address (in this case), you can log in as the user whose packets you captured.

Using a similar method, you can also capture rlogin and rsh sessions and determine the needed authentication data. For example, because rlogin and rsh use host authentication, you can determine the IP address, or fully qualified domain name (FQDN), and the username required to log in to the host. Once the host name and username for authentication are determined, they can be used for IP and Domain Name System (DNS) spoofing.

The SSH client is a replacement for Telnet, rlogin, and rsh. It provides a secure data channel between two hosts on a network. These hosts can be untrusted and the network can be unsecured. In order to work, both hosts must support SSH.

One host then connects to another host using an encrypted connection. Because the connection is encrypted, any hacker who captures the data will have an extremely difficult time decrypting it.

How SSH Works

The method for implementing SSH combines similar r-command concepts with a private and public key method. In order to understand how SSH works, it is a good idea to understand how the older r-commands work.

Insecure r-command Authentication

The following authentication method is used for r-commands, such as rlogin, rsh, or rcp, in Red Hat Linux. For the example, rlogin will be used. Any user logging on to a remote system must have a user account on the remote system. For this example, we will use the account susan. If Susan is logged on locally when she connects to a remote host, no password is needed to access the remote host.

No password is needed because her account is authenticated by an entry in the .rhosts file located in the remote systems $HOME/susan directory. The .rhosts file must be created in the susan home directory.

The .rhosts file contains the host name and username required for Susan to log in to the system. The host name of Susan's system is we-24-130-10-205.we.mediaone.net, and her username is susan. If her rlogin command matches the entry in the .rhosts file, she is allowed access to the system. No password is required. The .rhosts file is formatted as follows:

```
hostname username
```

The hostname should be the FQDN of the host, not the short host name.

For example, use we-24-130-10-205.we.mediaone.net instead of: we-24-130-10-205.

The username must be an account on the system. If a user account exists for this username on the system, the user can access all user accounts except root.

As mentioned earlier, for Susan to log in remotely, the root user of the remote host must create a .rhosts file in the $HOME/susan directory with her host name and username. For example, if Susan's machine were host name we-24-130-10-205.we.mediaone.net, the root user would enter the following:

```
we-24-130-10-205.we.mediaone.net susan
```

When Susan is ready to access the remote host, she would enter the following rlogin command:

```
rlogin -l susan we-24-130-8-170.we.mediaone.net
```

where we-24-130-8-170.we.mediaone.net is the remote host. The -l option indicates the account used for the login, which is susan. This method is not secure because the host name and username are sent to the remote host for authentication in clear text. This method opens the remote host to IP spoofing, DNS spoofing, and routing spoofing.

Because of these security vulnerabilities, it is recommended that you disable the r-command utilities. Once disabled, no one can access the machine via the r-command utilities.

1. To disable rlogin, you must edit the /etc/xinetd.d/rlogin file. Open the rlogin file using vi or an editor of your choice.

2. Comment out the service login line by adding a number sign (#) before it:

    ```
    #service login
    ```

3. Write and quit the file.

4. Next, you must restart xinetd by entering:

    ```
    /etc/rc.d/init.d/xinetd restart
    Stopping xinetd: [ OK }
    Starting xinetd: [ OK }
    ```

5. Disable the rsh service using the same method (e.g., edit the /etc/xinetd.d/rsh and /etc/xinetd.d/rexec files by commenting out the service shell line).

6. To provide additional security, disable the Telnet service using the same method (e.g., edit the /xinetd.d/telnet file by commenting out the service telnet line).

7. Restart xinetd.

You have disabled the remote client programs that send information without encryption. Because these programs are vulnerable to attacks, they should be replaced entirely by SSH. The following sections demonstrate how SSH replaces these programs.

Secure SSH Authentication

SSH is based on public-key cryptography. Versions before SSH 2.0 use RSA based authentication. Version SSH 2.0 and later use the unpatented DSA instead. Public-key cryptography uses private and public keys to ensure authentication. The private key is known only by the user, and the public key is available to everyone else, such as the remote host.

SSH can create a DSA private/public key pair for a user by using the **ssh-keygen -d** command. In SSH 2.0, the private DSA key is stored in the $HOME/.ssh/id_dsa file. The public key is placed in the $HOME/.ssh/id_dsa.pub file. The public key should be renamed and copied to the $HOME/.ssh/authorized_keys2 file on the remote system. The authorized_keys2 file contains one public key per line.

In SSH version 1, RSA authentication is used. An RSA private/public key is created in either OpenSSH version by entering the ssh-keygen command without the -d option. The private key is stored in the $HOME/.ssh/identity file, and the public key is stored in the $HOME/.ssh/identity.pub file of the user's home directory. The public key should be renamed and copied to the user's home directory on the remote system to the $HOME/.ssh/authorized_keys file.

SSH offers password authentication if the public-key authentication fails. It also provides password authentication if public-key authentication is not available. This flexibility allows the password to be encrypted and transmitted over the network so that data integrity persists, even if the public-key authentication does not work. Table 6.2 summarizes the locations of the private and public keys used in SSH.

Table 6.2 Public-Key Authentication Locations for SSH

SSH Version 2 Key	Local System Default Location	Remote Host Location
Private key	$HOME/.ssh/id_dsa	Not applicable
Public key	$HOME/.ssh/id_dsa.pub	$HOME/.ssh/authorized_keys2
SSH Version 1 key	Location system default location	Remote host location
Private key	$HOME/.ssh/identity	Not applicable
Public key	$HOME/.ssh/identity.pub	$HOME/.ssh/authorized_keys

Other important files used to identify public keys on a system are listed in Table 6.3.

Table 6.3 Additional Files Used in SSH

SSH File	Description
$HOME/.ssh/rc	Lists commands that will be executed during user login. These commands are run immediately prior to the opening of the user's shell.
$HOME/.ssh/known_hosts	Lists the public keys for all the hosts to which the user has logged in. The host public keys are listed here if they are not listed in /etc/ssh_known_hosts.
/etc/ssh_known_hosts	Lists the RSA- generated public keys for all the hosts that the system knows.
/etc/ssh_known_hosts2	Same as the ssh_known_hosts, except it lists the DSA-generated public keys for all known hosts.
$HOME/.ssh/config	Configuration file for the each user. Each user can have a specific configuration file (if needed), which is used by the SSH client.
/etc/ssh/ssh_config	The global configuration file used by SSH.
/etc/sshic	Simular to the $HOME/.ssh/rc, this file contains commands that must be run prior to shell creation for any user using SSH.

Implementing SSH to Secure Data

Before you implement SSH, you need to make sure both the local system and the remote system have SSH installed. It is also a good idea to use SSH 2.0 or later on each system. This ensures that the DSA algorithm is used instead of the RSA algorithm, which is patented in some countries. In the following examples, both systems are running Red Hat Linux with SSH 2.1 installed. Therefore, the DSA algorithm will be used, and no SSH installation is necessary because SSH is built into the operating system.

The **ssh-keygen** command is used to generate and manage SSH authentication keys. To implement SSH, you must first use **ssh-keygen** to create a private and public key on the client using either RSA or DSA authentication. The following steps demonstrate how to implement SSH to securely access a remote system.

1. Create a user on the client system. For example, create the user myaccountname. Enter:

   ```
   useradd myaccountname
   ```

2. Create a password for user myaccountname by entering:

   ```
   passwd myaccountname
   Changing password for user myaccountname
   New UNIX password:
   Retype new UNIX password:
   passwd: all authentication tokens updated successfully
   ```

3. Log on as user myaccountname.

4. Generate a public and private key (key pair) for myaccountname by entering the following command.

   ```
   ssh-keygen -d
   ```

TIP

By default, SSH generates an RSA key for SSH1.3 and 1.5. To generate a DSA key for SSH 2.0, you must specify the –d option when generating the key pair.

5. You will receive the following response:

   ```
   Generating DSA parameter and key.
   Enter file in which to save the key (/home/myaccountname/.ssh/id_dsa):
   ```

6. Press ENTER to save the key to the default directory and filename (/home/myaccountname/.ssh/id_dsa). You will then receive the following response:

   ```
   Created directory '/home/myaccountname/.ssh'.
   Enter passphrase (empty for no passphrase):
   ```

7. The program requests a passphrase. For this example, do not enter a passphrase. The passphrase is used by 3DES to encrypt the private portion of the private key. A passphrase must be empty for host keys. If you enter a passphrase, do not use simple sentences. Instead, make it at least 10 to 30 characters with numbers, symbols, and letters. Passphrases can later be changed using the -p option. Press **ENTER** twice for no passphrase.

> **NOTE**
>
> Passphrases are not recoverable. If you forget your passphrase, a new key must be generated. You must then distribute the new public key to all required systems.

8. The key generator summary will appear:

    ```
    Your identification has been saved in /home/myaccountname/.ssh/id_dsa.
    Your public key has been saved in /home/myaccountname/.ssh/id_dsa.pub.
    The key fingerprint is:
    ca:3b:f9:80:5a:91:e5:c1:1e:5b:30:02:2f:d5:53:13
    myaccountname@we-24-130-10-205.we.mediaone.net
    ```

9. The entire key-generation process is shown in Figure 6.3.

10. You have generated myaccountname's private and public keys. View myaccountname's private key by entering:

    ```
    cat /home/myaccountname/.ssh/id_dsa
    ```

Figure 6.3 Generating a Private and Public Key Using the ssh-keygen Command

```
Applications  Actions                              Sun Aug 3, 5:28 PM

                        root@localhost:/

File  Edit  View  Terminal  Tabs  Help
[root@localhost /]# ssh-keygen -d
Generating public/private dsa key pair.
Enter file in which to save the key (/root/.ssh/id_dsa): newkeygen
Enter passphrase (empty for no passphrase):
Enter same passphrase again:
Passphrases do not match.  Try again.
Enter passphrase (empty for no passphrase):
Enter same passphrase again:
Your identification has been saved in newkeygen.
Your public key has been saved in newkeygen.pub.
The key fingerprint is:
48:0c:0b:3a:da:a8:5f:f6:25:51:33:ae:38:01:7e:49 root@localhost.localdomain
[root@localhost /]#

    root@localhost:/
```

11. View myaccountname's public key by entering:

    cat /home/myaccountname/.ssh/id_dsa.pub

Myaccountname's public key can be distributed freely. Any system with which myaccountname needs to communicate securely will need to obtain its public key.

NOTE

You can rename the public key before you distribute it. For example, you can rename it "myaccountname.pub." This is much easier to remember, and it will be different from other user public keys created with DSA. You should always rename the public key after you generate a public and private key.

Distributing the Public Key

You must now activate the keys by placing the public key in the proper location on the remote server. The public key can be distributed freely; therefore, you can send it any way you want to the remote host. For example, VeriSign offers digital ID services for e-mail clients to transmit e-mail securely. The digital ID is a public key with ID information embedded. VeriSign automatically posts the user's public key on its Web site. Any user who needs to access a public key for a specific user can download the user's digital ID from the VeriSign Web site at https://digitalid.verisign.com/services/client. Figure 6.4 shows the information for downloading the public key (digital ID) for the user George Bush. It is doubtful that this George Bush is the President of the United States. The U.S. Federal Bureau of Investigations (FBI) would most likely have the President's public key unlisted, which is an option for all VeriSign users. If you needed to transmit e-mail securely with this user, you would download his public key. He would need to download your public key as well. When both of you had each other's public keys, you could transmit data to one another securely.

For this demonstration, you will upload myaccountname's private key to a Web server. The remote host will then download the public key and activate it. The public key is activated when placed into myaccountname's $HOME/.ssh/authorized_keys2 file on the remote system. The following steps demonstrate how to accomplish these tasks.

1. You will upload myaccountname's public key to the Apache Web server on your system. Make sure that Apache is installed by entering:

   ```
   rpm -qa | grep apache
   ```

2. You should receive a response similar to the following if Apache is installed:

   ```
   apache-manual-1.3.12-25
   apache-1.3.12-25
   apache-devel-1.3.12-25
   ```

Figure 6.4 Downloading Pubic Keys from the VeriSign Web Site

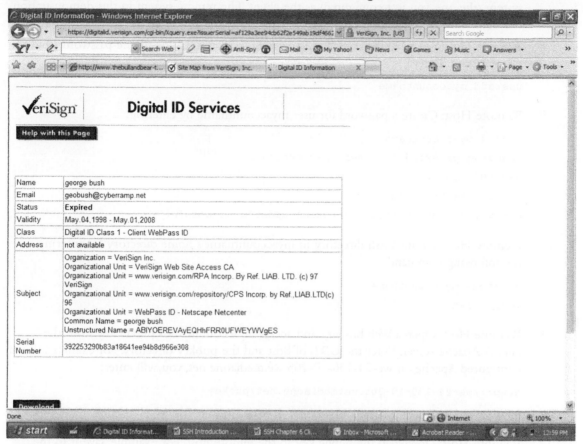

3. If you do not receive a response, you need to download and install Apache.

4. Create a *pubkeys* directory in the default apache root directory by entering the following:

    ```
    mkdir /var/www/html/pubkeys
    ```

5. Copy and rename myaccountname's public key to this Web directory by entering:

    ```
    cp /home/myaccountname/.ssh/id_dsa.pub
    /var/www/html/pubkeys/myaccountname.pub
    ```

6. You have uploaded the public key to your local Apache server. Verify it is uploaded by opening a browser, such as lynx or Netscape Navigator, and entering:

    ■ http://localhost/pubkeys/

The directory contents are listed by default. You should see myaccountname.pub listed. If not, confirm the root Web directory in Apache and make sure you copied the public key to the correct directory.

7. Remote Host: You need a second system to be the remote host. We will refer to the first system (the one you just configured) as the client. The remote system in this demonstration is a Red Hat Linux system located on the same network. Log in to the remote host as root.

8. Remote Host: You need to create a *myaccountname* account. Use the same password from the client system. Enter:

```
useradd myaccountname
```

9. Remote Host: Create a password for user myaccountname by entering:

```
passwd myaccountname
Changing password for user myaccountname
New UNIX password:
Retype new UNIX password:
passwd: all authentication tokens updated successfully
```

10. Remote Host: Create a .ssh directory in myaccountname's home directory by entering the following command:

```
cd /home/myaccountname
mkdir .ssh
```

11. Remote Host: Open a Web browser and access myaccountname's public key from the client's Apache server. Enter the URL of host and the pubkey directory. For example, if you configured Apache on we-24-130-10-205.we.mediaone.net, you will enter:

```
http://we-24-130-10-205.we.mediaone.net/pubkey
```

Your browser window will resemble Figure 6.5 in Navigator.

12. Remote Host: Download the public key to the remote host. For example, save it to the root user directory.

13. Remote Host: Next, you need to copy the contents of myaccountname's public key file to the /home/myaccountname/.ssh/authorized_keys2 file. This file does not currently exist. The simplest way to transfer the public key to this file is to copy myaccountname.pub and rename it as authorized_keys2. For example, if you downloaded myaccountname's public key to the root user directory, you would enter (from the root user directory):

```
cp myaccountname.pub /home/myaccountname/.ssh/authorized_keys2
```

The authorized_key2 file lists the public DSA keys that can be used for login by the user. Each public key must be listed as one line in the file. The id_dsa.pub file, when viewed in a text editor, is written as one line. Therefore, it is important that the key is copied as only one line when placed in the authorized_key2 file.

Figure 6.5 Accessing a Public Key from a Web Site

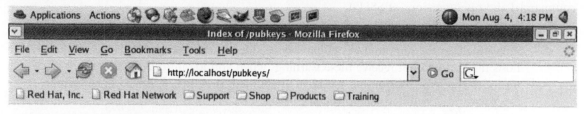

Index of /pubkeys

Name	Last modified	Size	Description
Parent Directory		-	
myaccountname.pub	04-Aug-2008 16:18	210	
root.pub	04-Aug-2008 15:45	210	

Apache/2.0.52 (Red Hat) Server at localhost Port 80

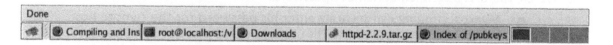

14.   Client Host: Physically access the client host.

15.   Client Host: Log on as myaccountname.

16.   Client Host: Log in to the remote host using ssh. If the remote host were we-24-130-8-170.
we.mediaone.net, you would enter:

```
ssh we-24-130-8-170.we.mediaone.net
```

17.   Client Host:You will receive a message similar to the following:

```
The authenticity of host 'we-24-130-8-170.we.mediaone.net' can't
be established.
DSA key fingerprint is
9a:e6:64:34:d5:fa:f7:e4:e9:fd:b7:e5:95:b0:1e:40.
Are you sure you want to continue connecting (yes/no)?
```

The message stating "The authenticity of host 'we-24-130-8-170.we.mediaone.net' can't
be established" is a standard message that informs you that a trust relationship has not yet been

established. This is standard for the first time a trust is established, and it is seen on both the commercial and open versions of SSH.

18. Client Host: Enter Yes to continue connecting. The following warning message appears, indicating that the remote host's public key is added to the client's $HOME/.ssh/known_ hosts file. You will not receive these warnings when you log in to the remote host in the future, as the trust relationship has been established. It is then followed by a prompt (no password is required due to the key pair):

```
Warning: Permanently added 'we-24-130-8-170.we.mediaone
.net,24.130.8.170' (DSA) to the list of known hosts.
[myaccountname@we-24-130-8-170 myaccountname]$
```

19. Client Host: You will receive a remote host command prompt for myaccountname.

All data transmitted between your system and the remote host are encrypted.

20. Client Host: Quit the session by entering the **exit** command.

NOTE

If public key authentication fails, or if you are logged on to the client system as a user other than myaccountname, ssh will request a password: myaccountname@ we-24-130-8-170.we.mediaone.net's password:

- Myaccountname can securely enter his password for the remote host, because he has an account. His username and password will be encrypted via SSH, so the transmission still is secure.
- If you are asked for a password, you need to retrace your steps. If public key authentication is set up properly, you will not be asked for a password.

The SSH Client

Initiating the SSH Client from Linux/UNIX is easy; from the shell prompt, type ssh –l username domain.ext and press Enter. For example if I wanted to connect to the talesfromtheterminal.com domain and the username of u35764221, I would type the following command:

- **Ssh –l u35764221 talesfromtheterminal.com**

I then would see the screen in Figure 6.6.

Figure 6.6 SSH Standard Session

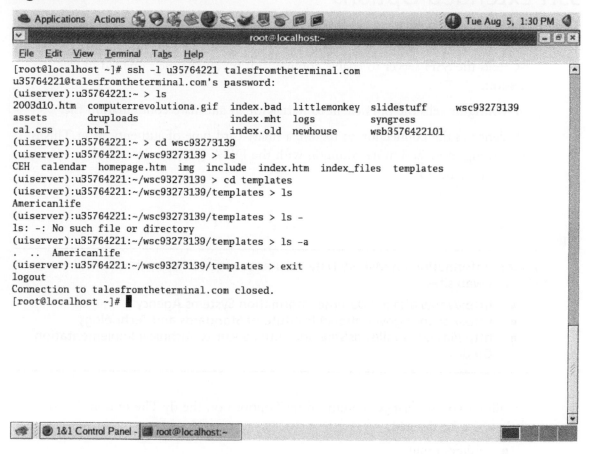

If it is the first time you have accessed the web site you may what is shown in Figure 6.7:

Figure 6.7 First time SSH Connection – Key Exchange

```
[root@localhost ~]# ssh talesfromtheterminal.com
The authenticity of host 'talesfromtheterminal.com (74.208.25.156)' can't be established.
DSA key fingerprint is 34:47:0f:e9:1a:c2:eb:56:eb:cc:58:59:3a:02:80:b6.
Are you sure you want to continue connecting (yes/no)? yes
Warning: Permanently added 'talesfromtheterminal.com,74.208.25.156' (DSA) to the list of known ho
sts.
```

Once connected (shown in Figure 6.6) you can execute shell commands as if you were at the console.

SSH Extended Options

There are a few extended options you can invoke when starting a standard SSH session. The following will give you an over view of these options.

-C tells the SSH server to enable compression on all channels opened in this session.

-F configfile tells the SSH client to start with an alternate configuration file.

-l identifies the connection to require a smart-card type of authentication. This is becoming more and more common with the DISA (Defense Information Systems Agency) standard.

TIP

For more information on Military Data Assurance requirements, check out the following web sites:

- http://www.disa.mil Defense Information Systems Agency
- http://csrc.nist.gov/ National Institute of Standards and Technology
- http://iase.disa.mil/stigs/stig/index.html Security Technical Implementation Guides

-o allows you to change "command file" options on the fly. The options listed below can be defined:

- AddressFamily
- BatchMode
- BindAddress
- ChallengeResponseAuthentication
- CheckHostIP
- Cipher
- Ciphers
- ClearAllForwardings
- Compression
- CompressionLevel
- ConnectionAttempts
- ConnectTimeout
- ControlMaster

- ControlPath
- DynamicForward
- EscapeChar
- ForwardAgent
- ForwardX11
- ForwardX11Trusted
- GatewayPorts
- GlobalKnownHostsFile
- GSSAPIAuthentication
- GSSAPIDelegateCredentials
- Host
- HostbasedAuthentication
- HostKeyAlgorithms
- HostKeyAlias
- HostName
- IdentityFile
- IdentitiesOnly
- LocalForward
- LogLevel
- MACs
- NoHostAuthenticationForLocalhost
- NumberOfPasswordPrompts
- PasswordAuthentication
- Port
- PreferredAuthentications
- Protocol
- ProxyCommand
- PubkeyAuthentication
- RemoteForward
- RhostsRSAAuthentication
- RSAAuthentication
- SendEnv

- ServerAliveInterval

- ServerAliveCountMax

- SmartcardDevice

- StrictHostKeyChecking

- TCPKeepAlive

- UsePrivilegedPort

- User

- UserKnownHostsFile

- VerifyHostKeyDNS

- XAuthLocation

–V gives you the version number of SSH and exits (see Figure 6.8).

–v shows all messages (see Figure 6.8).

Figure 6.8 –V Version Option and –v Verbose Option

The –X option starts X11 forwarding so that you can run the X windows GUI in a SSH session. However, if you are logging in as a user already logged into the console with X-windows running, you will see the screen shown in Figure 6.9:

Figure 6.9 – SSH –X (Start X11 Port Forwarding) Example with Error

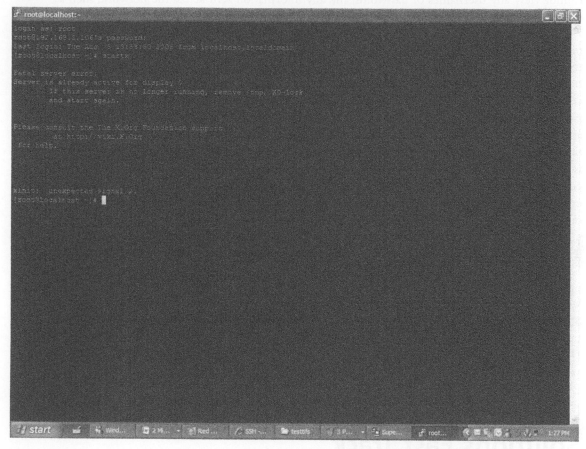

Summary

In this chapter, we discussed network encryption and why it is essential to the security of your network. Network encryption ensures that data sent across a network from one host to another is secure. If a sniffer intercepts the data, it is unusable because the data is encrypted. Therefore, a hacker cannot view any usernames or passwords, and any information sent across the network, such as confidential data, is safe.

To display the problems associated with unencrypted data transmission, you captured unencrypted network traffic and analyzed it for security vulnerabilities. You learned that rlogin, rsh, and Telnet are three notoriously unsafe protocols. They do not use encryption for remote logins or any type of data transmission. You discovered that Telnet sends each password character as a separate packet. If you continue to scroll down the packet capture and view each Telnet data packet, you will discover the password. An easier way to discover the Telnet password is to follow the TCP stream. The username and password are displayed in clear text, as well as all of the data contained in the transmission. To solve this problem, you learned how to encrypt network traffic with OpenSSH. OpenSSH (www.openssh.org) is an open source program that encrypts all traffic between hosts. It is a secure replacement for common Internet programs used for remote connectivity, such as Telnet, rlogin, and FTP. Because it encrypts all traffic, it always hides usernames and passwords used for remote logins. After the login occurs, it continues to encrypt all data traffic between the hosts.

You implemented secure data transmissions using OpenSSH over an unsecured network. This required ensuring that OpenSSH was installed on two different hosts. One system was the SSH remote host, and the other was the SSH client. SSH provides authentication by creating a private/public key pair for a user by using the ssh-keygen command. In SSH 2.0, the private DSA key is stored in the $HOME/.ssh/id_dsa file. The public key should be copied and stored in the $HOME/.ssh/authorized_keys2 file on the remote system. The authorized_keys2 file contains one public key per line. SSH 2.0 sessions are encrypted using ArcFour, CAST128, Blowfish, or 3DES. Data integrity is ensured using hmac-md5 and hmac-sha1. SSH 2.0 is superior and should be used whenever possible.

We then looked at the client and options for OpenSSH and how to establish different types of sessions, with options that give more flexibility.

Solutions Fast Track

Understanding Network Encryption

☑ Network encryption is used for any data transfer that requires confidentiality.

☑ Encryption ensures that data sent across a network from one host to another is unreadable to a third party.

☑ Rlogin, remote shell (rsh), and Telnet are three notoriously unsafe protocols. They do not use encryption for remote logins or any type of data transmission. If a malicious hacker captured this traffic, it would display the data, such as usernames or any passwords, in clear text.

Using OpenSSH to Encrypt Network Traffic Between Two Hosts

- ☑ OpenSSH encrypts all traffic between two hosts using Secure SHell (SSH). It is a secure replacement for common Internet programs used for remote connectivity, such as Telnet, rlogin, and rsh.

- ☑ It features strong encryption using Triple Data Encryption Standard (3DES) and Blowfish, as well as strong authentication using public keys, one-time passwords (OTPs), and Kerberos authentication.

Installing OpenSSH

- ☑ OpenSSH implementations are significantly different between operating systems. The OpenSSH Portability Team uses the OpenBSD OpenSSH code to develop portable versions for other operating systems. You must make sure a specific version exists for your operating system at www.openssh.org.

- ☑ The method for implementing SSH combines similar r-command concepts with a private and public key method.

- ☑ SSH can create a DSA private/public key pair for a user by using the ssh-keygen -d command. In SSH 2.0, the private DSA key is placed in the $HOME/.ssh/id_dsa file. The public key is placed in the $HOME/.ssh/id_dsa.pub file. The public key should be renamed and copied to the $HOME/.ssh/authorized_keys2 file on the remote system.

Configuring SSH

- ☑ Both hosts must have SSH installed to transmit data securely. The SSH Client installed on one end and the SSH Server on the other end.

- ☑ You must first use **ssh-keygen** to create a private and public key on each host using either RSA or DSA authentication. Then, distribute the public key to the host with which you wish to communicate, and vice versa.

- ☑ To establish the connection using SSH, the **ssh** command is used in the format **ssh remotehost**. Remotehost is the name of the host you will connect to using SSH.

Implementing SSH to Secure Data

- ☑ ssh-keygen is the command used to generate and manage SSH authentication keys.

- ☑ Default file for keys are /home/username/.ssh/id_dsa.

- ☑ Passphrases are used to create keys and they should be changed once a year.

Distributing the Public Key

☑ If you use a public service (like Verisign), they will handle the public key.

☑ If you are using internal public keys, copy the file to /var/www/html/publickeys.

☑ To access the keys, go to http://serverlocation/publickeys.

☑ Once the public key is added, you can SSH to that device (if you have username and password).

The SSH Client

☑ The two most popular SSH Clients are OpenSSH for Linux and PuTTY for Windows.

☑ There are many options for both the GUI Windows and OpenSSH client for Linux.

☑ Keys must be shared before a client can connect to a server device.

Frequently Asked Questions

Q: I am receiving warning messages regarding key lengths. What do these messages mean, and how can I prevent them?

A: The key-length warning messages you see are sent by OpenSSH when it encounters certain defective RSA or DSA keys that are sometimes generated by a bug in the ssh-keygen program (in commercial SSH). These defective keys are Pubkey Authentication keys whose Most Significant Bit (MSB) is not set. Thus, these keys are frequently half as long as advertised (they advertise as full length). The warning messages alert you that OpenSSH has detected this type of defective key. You can prevent this type of warning message by editing the known_hosts file. Find the entry listing the incorrect key length value (often 1024), and change the entry to list the correct key length value (generally 1023). Another solution is to simply create new keys. This approach is preferable because even after correction, the modified keys are generally less secure.

Q: Why did I lose support for SSH2 after I upgraded to OpenSSH 2.5.1?

A: When you upgrade OpenSSH versions, your sshd_config or ssh_config programs may incur some modifications. It is advisable to verify the settings in these files whenever you upgrade OpenSSH. If you are upgrading from OpenSSH 2.3.0 to 2.5.1, you can add HostKey /etc/ssh_host_dsa_key to your sshd_config file. This modification will retain your SSH2 support.

Q: Why does it take so long for SSH to connect with Linux glibc 2.1?

A: The Red Hat implementation of glibc offers a universal "IPv6 or IPv4" resolution capability. Although this feature can be convenient, it requires more time to resolve IP addresses from domain names because it must make the IP version determination on a case-by-case basis. To speed up resolution, you can use the **–with-ipv4-default configure** option. When you enter this option, OpenSSH will resolve only IPv4 addresses. Similarly, you can use the **–6** option to instruct OpenSSH to resolve only IPv6 addresses.

Q: Why does SSHD in the file sometimes state they do not have support for RSA or DSA?

A: Your OpenSSH libraries must be constructed to include this support. You can verify that RSA and DSA are supported in your program files by checking internally or by using the RSAref.

Q: The configure file is missing from my distribution, and the **make** command fails when executed. Why?

A: If you receive a missing separator error when the **make** command fails, or you are missing the configure file in your downloaded tar.gz, you probably have the same problem: You may be trying to compile the OpenBSD distribution of OpenSSH on a platform other than the one you used to download it. You must use a portable version of OpenSSH in order to do this without error.

Q: OpenSSH hangs when I exit SSH. Why?

A: Linux and HP-UX systems have been noted to hang when exiting OpenSSH. This bug appears in current OpenSSH versions and occurs primarily when a background process is active. You can enter **sleep 20&exit** to test for this problem. The man page for your shell should list an option you can use to send a HUP signal to active processes upon exit. Bash users can use the following entry in either /etc/bashrc or ~/.bashrc:

```
shopt -s huponexit
```

Q: What are the two most accepted SSH clients?

A: OpenSSH for Linux and PuTTY for Windows.

Q: Can I change my SSH Public Key?

A: Yes. You should change it once a year (at least). The command to change your SSH Key is as follows:

```
ssh-keygen -p -t dsa
```

We fully acknowledge use of chapter 07, *"Avoiding Sniffing Attacks through Encryption," from Hack Proofing Linux: A Guide to Open Source Security, 978-1-928994-34-3*

Chapter 7

The Components That
Make Up the SSH Server

The SSH Server Basics

Solutions in this chapter:

- **The Components That
  Make Up the SSH Server**

- **Protocols in Use**

- **Randomness of Cryptography**

- **Which Communication Is Protected with SSH**

- **F-Secure SSH Server**

- **Other SSH Server Types**

- **Compiling SSH**

- **Server Options**

- **Running the Server**

- **Authentication**

- ☑ **Summary**

- ☑ **Solutions Fast Track**

- ☑ **Frequently Asked Questions**

The Components That Make Up the SSH Server

Before detailing the SSH protocol and the function of its single parts, it is suitable to list and describe the components making up the server and the service in general. An initial note that could be misleading, but which is useful to lay the basis for the following paragraphs, is that, within a SSH service, the existing components may not necessarily be translated into programs. They can, however, represent logical and abstract entities. Here is a list of components making up the SSH server.

- Server: Program that can manage the SSH requests according to the standards specified within the RFCs. In practice, in UNIX environments, it corresponds to sshd (where sshd is the SSH service daemon on the *NIX environment).

- Client: Program that performs the connections to the SSH server in order to use its implemented services. The most famous ssh clients are ssh on UNIX and PuTTY on Windows.

- Session: A lasting connection between a client and a server. It is initialized after a successful authentication and ends when the connection is interrupted.

- Key: It includes a small quantity of data and is used as parameter for the cryptographic algorithms used when protecting a message or during authentication. The use of a key ensures that only the legitimate owner is able to decode a massage sent to him or her. SSH manages four types of keys, as shown in Table 7.1.

Table 7.1 Key Types Created and Purpose for SSH

Keys Used				
Name	Duration	Created By	Type	Purpose
User key	Persistent	User	Public	Identify a user to the server
Session key	A session	Client and server	Private	Protect the communication
Host key	Persistent	Administrator	Public	Identify the server
Server key	1 hour	Server	Public	Encode the session key (SSH1)

- User key: The asymmetric and persistent key used by the client to verify the user's identity.

- Host key: The asymmetric and persistent key used by the server to verify its identity. If a machine runs a single SSH server, its key will be unique; if a host runs multiple SSH servers, it could have, for each server, its specific key.

- Server key: A temporary asymmetric key. It is regenerated regularly, usually each hour, and is used to protect the sessions. This component remains absolutely reserved, is not saved on a disk, and is not transmitted for any reason.

- Session key: A symmetric key used to encrypt communications between a client and a server. Its sharing occurs securely during the initial setup of the SSH connection. Both communication sides own this key, and it is destroyed as soon as the communication ends.

- Key generator: Program generating the keys with persistent validity. ssh-keygen is an example.

- Known hosts database: A host collection that is used during authentication.

- Agent: Program saving the user key within the cache memory. It allows the end user to avoid continuously entering his or her passphrases.

- Signer: Program signing the packets based on the host-based authentication method.

- Random seed: Set of random data whose function is to initialize the part of software generating random numbers.

- Configuration file: As the name suggests, it includes all parameters used to correctly run the server-side and client-side of the SSH protocol.

It is helpful to note that a server could not have its own key or could manage multiple keys. From the mere implementation point of view, the components in Table 7.2 are noticed:

Table 7.2 Components of the SSH Key

Software Components	
Name	**Description**
ssh	It is the client side of the protocol. It performs the connection requests to the server.
sshd	It is the server side of the protocol. It accepts the connection requests carried out by the different clients.
ssh-keygen	It generates and converts the keys
ssh-agent, ssh-add	It saves the private key in the memory
ssh-keyscan	It shows the host keys existing on an ssh server.

Protocols in Use

SSH (Secure Shell) is a protocol to ensure the possibility to login remotely or access services, all by focusing the attention on the security concept. It is made up of three key elements (see Chapter 4 for more information):

- Transport Layer Protocol (SSH-TRANS), whose function is as server for authentication, confidentiality, and integrity. In some servers, the compression service also could be provided. The transport layer is based on the TCP/IP protocol; this does not exclude the fact that we could find specific cases where the underlying element is represented by an alternative but reliable data flow.

- User Authentication Protocol (SSH-USERAUTH), whose task is to authenticate the client to the server. Its operation is based on the transport layer protocol.

- Connection Protocol (SSH-CONNECT), whose task is to manage the encrypted tunnels within the different logical channels. Its operation bases on the user authentication protocol.

Once a secure connection has been established through the transport layer, the client sends a request to get the service. After authentication by the user, a new request is sent. This way of operating allows ssh to coexist with the protocols defined at a higher level and thus use ssh inside them. The connection protocol provides a series of channels in order to meet the most various purposes. Currently the most common uses are for a remote control of the sessions regarding the shells, for the forwarding (tunneling) of arbitrary TCP/IP ports, and for the forwarding of X11 connections. The primary aim of the SSH protocol is to improve security within the Internet; all this is performed while taking into account the implementation complexity and without ever stooping to compromises of security, as follows:

- All algorithms for integrity, cryptography, and generation of public keys are well known.

- All algorithms are used to protect from the strongest cryptoanalysis attacks.

- If an algorithm is "broken," its substitution does not involve the protocol bases.

During the protocol development, some concessions have been made in order to facilitate the spread and accelerate the initial development. Initially the protocol allowed for not checking the actual fatherhood confirmed of the key used by the server offering the service. This solution enabled the rapid protocol spread and the increase of usability until the first network infrastructures for public key validation appeared. It is possible to end this introduction to the protocol with the following considerations, all of which involve security aspects. The transport protocol (SSH-TRANS) provides a reserved channel through a nonsecure network. Its function is to authenticate, exchange key, encode, and protect integrity. It also offers the possibility to obtain a session ID, which can be used by the protocols at a higher level. The authentication protocol (SSH-USERAUTH) provides a suite of mechanisms so that a client can authenticate itself to a server. Each mechanism used in the authentication protocol uses the session ID generated by the transport layer protocol. We repeat that the constraints of security and uniqueness of the ID must be guaranteed by the protocol that generated it, thus by the transport layer protocol (SSH-TRANS). The connect protocol (SSH-CONNECT) specifies the mechanisms to perform the multiple multiplex of data flows (channels) through an authenticated and confidential transport. Furthermore it specifies the channels for the access to the interactive shell, for the proxy-forwarding of the various protocols requiring a secure means of transport (e.g., some TCP/IP implementations), and for the secure access to subsystems existing on a server. Let's see now for each section of the ssh protocol the relevant characteristics.

SSH Authentication Protocol

The ssh authentication protocol is a general-purpose authentication protocol. It must lie above the transport layer protocol. For this protocol, integrity and confidentiality must be guaranteed by the underlying protocol. The name of the service for this protocol is "ssh-userauth." When the protocol starts, it receives the session ID from the underlying protocol (through the exchange of a hash H value during the first key exchange). The session ID allows us to univocally identify the session and can be used as signature to establish the correct fatherhood of a specific private key. This protocol must also know whether the underlying protocol offers the confidentiality protection service. Let's see now the structure of the authentication protocol framework. The server manages the authentication by suggesting to the client which authentication methods are supported to continue the data exchange. In turn the client is free to test the authentication methods listed by the server in any order. Thus, the server completely controls the authentication process used, and the client has the flexibility to choose the supported method or the one most convenient for the user.

The authentication methods are identified by their name as described in the shh architecture. However, there is a supported method that should not be in the list of the available ones: the "none" authentication method. Despite this premise, it happens that the list of the supported methods sent to the client can contain "none." The server must always reject this kind of requests, unless the client has the privileges of an access without authentication. The advantage of this type of request is to get the authentication methods implemented in the server. Furthermore, the server should consider a timeout within which it should end the not accepted authentications (ten minutes is recommended). Moreover, it should limit the number of attempts after failed authentications (the count of twenty attempts is recommended). All authentication requests must have a fixed structure; the only variant allowed is the one related to the authentication method. Within the authentication message structure, we find fields such as user name (coded according to the ISO-10646 UTF-8 standard), service name (coded in US-ASCII), and the method name (coded in US-ASCII). The "user name" and "service name" fields are repeated at each new authentication attempt; we point out that they can change each time. The server implementation must check that for each attempt, these fields are provided and the flush of the previous requests must be performed if these values change over time. If the server is not able to perform the flush, it must perform the disconnection.

The "service name" specifies the services to be started after the successful authentication attempt. This field includes a series of values that correspond to the services the server could offer. If the service requested by the client is not available, the server could immediately disconnect the client. However, it is advisable that the server send a "formal" disconnection." In any case, if the server does not meet the request made by the client, it must absolutely refuse the connection.

If the "user name" does not exist, the server could disconnect the client or send a list of "method names" it can accept. For this purpose, the server avoids any information release about the accounts in it. In any case, if the "user name" does not exist, the authentication request must not be accepted. An authentication request can also occur after a series of messages. All messages depend on the "method name" used; in turn the client could send a request again and in that case the server must abandon the previous connection attempt to manage the new one. For the "method name" the following fields are specified: public key (required), password (optional), hostbased (optional), and none (not recommended). If the server refuses an authentication request, it must respond with the SSH_MSG_USERAUTH_FAILURE message.

If the server accepts the authentication, it will send a list (comma-separated values) of the "method names" that could fulfill the client's request and then continue the authentication process. It is advisable that the server include only the "method names" that really are supported. When the server accepts the authentication, it will respond with SSH_MSG_USERAUTH_SUCCESS. It is helpful to consider that the client could send several authentication attempts without waiting for the individual results. In this case the server shall, however, send a SSH_MSG_USERAUTH_FAILURE message before managing the following request. Before going on with the analysis, it is useful to consider how in some jurisdictions sending warning messages before the authentication can be used in order to have a legal protection. Some Unix machines display a text from /etc/issue by using TCP wrappers or similar software to issue a text before the login prompt. The SSH server can send a SSH_MSG_USERAUTH_BANNER message in any moment between the beginning of the authentication phase and its end. Despite the importance of this message, some clients tend to hide it or give the user the possibility to hide it as it would be defaulted for each login attempt. Let's see now the authentication request types. The first considered is the "none" one. A client could request the list of the authentication method names by using the "none" authentication method. If there is no request of authentication by the user, the server will respond with SSH_MSG_USERAUTH_SUCCESS; otherwise, it responds with SSH_MSG_USERAUTH_FAILURE and could send the list of the supported authentication methods. The method in question should not appear in the list of the supported methods. The second request method considered is "public key." The only server-side requested authentication method is the public key-based method; it goes without saying that this method must be implemented. It is useful to point out that this method does not require that the clients have a public key. This method requires the client to forward its signature based on its own private key. In turn, the server controls that the key sent is valid for that user and must control that the key has a valid signature. If both pieces of information are correct, the server accepts the authentication; otherwise, it refuses it. The server could also require the following authentications in order to ensure the actual presence of the client during time. For the initial key exchange, there is list of algorithms supported by the server. If the server does not support the type of algorithm chosen by the client, it must simply refuse the request. In short, the necessary steps for the authentication are as follows:

- The client sends its signature generated from its primary key.

- The server receives the message and controls the requirements previously defined.

- After the ownership validation, the server will send SSH_MSG_USERAUTH_SUCCESS or SSH_MSH_USERAUTH_FAILURE.

The "password" authentication request method, as the name suggests, bases everything on the password. Remember that the server could require the user to change the password. The password will be stored within the password database existing on the server. All passwords must be transmitted according to the ISO-10646 UTF-8 coding. The clients accepting input values not coded according to the server standard must perform a coding and then a forwarding to the server. In turn, the server shall convert the password according to the standard with which the passwords are stored within the database. This decision is very important as it allows us to disregard which operating system or application the user is using. As for security, the SSH protocol relies on a cryptography at transport layer level; thus, it does not wonder whether the password is transmitted in clear. If there is no guarantee that the packet is encrypted before being sent, the password authentication method must be disabled. The server shall respond with the following:

- SSH_MSG_USERAUTH_SUCCESS: If the authentication was successful;

- SSH_MSG_USERAUTH_FAILURE: If the authentication was not successful;

- SSH_MSG_USERAUTH_PASSWD_CHANGEREQ: If the user password is expired. In this case, the authentication could be rejected.

Let's analyze the "host based" authentication request. Some sites could enable an authentication based on the host and the user existing in the remote host. This type of authentication is not suitable for systems where a high security control is required, but could be useful in other operating environments. The implementation of this method is optional and if it is the preferred one, it is necessary to check that the user does not get the private key of the host used. This method requires the client to send a signature generated with the host private key which, in turn, will be checked by the server. The authentication is accepted once the host identity has been validated. When possible, it is useful that the server perform new checks in order to verify the client's identity. For the correct operation of this method, sometimes it is necessary to change the firewall rules.

SSH Transport Layer Protocol

The transport layer is defined as a secure and low-level protocol. The main operation is to provide services of strong cryptography, data integrity protection, and security within the password authentication method. The authentication method implemented at this level is host-based and does not require any action by the user. The protocol was designed to be easy and flexible and to enable the parameter negotiation and minimize the number of messages exchanged between the server and the client. The key exchange method, the algorithms for the generation of the public keys, the algorithms for the symmetric cryptography, and the hash algorithms are all parameters negotiated with this protocol. In most environments, only two key exchanges are necessary to have the complete key exchange: the authentication to the server and the notification of the requested services. At worst, three exchanges are needed.

The SSH protocol works by using a binary-transparent transport using 8-bit clean. The underlying transport protocol should ensure the protection from transmission errors, which would close the ssh connections. If TCP/IP is used as underlying protocol, the server listens for new connections on TCP port 22. This port was reversed by IANA for the SSH service. Once the connection has been established, both members, the client and the server, must send a string regarding the version of the implemented protocol. Any string the server sends to the client must be duly coded in order to allow any client to perform a correct interpretation. The key exchange starts as soon as the protocol version identifier is sent.

As services and protocols are continuously generated, some people could object to the increasing size of the transmitted packets due to new headers, padding operations, or the message authentication code (MAC). The minimum packet size is 28 bytes (according to the negotiation algorithm used). If we consider the size increase for packets already having considerable sizes, this parameter is irrelevant; sessions like telnet have to be described specifically. In addition, in these cases, we are supported by the limits of the underlying protocols. The sole environment where we could find problems is the PPP protocol for the slow modem lines. Going back to the parameters negotiated during the key exchange, we mention the compression (by using zlib) and the cryptography algorithms. In this regard, it is useful to make some observations. After choosing the cryptography method, it is applied to the message length, the padding length, the payload, and the padding itself. An interesting observation involving the use of cryptography algorithms is their duplicity. The ciphers used are considered in each communication direction; that is, the server could use a cryptography method whereas the client could use another one; although this is possible, we suggest using the same method for both directions.

An important aspect of communication regards the integrity of transmitted data. Within the SSH protocol, the integrity is protected. In each packet, protected elements include the MAC generated by the public key, the packet sequence number, and the content of the packet transmitted. As said for the cryptography algorithms, those of the MAC generation can be distinguished for the two communicating entities; however, also in this case, the same observation is valid: we suggest that the choice be the same both for the server and the client. The actual key exchange starts as soon as the lists of the algorithms supported have been exchanged. Each communication side will have its "preferred" algorithm; however, we assume they are the same for both. The key exchange methods can use an explicit or implicit authentication. In the first case, the message sent for the key exchange contains the signature or other parameters to check for the server authenticity; in the second case, the server, in order to demonstrate it knows the public key of the client, sends a message and the corresponding MAC the client can check. The negotiation algorithms complete the picture concerning the parameter negotiation. Each algorithm supported must be contained in a properly formatted list. The order in which they appear represents also the order they are preferably used. The first algorithm is the preferred one. Among the existing algorithms, the first algorithm fulfilling the following conditions is chosen:

- The server supports the algorithm;

- If the algorithm requires encryption-capable host key, there must be a server_host_key_ algorithm algorithm which has to be supported also by the client;

- If the algorithm requires signature-capable host key, there must be a server_host_key_ algorithm algorithm which has to be supported also by the client.

If there are no algorithms fulfilling these conditions, the connection is interrupted. The successful key exchange will produce two values: the secret key and the hash value. The cryptography and the authentication keys derive from these values. The hash is the first value used as session identifier, which is unique for the connection underway. During a connection, it is possible to request a further key exchange by simply sending the SSH_MSG_KEXINIT packet. Following the message, each part involved re-starts the key exchange process by maintaining the role of the individual parts (the server will continue to act as the server and the client will do the same). The methods of cryptography, compression, and generation of the MAC will not change until the new key exchange is successfully completed (before a new SSH_MSG_ NEWKEYS). The key renewal is suggested after the transmission of a huge amount of data (GB) or after hours of connection. Both after the first exchange and after the renewal, the client can request the list of services available on the server. If the server rejects the request, it must disconnect the client. The disconnection message (SSH_MSG_DISCONNECT) requires the server not to send or receive any type of data. All implementations must be able to adequately process this type of message.

Connection Protocol

The connection protocol was designed to operate over the transport layer protocol and the user authentication protocol. It manages the interactive login sessions, remotely executes commands, and the forwarding of the TCP/IP and X11 connections. Note that all previous examples require the opening of a channel. Multiple channels can be multiplexed in a single connection. Each channel is characterized by two numbers, which represent the ends of the channel. The request to open a channel includes the number the sender uses for that channel. Once the numbers for the communications have been established, it is necessary that the window size be exchanged. When a new channel is opened, the operations to be carried out are the following:

- Sending of a request together with the number locally chosen to manage the channel;

- The receiver decides whether to accept the channel-opening request; if yes, it responds by giving its identification number for the open channel.

After the connection of the two ends, there is the actual data transfer. As anticipated, the window size is sent so that the part involved in the communication can send the data without changing the size of this window. After the reception of the first message, it is possible to change the window size by sending a new message containing the exact number of bytes to be sent. The connection layer implementation works it so that:

- It must not publish a size that is not able to manage the transport layer;

- It must not generate packets bigger than those the transport layer protocol can manage.

When the communication must be ended, a message for closing the SSH_MSG_CHANNEL_ EOF channel is sent. For this type of message, no response is specified; however, the applications prefer sending an EOF. Remember that following this message, it is possible to continuously send data. To cause the actual closing, it is necessary to send the SSH_MSG_CHANNEL_CLOSE message. With this message, the channel has to be considered as closed and the number associated with the channel could be used for another communication. These messages do not occupy the space of the available window. Now let's return to the previous examples on the uses of the connection protocol. A session is the remote running of a program, such as a shell, an application, a system command, or any type of subsystem. The program in question could have a tty or it could involve the X11 forwarding. For the last one, we recommend that the cookie sent for the X11 authentication be false and random, but controlled and replaced with the real cookie once the connection has been established. The X11 channels do not depend upon the session, and the session closing does not imply the closing of the X11 channel. The server implementation must reject the requests to open an X11 channel without their having performed an X11 forwarding request. Another example involves the remote execution of shells or commands. To complete this analysis, there is still the topic concerning the port forwarding on the TCP/IP protocol. When the port forwarding is performed, it is not necessary to specify the end point (i.e., the service user), but within the SSH protocol a specific request must be made, also defining the end user. The address and the port towards which the bind must be performed are thus to be specified. The implementations should enable the port forwarding of users that have carried out an authentication as privileged users. In the case of an incoming connection on a port on which a TCP/IP forwarding request has been made, a channel is opened. The implementations must reject the messages that have not made a forwarding TCP/IP request beforehand by giving the port number.

Randomness of Cryptography

Before considering the randomness within ssh, it is useful to remember the concept underlying a cipher, as shown in Figure 7.1:

Figure 7.1 Process of a Block Cipher, Using Basic Encryption: Combining Block Text to Plain Text to Create Cipher Text

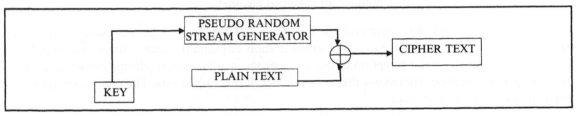

Generating pseudo random sequences having adequate randomness properties is one of the current problems of cryptography. Cryptography algorithms and protocols require a good source of random bits. The randomness within the SSH protocol is used:

- To generate the keys for data encryption ;

- As text for the source message padding and as the initialization vector of the encryption algorithms

- To carry out controls on the bytes or cookies exchanged within the protocol as counter-measure for packet-spoofing attacks.

Achieving randomness is more difficult than one can imagine. Furthermore it is necessary to remember how the good generation of a random number varies according to the context in which the number is used. For example, a random number is effective for a situation regarding statistics, but the same generation method could be completely ineffective in a cryptographic context. Each application requires properties that are to be considered a priori in input. An example of this constraint is distribution. Going back to cryptography, the required constraint is the one of unpredictability; an ill-intentioned user, when reading our data or the information in transit on a channel, must not be able to "guess" the keys used for the encryption or decryption of the message.

Randomness, in the real meaning of the term, is a result that cannot be achieved by using a computer. Any bit sequence produced as output of a program can easily be reproduced; in most cases, for the same inputs, we have the same results. In order to have a real randomness, we have to turn to physical processes or phenomena such as the behavior of a liquid, turbulence, or radioactive decay. Even though these phenomena are a clear example of randomness, we have to pay attention not to introduce structure constraints.

Going back to mere IT issues, we point out that there are algorithms that output long and practically unpredictable bit sequences having good statistic randomness properties. These algorithms are used within cryptography-related applications. The algorithms under examination are classified are PRNGs (pseudo-random number generators). A PRNG requires a small quantity of input data called seed so that the output result is always different. Starting from the seed provided in input, the algorithm generates a string longer than the source seed. The string in output has a good randomness property and is defined as "randomness stretcher." After these considerations, we notice that a program using a PRNG algorithm must find a random sequence of smaller size and with a good unpredictability property.

It is not in cryptographic contexts that the use of random numbers is required; some operating systems include some generators. Some variants of Unix operating systems such as Linux and OpenBSD encapsulate a device driver, accessible via /dev/random and /dev/unrandom, which provides a series of random bits. The reading of these devices and thus of the generated bits is carried out simply through the usual file opening and reading routines. The bits included in these devices are generated by using a series of methods, some of which are very efficient. Going back to the previous examples, the disk access request time can be considered as a set of fluctuations due to turbulences detected on a body. Another technique considers the less significant bit coming from the noise received on the microphone port. Going on with the examples, we cannot forget units such as the network packet fluctuation, the events associated with the keyboard, the interrupts, and so on. SSH implementations use random elements; their use is completely hidden to the end user. Here we describe what happens within the SSH implementations. OpenSSH and Tectia use the randomness functions implemented in the kernel together with a series of samples regarding fluctuating parameters, such as the ps or nestat commands, taken from the system. These commands are used as seed in the PRNG algorithms because they have a good randomness property. Because generating random bit sequences is time-intensive, SSH stores a pool of random bits within a file, as shown in Table 7.3:

Table 7.3 Stored Pool of Random (Seed) Bits for SSH in UNIX

| | Examples | |
	OpenSSH	Tectia
Server	/etc/ssh/ssh_random_seed	/etc/ssh2/random_seed
Client	~/.ssh/random_seed	~/.ssh2/random_seed

These files should be protected because they contain sensitive information whose release could weaken the SSH security, giving an opening to an attacker. Although this risk has been contemplated, SSH puts into action a series of countermeasures that can control this possible file violation. The information contained in the seed is, however, always mixed with other random bits before being provided as input to the PRNG algorithm. Note that only the first part of the seed is saved on the disk. This reduces the impact of accidentally released sensitive information.

Within implementations like OpenSSH and Tectia, all this is automatically made invisible. OpenSSH makes a link to the OpenSSL library and uses its own source of random numbers or leans on the one provided by the kernel, if made available. When OpenSSH is installed on a platform that does not provide for the use of the /dev/random device, it is possible to follow another way. The alternative is to install a plug-in like Entropy Gathering Daemon (EGD) and compile OpenSSH through the --with-EGD option. A further alternative is to use the entropy-gathering mechanism existing within OpenSSH. However, it is possible to customize the choice of the program that serves as the generator of random numbers and the choice has to be specified within the /etc/ssh/ssh_prng_cmds file. Remember that the seed is stored within the ~/.ssh/prng_seed file. In the last OpenSSH implementations, this method is automatically adopted if there is no /dev/random device. The OpenSSH 3.8 and later versions have the random bit generator (ssh-rand-helper) separated from the main program and its use must be activated through the --wih-rand-helper compilation option.

Which Communication Is Protected with SSH

We describe here some uses for when the SSH protocol finds an application.

X11 Forwarding

Often there is the need to remotely control a specific application. To reach this objective, two methods are available: the first one by executing X11-forwarding only and the second one by using SSH. See Figures 7.2 and 7.3 for further explanation.

Figure 7.2 Clear Text Method of Using GUI X-Windows to Access Remote Host

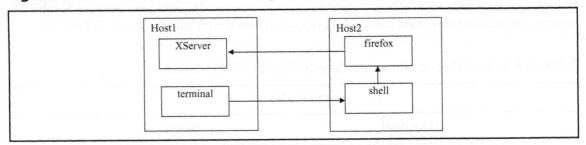

With SSH:

Figure 7.3 Encrypted (SSH) Method of Accessing Remote Host with GUI/X.11 Forwarding

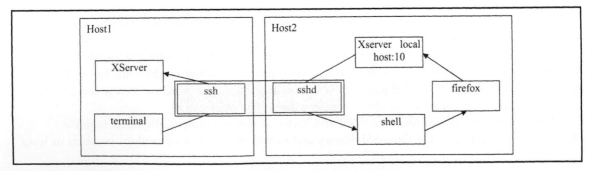

In order to take into account the advantages that would come from using SSH, Table 7.4 summarizes the advantages and disadvantages of this solution.

Table 7.4 Benefits of SSH Versus Clear Text Between Client and Server

	X11 Forwarding Comparison	
Criterion	**With SSH**	**Without SSH**
Cryptography	All communication is encrypted. The time used to encode and decode the message is made up with compression.	All communication occurs by leaving the message transmitted in clear text, enabling ill-intended users to recover the transmitted passwords.
X11-security	The X-Server could be running with the -nolisten TCP option, negating the possibility of non-authorized accesses.	The server must accept the connections on the TCP 6000 port so that everybody has access.
Firewall/NAT	No problems have been found.	This method does not work in the case of a firewall between the ssh server and the ssh client.

Pipes

In some occasions, pipes could be useful to redirect the output of a command, invoked through ssh, to the shell from which it was invoked. To do this, it is necessary to invoke the ssh command without including the –t parameter. This need generates a series of examples, as follows:

- imap (fetchmail, mutt): Protocol used to exchange mails. Unfortunately this command transfers the mails without applying a cryptography method. By accessing the server through ssh, it is possible to perform an imap tunnel on ssh in order to make the transfer more secure, by introducing the cryptography and authentications methods of SSH, and faster, thanks to the compression.

- smtp (exim): Because some domains refuse mails from dial-up system, with ssh it is possible to bypass this problem.

- rsync: Tool to perform the incremental backup of two folders, such as from a local disk. If it is performed with the –e ssh parameter, it will tunnel the communication.

- scp, sftp: Commands used to securely transfer files.

- uucp: Protocol used to exchange files, mail, or usenet news. Because the authentication is performed without cryptography, it is suitable to tunnel uucp with ssh.

■ cvs: File versioning system. Synchronization is made through a directory shared on the file system (local, nfs, samba, and so on) or on a CVS server, which can be connected through ssh.

Portforwarding

Figure 7.4 Encrypting HTTP (port 80) Data Between Secure Client and Server Proxy Using SSH Over Port 22

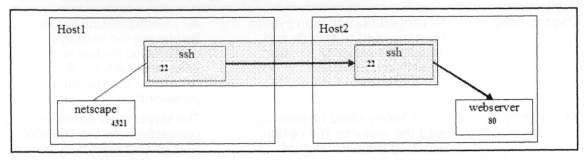

From Figure 7.4, it is possible to notice the port forwarding of port 22 with port 4321 and then of port 22 with port 80. From the browser in use, the address http://localhost:4321 will correspond to the web server.

Telescopic Tunnel

It is possible to invoke the ssh client by specifying a port different from 22 by using the –p parameter. This way of operating allows one to manage ssh sessions within other ssh sessions already started.

PPP over SSH

The point-to-point-protocol describes the connection and the following communication steps between two virtual network interfaces. Through a simple configuration, it is possible to tunnel communications through ssh.

As you can see, ssh represents a plus, which allows most services to add the security concept in the transmission and authentication without turning to compromises other than that of the time required for the initial setup of the environment. We can protect any type of service by differentiating which communications are protected from ssh and which are not. The use of ssh is therefore recommended for all services that do not natively offer the protection and check for the integrity of the media.

F-Secure SSH Server

Up to version 5, the tool was called F-Secure; from version 6 on, the tool started to be called Reflection for Secure IT. In particular, Reflection for Secure IT is a family of products made up of client and server components and based on the secure shell protocol. These are available both for UNIX and Windows. The purpose of the suite of tools is to protect data transfers through encryption. The features that allow for authenticating the parts involved in the communication and checking for the integrity of transmitted data have been implemented.

Tools & Traps...

Reflection for IT Security

You can learn more about this product and find evaluation versions as well as commercial license versions at http://www.attachmate.com/Products/Host+Connectivity/Security/Reflection+for+Secure+IT/rsit.htm.

Reflection for Secure IT Protocol

The protocol implemented by the tool is SSH2 (IETF SecSh Internet drafts and RFCs 4250–4254, 4256, 4462, 4344, 4345, and 4716). As for transfers, in the Microsoft world, SCP1 (for compatibility with OpenSSH servers), SCP, and SFTP are supported; the server in the UNIX environment supports instead SCP2 and SFTP2. The cryptography algorithms supported are many and are listed below:

- Ciphers:
    - AES (128, 192, and 256 bit)
    - 3DES (three 56-bit key EDE)
    - Blowfish (128 bit)
    - CAST (128 bit)
    - Arcfour (128 bit)
- HASHing algorithms:
    - MD5
    - SHA-1
    - RIPEMD (RACE Integrity Primitives Evaluation Message Digest)

- Key exchange:

    - RSA DSA

    - Diffie-Hellman

The validation of the cryptographic libraries is FIPS 140-2, Level 1 (certificate #766).

Reflection for Secure IT Authentication

The strong integration with the Microsoft world enabled Reflection for Secure IT to interface with the authentication mechanisms based on Microsoft domains. The possible authentications are as follows:

- Password:

    - Local (Microsoft)

    - Traditional password (UNIX)

    - Windows domain authentication (Microsoft)

- Keyboard interactive:

    - Traditional password

    - PAM (Pluggable Authentication Module for UNIX)

- SSH user keys:

    - Support for RSA and DSA keys

    - Support for key agent forwarding

- GSSAPI (Generic Security Services Application Program Interface):

    - Microsoft SSPI (Security Support Provider Interface) logon credentials (Microsoft)

    - Supports both user and host authentication using GSSAPI (Microsoft)

Reflection for Secure IT ensures the highest US government standard levels and allows the administrator to remotely administer critical servers or systems in untrusted networks, to securely transfer data with the guarantee that the transfer occurred correctly, and to access TCP/IP-based applications through ad-hoc created tunnels. It replaces thus all situations where old and insecure protocols like Telnet and FTP are used.

Both Windows and Unix versions of the Reflection for Secure IT server allow tunneling in different ways:

- Local

- Remote

- X11 protocol (UNIX)

- FTP protocol (Windows)

- RDP protocol (Windows)

Reflection for Secure IT Logging

Are You Owned?

Security and Logs

All services can generate logging information in Linux/UNIX; this data is directed to the syslog service daemon (UDP Port 514), and in Windows, this information is directed at the Windows Event Logs. You are aware of your security profile only to the frequency and depth that the files are viewed. There are tools to automate this task. Log Parser™ is a free windows utility, and the **grep** command exists in UNIX. (See Syngress title *Microsoft Log Parser Toolkit, ISBN 978-1-932266-52-8,* for more ways to use the tool.)

The logging characteristics of the tool can be refined; indeed, based on the platform on which the server is installed, it is possible to decide whether to write the logs directly within the Microsoft Event or on text files. It is also possible to define the adequate logging level by choosing among Errors, Warnings, Information, Protocol details, and Hex-dump. One particular logging level is called Custom; with this it is possible to specify an event or specific group of events that can be logged. Log file names are generated automatically using the format RSSHD-YYYYMMDD-HHMMSSmmm. log, where YYYYMMDD indicates the date and HHMMSSmmm indicates the GMT time of log file creation. Obviously it is possible to define rotation parameters with the items, as follows:

- Log file rollover (by size)
- Log file rollover (by time)

This type of feature is important when the log activity is to be stored on a remote log farm; indeed it is a task of Reflection for Secure IT to rotate the files and correctly name them according to their date and time. Tables 7.5 and 7.6 show the compatibility with the operating systems.

TIP

The gathering of system log information is critical to your IT security, however, if you do not view these logs, they are just taking up space and you will be unaware of any attacks. You should have a process and policy for the frequency of reviewing these logs.

Table 7.5 Supported Platforms: Linux/UNIX

Unix Systems	
HP-UX 11i v1 (PA-RISC)	SUSE Linux Enterprise Server 9 (Itanium)
HP-UX 11i v2 (Itanium)	SUSE Linux Enterprise Server 9 (x86)
IBM AIX 5.2 (POWER)	SUSE Linux Enterprise Server 9 (x86-64)
IBM AIX 5.3 (POWER)	SUSE Linux Enterprise Server 10 (x86)
Red Hat Enterprise Linux 4 (Itanium)	SUSE Linux Enterprise Server 10 (x86-64)
Red Hat Enterprise Linux 4 (x86)	Sun Solaris 8 (SPARC)
Red Hat Enterprise Linux 4 (x86-64)	Sun Solaris 9 (SPARC)
Red Hat Enterprise Linux 5 (x86)	Sun Solaris 10 (SPARC)
Red Hat Enterprise Linux 5 (x86-64)	

Table 7.6 Supported Platforms Windows

Microsoft Systems
Microsoft Windows Vista
Microsoft Windows XP
Microsoft Windows Server 2003
Microsoft Windows 2000 Server

Other SSH Server Types

There are different SSH implementations, both for the client side and the server side; some are dedicated to specific operating systems, such as Linux, Unix, and Windows; others are dedicated to specific purposes or applications. Among the most famous SSH suites, we will discuss the following:

- SSH1 e SSH2 (SSH communications limited solution)
- OpenSSH (free open solution)
- F-Secure or Reflection for Secure IT (commercial solution)
- Dropbear SSH (free open solution)

The F-Secure or Reflection for Secure IT solution has already been described in the previous paragraphs; that is why it is not described in this section.

OpenSSH

OpenSSH has been released for the first time within OpenBSD 2.6; indeed it was created with the open source BSD license by effectively removing any restriction applied to the SSH version of

Tatu Ylönen. To date, the OpenSSH suite is the most common among the available open solutions. The key components of the OpenSSH suite are:

NOTE

OpenSSH can be downloaded from http://www.openssh.org/.

- ssh, which replaces rlogin and telnet
- scp, for file transfer
- sftp, in place of ftp
- sshd, the SSH daemon

The possible authentications are:

- With public key
- Through passwords and challenge-responses with keyboard interaction
- With the use of Kerberos/GSSAPI

In addition, other authentication methods can be enabled, such as BSD (bsd_auth) or PAM, to enable the authentication through methods such as the one-time password.

SSH1 e SSH2

SSH1 e SSH2 (generally called SSH) has been written for Unix systems and then transferred onto other operating systems. This implementation differs from a completely open source one like OpenSSH because, although the source code is released openly, its free use is allowed only for non-commercial uses. If you want to use SSH for commercial purposes, it is necessary to buy it; the product is marketed by SSH Communication Security, Ltd., and by Attachmate, which markets the product with the name Reflection for Secure IT. Because it is distributed as SSH source code, it must be compiled; however, precompiled packages are available for the most popular systems.

NOTE

At the time of this writing, the commercial version of SSH can be purchased from http://www.ssh.com.

The retail prices at the time of writing were $159.00 for the client and $829.00 for the server (for small/home business use).

OpenSSH Features

OpenSSH is the best and most used open solution because of good implementation, code strictness and cleaning, and the presence of various features that provide high product compatibility and flexibility. These characteristics have made the software very versatile and adaptive to the different environments where it is installed. Indeed, OpenSSH supports numerous encryption algorithms, including 3DES, Blowfish, AES, and Arcfour. It also provides full compatibility with the SSH 1.3, 1.5, and 2.0 standard protocols. Both the client side and the server side of SFTP completely support SSH1 and SSH2. The other key features of the product are listed below:

- X11 forwarding (encrypts X Window System traffic)
- Port forwarding (encrypted channels for legacy protocols)
- Strong authentication (public key, one-time password, and Kerberos authentication)
- Agent forwarding (single-sign-on)
- Kerberos and AFS ticket passing
- Data compression

While we were writing this book, the last version was OpenSSH 5.0; its diffusion characteristics make OpenSSH the most maintained and monitored product from the security profile point of view. Vulnerabilities, once found, are often corrected quickly.

Dropbear SSH Server and Client

Dropbear represents a minimized SSH 2 solution and is distributed under an open-source license; in particular the MIT-style license is applied. It is particularly suitable for "embedded" Linux (or in general Unix) systems in which hardware resources are limited. The key features include the possibility to statically compile Dropbear in a 110kB file; it provides the support to X11 forwarding and for the authentication-agent forwarding for OpenSSH clients. The Dropbear software is compatible with the ~/.ssh/authorized_keys created by OpenSSH It is possible to enable the forwarding of TCP-based communications. Because it was designed to ensure maximum portability on highly customized systems, the platforms on which it was tested are numerous; the main ones are the following:

NOTE

DropBear SSH can be downloaded from the following web site: http://matt.ucc.asn.au/ dropbear/dropbear.html.

- Linux: Standard distributions
- Mac OS X (compile with PAM support)
- FreeBSD, NetBSD, and OpenBSD

- Solaris: Tested v8 x86 and v9 Sparc
- IRIX 6.5 (with /dev/urandom; prngd also should work)
- Tru64 5.1 (using prngd for entropy)
- AIX 4.3.3 (with gcc and Linux Affinity Toolkit); AIX 5.2 (with /dev/[u]random).
- HPUX 11.00 (+prngd); TCP forwarding doesn't work
- Cygwin: tested 1.5.19 on Windows XP

Compiling SSH

First of all it is necessary to download the last stable version of the SSH packet from the official site, ftp://ftp.ssh.com, and then extract it:

```
$ tar zxvf ssh-version-number.tar.gz
```

Usually it is possible to find the signature, in PGP format, of the just-downloaded packet in order to check that the downloaded archive is the same as the original one. The validation procedure requires that the public key is added to the local keyring; usually it is called:

```
$ SSH-DISTRIBUTION-KEY-RSA.asc
```

Further, the signature file with the .sig extension has to be downloaded and then you have to check the packet by digiting:

```
$ pgp ssh-version-number.tar.gz
```

If no warning message is output, then the packet can be considered as valid. The compilation and installation part of the SSH tool requires, as usual, the execution of three key commands within the directory produced by the extraction process; the commands are listed below:

```
$ ./configure
$ make
$ make install
```

The third command must be executed with root privileges because some of the necessary files to run the SSH components will be installed on the file system within some system directories.

The compilation options are different and can be used to refine the product installation by excluding some features, enabled by default, or activating others for specific purposes. The main compilation options are mentioned below; however, it is possible to display the complete list by using the following command:

```
$ configure -help
```

WAN – LAN Connections

If you want to use SSH on the geographical instead of local network, it is advisable to disable the tcp-nodelay option, which allows reducing packet fragmentation:

```
# SSH1, SSH2
$ configure ... --disable-tcp-nodelay ...
```

TCP-Wrappers

TCP-wrappers are security features that allow the filtering and blocking of incoming communications on the basis of the source address generating them. SSh includes the possibility to enable this feature or not through a switch, described below, at compile time:

```
# SSH1, SSH2
$ configure ... --with-libwrap=/usr/local/lib ...
```

X Forwarding

You can inhibit the running of X forwarding, which is the feature that starts applications using a graphic interface on the server and displays the application GUI on the client. To disable it, it is necessary to use the following switch:

```
# SSH1 only
$ configure ... --disable-server-x11-forwarding ...
$ configure ... --disable-client-x11-forwarding ...
# SSH2 only
$ configure ... --disable-x11-forwarding ...
```

Port Forwarding

At compile time, it is also possible to disable the port forwarding capability, which is the feature that encrypts communications traveling over the TCP/IP protocol:

```
# SSH1 only
configure ... —disable-server-portforwarding
# SSH2 only
configure ... —disable-tcp-portforwarding
```

Encryption Algorithms

Obviously it is possible to define which encryption algorithms can be compiled and installed. To add a specific algorithm, it is necessary to add the strings —with-idea, —with-blowfish, —with-des, —with-arcfour, —with-none to the compile command. To exclude the support, the —without keyword has to be used.

Authentications

Your next step is to define the authentication mechanisms supported once SSH has been compiled. There are different types of authentication; the main ones include Kerberos, SecurID, and in version 2 of SSH, those based on OpenPGP. To enable the Kerberos-based authentication, it is necessary to use the previously described syntax as follows: —without-kerberos5. For SecureID, use —with-securid. You can choose to enable the authentication based on PGP with the syntax —with-pgp.

Server Options

After successfully compiling the OpenSSH (sshd) daemon, it is possible to determine some aspects of its behavior by acting on specific options. OpenSSH allows specifying options at two different levels:

- Within the configuration file
- Via the command line when invoking the daemon

It is important to notice how the selectable options depend upon the choices made at compile time (*compile-time flags*); if an option whose support was omitted at compile time is specified, it will not be effective. In the first case, by acting on the configuration file existing in */etc/ssh/sshd_config*, it is possible to declare a series of options, each on separate lines, specified through the *keyword value* pair; if the value string contains spaces, it must be enclosed in double quotes (""). When the sshd daemon processes the configuration file, blank lines and the lines starting with # are considered as comments. The configuration file content is processed by the daemon when started or when it receives a hangup signal (posix's SIGHUP); thus, it is possible to force the daemon to reread the content of its configuration file without ending the process and the active connections. In the configuration file, there can be other two keywords worthy of attention: *subsystem* and *match*. With the *subsystem* keyword, it is possible to configure an external module; by default, no subsystem is enabled. The typical example of a subsystem used to enable the secure file transfer is sftp-server. This module is invoked when the file transfer is requested by a client. On the contrary the *match* keyword introduces a conditional block. If the arguments specified after the keyword are fulfilled, the directives on the following lines overwrite the ones defined in the global configuration file section; this happens until a new conditional block or the file end. The arguments of a match block are defined as criteria–pattern pairs; the available criteria are *User*, *Group*, *Host*, and *Address*. It is possible to define individual or multiple criteria by separating the last ones through a comma, and they are accepted in the definition of the wildcard pattern and logical NOT operators.

NOTE

A pattern consists of zero or more non-whitespace characters. A pattern-list is a comma-separated list of patterns. Patterns within pattern-lists may be negated by preceding them with an exclamation mark ('!'). Note the following:

- * is a wildcard that matches zero or more characters.
- ? is a wildcard that matches exactly one character.

It is important to remember that only a subset of all available keywords can be used within the *match* block. To clarify both concepts, we provide a practical example using both directives in order to restrict, for each user in the system, the access to his or her own home directory only. To achieve this result, it is sufficient to edit and add the following directives, paying attention that they are at the end of the configuration file:

```
Subsystem    sftp    internal-sftp
Match Group sftp
   ChrootDirectory %h
   ForceCommand internal-sftp
   AllowTcpForwarding no
```

These options enable the file transfer subsystem by chrooting the users belonging to the sftp group in their own home directories (%h); furthermore, the possibility of port forwarding is suppressed, which, together with the impossibility to dispose of a shell, increases the overall security level of the implementation. Table 7.7 gives the relevant descriptions and default values of the main keywords that can be declared in the configuration file; for the complete list of the definable options, refer to the relevant page of the online manual (man sshd_config).

Table 7.7 SSH Server Configuration File Variables

Keyword	Description	Value (Default in Bold)	Apply Only for Protocol 2
AddressFamily	Specifies which address family should be used by sshd(8).	**any** inet inet6	
AuthorizedKeysFile	Specifies the file that contains the public keys that can be used for user authentication. AuthorizedKeysFile may contain tokens of the form %T, which are substituted during connection setup.	**.ssh/authorized_keys**	
Banner	The contents of the specified file are sent to the remote user before authentication is allowed. By default, no banner is displayed	File_path	Yes
ChrootDirectory	Specifies a path to chroot(2) to after authentication. This path, and all its components, must be root-owned directories that are not writable by any other user or group.		

Continued

Table 7.7 Continued. SSH Server Configuration File Variables

Keyword	Description	Value (Default in Bold)	Apply Only for Protocol 2
HostKey	Specifies a file containing a private host key used by SSH	**/etc/ssh/ssh_ host_key** (protocol 1) etc/ssh/ssh_host_ rsa_key and /etc/ssh/ssh_ host_dsa_key (protocol 2)	
ListenAddress	Specifies the local addresses on which sshd(8) should listen. Multiple ListenAddress options are permitted. Additionally, any Port options must precede this option for non-port qualified addresses.	**0.0.0.0**	
Match	Introduces a conditional block.		
PasswordAuthentication	Specifies whether password authentication is allowed.	**yes** no	
PermitEmptyPasswords	When password authentication is allowed, it specifies whether the server allows login to accounts with empty password strings.	yes **no**	
PidFile	Specifies the file that contains the process ID of the SSH daemon.	**/var/run/ sshd.pid**	
Port	Specifies the port number on which sshd(8) listens. Multiple options of this type are permitted.	**22**	
Protocol	Specifies the protocol versions sshd(8) supports. The possible values are 1 and 2. Multiple versions must be comma-separated.	1 2 **2,1**	
PubkeyAuthentication	Specifies whether public key authentication is allowed.	**yes** no	yes

In addition to the options definable in the configuration file, it is possible to specify options when invoking the daemon by using parameters passed via command line. In many cases, these options are the counterpart of options that can be specified through the configuration file; on the contrary, the options declarable in the configuration file do not always have an equivalent definable via the command line. However, for all keywords without a corresponding command line parameter, there is also the possibility to use the –o option to specify it. For example, it is possible to specify the support for version two of the protocol through the following command line:

```
# sshd -o "Protocol 2"
```

If the same option exists both in the configuration file and specified through command line, the last one has the priority. Table 7.8 includes some main options that can be set via the command line:

Table 7.8 SSH Server Command Line Variable Options

Command-Line Option	Description	Value (Default in Bold)
-f config_file	Specifies the name of the configuration file sshd refuses to start if there is no configuration file.	**/etc/ssh/sshd_config**
-p port	Specifies the port on which the server listens for connections. Multiple port options are permitted.	**22**
-o option	Can be used to give options in the format used in the configuration file. This is useful for specifying options for which there is no separate command-line flag.	
-d	Debug mode. The server sends verbose debug output to the system log and does not put itself in the background. Multiple -d options increase the debugging level. The maximum is 3.	

OpenSSH needs the existence of some files, in addition to the configuration file, to run correctly. At the daemon start, default paths are used where this information can be searched; it is possible to specify, as described before, alternative paths via the configuration file or command line. In particular, the files that play a specific role for the correct daemon running, besides the already mentioned configuration file, are the following ones:

- Host key files
- Per-account authorization files

The host key files contain information that uniquely identifies the ssh server to the clients. This information is stored in the form of a pair of keys, a public and a private one, which are within the `/etc/ssh/ssh_host_key` path. It is possible to distinguish the public key from the private one from the `.pub` extension associated to it. For the use of version 2 of the protocol, there is a second location where the pairs of keys used for the operation: `/etc/ssh/ssh_host_dsa_key`. The per-account authorization files specify the file path where the public keys to be used for the user authentication are to be searched. For the definition of these paths, it is possible to use special tokens that allow selecting between absolute and relative paths with regard to the home directory of each user.

NOTE

The Following Tokens are Defined:

- `%%` is equivalent to the literal %.
- `%h` is replaced by the home directory of the user being authenticated.
- `%u` is replaced by the username of the user being authenticated.

Running the Server

Usually the OpenSSH server is run as a daemon and invoked at the system start. Each time the service is requested by a client, the daemon simply allocates a new child process to manage the request; the process so created will manage the keys, cryptography, authentication, and execution of commands; it will also manage the data exchange. Alternatively it is also possible to invoke the sshd daemon via the command line; this type of use contrasts with the one seen before, which usually uses inetd (or xinetd) or startup scripts existing in the /etc/rc.d directories. Notice also that an ordinary system user, i.e., without administration privileges, can invoke the sshd daemon, provided that some preliminary operations are completed.

It is possible to launch the OpenSSH daemon in one of the following ways:

- Server start through invocation from the command line
- Server start via init script or inetd (xinetd in alternative)

In the first case it is possible to start the server by typing sshd from the command prompt; as mentioned before, this network service can be executed both by an administrator user, usually root, and a privileged user. In this second case, some preliminary settings are necessary in order to successfully start the server. If the command is started by a root user, OpenSSH will automatically start in the background, listening for requests by the clients. The settings and paths used are those by default. If the server is to be run by a non-privileged user, it is necessary to complete the following steps:

1. Creation of a configuration file (optional);
2. Generation of a host key;
3. Choice of a non-privileged port (>1024).

First of all it is necessary to create a configuration file; this file will be specified, through the -f option, as a parameter at the server start. If this parameter is omitted, the default options or those specified in the global configuration file of the daemon, existing in /etc/ssh/sshd_config, will be used; it is important to stress this condition in order to avoid unexpected behaviors. Secondly, after the creation of a configuration file according to the user specifications, it is necessary to create a set of keys to be used to identify the server. This step is unavoidable because other keys defined within the system are inside paths a common user cannot access. To complete the generation of the key pair for the identification of the server, which is used at different levels in order to run it, the ssh-keygen. ssh-keygen command is used. It allows one to generate, manage, and convert authentication keys for OpenSSH; the utility generates key pairs for use with the first protocol version (RSA) and version 2 (RSA or DSA). The invocation of this command, which is independent of the parameters used, generates a key pair, a private and a public one. The last one is identified with the .pub extension. The main options, besides defining the output file name, give the pair of keys (-f), specifying the type of key (-t) and its length (-b).

Finally, because the user does not have the privileges necessary to use the privileged ports, he or she has to indicate to the daemon, through the –p option, the port on which to listen for incoming connections. The specification of a port lower than 1024 or of a port already used by another service will stop the daemon with the corresponding display of an error message.

> **NOTE**
>
> Regardless of the choice made, in order to allow clients to connect to the OpenSSH server, it is necessary to ensure that the port on which the service is listening can be reached and the connections directed to this port are not blocked by the packet filter devices.

If the daemon setup is performed by a standard user, it is particularly convenient to use the -d option to get additional information useful for the diagnosis of problems that prevent the server start. If you want to perform the service at the system start, it is possible to opt, as mentioned at the beginning of the section, one of the following ways: use an init script or use inetd (or the xinetd version). In the first case, it is possible to use a script among the existing ones in many Linux and BSD distributions and add it at the initial run level of the system in order to start the daemon at system boot. If this script is not available, it is possible to take cue from those provided together with the daemon source (/contrib directory within the source packet). Furthermore, in this script, a check is often carried out in order to verify the existence of specific objects necessary to run the server. These objects include the cryptographic keys; if they do not exist, the ssh-keygen utility is invoked in order to create them.

If instead you want to use the inetd daemon to perform the service, simply edit the configuration file, usually present in /etc/inetd.conf (or /etc/xxinetd.conf), making sure to enter, or in some cases decomment, the following lines:

```
ssh stream tcp nowait root /usr/local/sbin/sshd sshd -i
```

Moreover it is necessary to check that in the /etc/service file of the system there is an entry for OpenSSH with the relevant port associated; by default, the port is 22. The change of these files requires root privileges on the system.

WARNING

Note that when the OpenSSH service is started by a non-privileged user, there are some limitations. These limitations include the impossibility to connect to users other than those with which the process has been executed and the impossibility to access diagnostic information stored in the system logs. It is also important to remember that, as the daemon start is a manual step, it is necessary to dispose of a second access method to start the service. Some of these limitations can be overcome by using specific options.

Basic Server Configuration

We have already described the format and main options definable within the configuration file; furthermore, we have seen how it is possible to require the OpenSSH daemon to use an alternative configuration file through options specifiable from the command line. Now it is time to talk about the configuration file structure. Together with the source one, a standard configuration file is provided. It contains some default directives; however, it is possible to specify specific options in the configuration file in order to overwrite the built-in options and ensure a good security level to the service. The example in Figure 7.5 allows:

- Limiting the login capabilities only to the users who need it.

- Avoiding the login by the administrator and obliging him or her to access as a non-privileged user and to switch to root later.

- Restricting the number of interfaces on which the daemon has to listen.

- Disabling of possible spoofing of sessions; client-alive checks are sent using the encrypted channel.

Figure 7.5 Contents of the SSH Server Configuration File

AllowGroups	Users
AllowUsers	*‹list of users, comma separated.›*
ChallengeResponseAuthentication	No
ClientAliveInterval	15
DenyGroups	Root
DenyUsers	Root
KeepAlive	No
ListenAddress	*‹IP_address.›*
LoginGraceTime	60
MaxStartups	2:50:10
PasswordAuthentication	No
PermitRootLogin	No
Protocol	2
PubkeyAuthentication	Yes

The standard SSH configuration file is not an unchangeable part of the system. If fact this file is likely to be updated and changed to follow the company's security policy and other security needs. This file, however, is a good place for new administrators and users to start learning about the options available to SSH.

WARNING

OpenSSH is made to be as secure as possible, but an improper configuration can expose it to risks.

Authentication

OpenSSH supports different techniques for the authentication; these can be enabled or disabled by acting on the daemon configuration file. At the time this book was written, the main authentication mechanisms supported by OpenSSH for the authentication were:

- password
- publickey (DSA, RSA, OpenPGP)
- hostbased

The simplest method for the authentication to the server is to provide one's identity through the user name-password pair. Similarly to what happens for other authentication mechanisms, after establishing a connection to the OpenSSH daemon, this authenticates that the credentials to access are provided in the form of the username and password. Besides using the local repository of the system users, usually defined in /etc/passwd, it is possible to authenticate the request to a Kerberos KDC.

Instead of providing a password, it is possible to use a pair of keys for the authentication to the server. Furthermore, the private part of the key can further be protected by a password. The public key-based authentication bases on the principle of the asymmetric ciphers. The client and the server have a key; each encrypts the messages that only the other end of the communication can decrypt. Thus, by keeping one's key secure from prying eyes (private key), the other end can assume the authenticity, as well as read the communication content using its key (public key). To that end it is possible to use three different algorithms, as discussed in Table 7.9:

Table 7.9 Algorithms and Options for SSH Authentication

Algorithm	Parameter to ssh-keygen	Default Output Filename	Public Key Starting with
RSA (SSH version 2)	-t rsa	~/.ssh/id_rsa ~/.ssh/id_rsa.pub	ssh-rsa
RSA (SSH version 1)	-t rsa1	~/.ssh/identity ~/.ssh/identity.pub	2048 35
DSA	-t dsa	~/.ssh/id_dsa ~/.ssh/id_dsa.pub	ssh-dsa

Each public key, e.g. ~/.ssh/id_dsa.pub, is made up of the following parts:

- An identifier on the type
- A space
- The modulus (the alphanumeric string)
- A space, followed by a comment (optional)

The modulus is the textual, Unicode representation of the key; this representation of the keys allows one to manage them more easily. Displayed below is an example of what a person capturing your authentication data that is being sent via SSH (Figure 7.6). Note that none of the data is readable, due to the encryption.

Figure 7.6 Display of Encrypted Authentication Data Generated by SSH

```
Ssh-dss AAAAB3NzaC1kc3MAAACBAPqxNrKasR6zUGxFE/B61b4sjrEZCNrPgoaTht RhjGV+1pD4UUW3jMefvefI2j26
dvHLoEGe9DJ3wfj71RWEFFYoIL1rRJF4Tn9Isej0g69aKY7PcaCLLpJPSbJCNyXDSyL1qRK8ROgX+F34uvet/3kuJ4Fo
IgH2//d/tJE5LifBAAAAFQDAy/zuHqLYk/4DLyboYqJP77UkLQAAAIAoUrfZkgo3GKXQn06qTbF1UuMf1RMz/BHBrFjp
+bUI1xCnde8u6wOFn+2HWZimU0LfR2UbrnAcvjGwYo0COj8vWZKEOuHzY+e1xzgHxwrx3BJ5R02B9ASwv4GA5hRqLwUq
wHxuQz7PpoSgsRLdhRbJmhZiACG1VHZg+pOkT6zeOAAAAIAi11TBIPRrKOqDHzOeX1CZmwBXnRs1MZQV2AKOb1NN2UY1
1AwmnwJpC+bFB93RhN/aaZi8f2W7Z0Gncp8J6WSAfRFggqwryhYDQX5c2ze4E6AROqAD1/b7XwGJyhwP+J4h78CP5y8b
RuJNUkrA2vfQfpsmSjiIRB7PXAUXR80vOq== root@netherworld
```

The use of this technique has some advantages compared to the previous one, including:

- It is more difficult to perform attacks of brute force and credential cracking
- Leaving the public key on the server system is more secure than setting the credentials on the system within /etc/shadow.
- A passphrase to be remembered with the possibility to connect to multiple systems.

At last, through the host-based authentication mechanism, it is possible to enable the access from a client system to the server system if the username used exists in both systems. This method is useful in small realities where there are trust relations among the different systems; moreover the passwords are not to be transferred to the different systems as the key mechanism described in the previous point is used. However there are some security implications derived from the use of this method that are to be taken into account: the compromise of one of the clients within the hosts authorized to access the ssh server lets the attacker access a subsequent system.

Summary

In this chapter we looked at the available options for SSH servers, both commercial and open source. We overviewed the protocols and standards that document the servers function as well as how we can customize the server services to meet changing needs. The files and variables associated with the creation of the server were discussed.

The configuration of the server post compile, we investigated and saw the methods to generate key pairs for authentication. Two commercial options were examined. One is compatible with the original SSH standard. It provides legacy compatibility and technical support and stable patch management.

Solutions Fast Track

The Components That Make Up the SSH Server

- ☑ The SSH server service daemon is called sshd.
- ☑ sshd is a manually loaded service.
- ☑ The standard sshd service supports ssh clients and scp and sftp commands.

Protocols in Use

- ☑ The Transport layer protocol (SSH-TRANS) creates the encrypted session.
- ☑ The (SSH-USERAUTH) authenticates the user to the server.
- ☑ The connection protocol (SSH-CONNECT) handles the sessions and channels used between the client and server.

Randomness of Cryptography

- ☑ Generating encryption keys requires a random number generator.
- ☑ Block ciphers apply block text, with clear text using the key to generate cipher text.
- ☑ PRNG stands for Pseudo-Random Number Generator.
- ☑ PRNGs require a small amount of text to seed the key generation.
- ☑ The seed text can be a stored file or some other event, such as seconds idle for the harddrive.

Which Communication Is Protected with SSH

- ☑ Traffic between the UNIX client and server using X-Windows is clear text.
- ☑ Traffic using telnet, rlogin, rsh and http, are clear text by default.

   ☑ Port forwarding allows unsecure traffic to go over an SSH tunnel to the server, providing encryption for X-Windows, http, and other clear text protocols.

   ☑ SSH client replaces telnet, rlogin, rsh and ftp.

F-Secure SSH Server

   ☑ F-Secure SSH is a commercial product called Reflection for Secure IT.

   ☑ The location for this software is http://www.attachmate.com.

Other SSH Server Types

   ☑ OpenSSH is the most popular server, as it is open source and supports multiple platforms.

   ☑ SSH1 e SSH2 is a commercial program located at http://www.ssh.com.

   ☑ Dropbear is a minimized SSH protocol used when hardware is minimal.

Compiling SSH

   ☑ All SSH versions come in source code and must be compiled on the server on which you plan to run it.

   ☑ Command line and configuration file options are available to control how SSHd compiles.

   ☑ Once the sshd service daemon is compiled, it must be manually started.

Server Options

   ☑ The traffic between the UNIX client and server using X-Windows is clear text.

   ☑ Traffic using telnet, rlogin, rsh and http, is clear text by default.

   ☑ Port forwarding allows unsecure traffic to go over an SSH tunnel to the server, providing encryption for X-Windows, http, and other clear text protocols.

   ☑ The SSH client replaces telnet, rlogin, rsh, and ftp.

Running the Server

   ☑ Command line and configuration file options can be invoked to customize SSH.

   ☑ The configuration file is a starting point for configuration.

   ☑ This file should be reviewed against your company's security policy.

   ☑ Logging is a valuable tool in monitoring against security breaches.

Authentication

- ☑ The three methods of authentication are:
  - ☑ Password
  - ☑ Public key (RSA, OpenPGP, and DSA)
  - ☑ Host based (stored key)
- ☑ Generated RSA and DSA keys are stored in files in the ~/.ssh/ folders.
- ☑ When connecting to multiple systems, pass phrases can be used.

Frequently Asked Questions

Q: What RFC's apply to SSH server?

A: IETF RFC's 4250, 4251, 4252, 4253, and 4254 (see Chapter 4 for more details).

Q: What is the most popular SSH server available today?

A: OpenSSH (from the OpenSSH Group http://www.openssh.org) is the most popular in use today.

Q: How strong are the encryption algorithms in use today?

A: 3DES and AES can use up to a 256-bit key. These algorithms are industry standards and are currently susceptible to breach.

Q: Where can I learn more about these encryption standards?

A: *Cryptography for Developers,* published by Syngress Publishers in 2006, will help you understand the cryptography standards in use, both in SSH and in other security protocols.

Q: Are there packages of SSH server that I don't have to compile myself?

A: Yes, OpenSSH has a compiled version for most platforms as well as the two commercial packages.

Q: Why would you choose Dropbear over OpenSSH?

A: If you are running a small hardware platform and resources are scarce, you may need SSH but not have the resources to run the full OpenSSH version.

Q: If we can use AES or 3DES, why would we use older encryption methods that are not as strong?

A: Some legacy clients do not have the latest additions, so to maintain backward compatibility, we had to leave them in.

## Chapter 8

SSH on Windows

Solutions in this chapter:

- **Using Windows SSH Clients**
- **Selecting an SSH Server for Windows**
- **Using SUA SSH Servers**
- **Using Cygwin SSH Servers**
- **Using Native Windows SSH Servers**

☑ **Summary**

☑ **Solutions Fast Track**

☑ **Frequently Asked Questions**

Introduction

Historically, Windows has been a graphical operating system. The initial 16-bit versions of Windows were overlays over MS-DOS. However, Microsoft developed a comprehensive set of native 32-bit Windows APIs, collectively known as Win32, designed to be the core of a family of native Windows operating systems. The first of these systems, Windows NT, offered Win32 as the main environment; a subset of these APIs, Win32s, was back-ported to Windows for Workgroups. Windows 95 provided native support for Win32 even though some operating system components were still 16-bit.

Once the Win32 environment was introduced, most Windows users quickly came to see the command line as a legacy interface for DOS programs and for some scripting environments. Almost all of the user applications and management tools were developed as GUI programs. Until Windows NT 4.0 Terminal Server edition, there was no facility for remote login built in to Windows; administrators and users needed to physically log on to a Windows machine to run applications and utilities on it. To work around this problem, Microsoft used the MS-RPC protocol and graphical frameworks such as the MMC to provide centralized, distributed administrative tools. These tools continue to be the main thrust behind Microsoft's administration philosophy, even as support for the Remote Desktop Protocol (RDP) was added to Windows 2000 to reduce the need for physical console access.

Over the years, however, administrators and power users have asked for the increased flexibility offered by command line management tools and scripting interfaces. In answer, Microsoft has been slowly introducing more command-line tools in each new version of Windows, as well as increasing the options available in existing tools and utilities. As more of these tools and applications become readily available, and as more Windows administrators learn about them and become comfortable using them, the need for a secure connection grows. While RDP and the MS-RPC protocol suite address many of these needs, it doesn't solve them all – and they do not address the needs of users and administrators in heterogeneous environments.

Using Windows SSH Clients

Let's start our exploration of Windows SSH software by taking a look at the clients available. In general, Windows SSH clients do more than their counterparts on Unix, Linux, and Mac systems because Windows doesn't have a native terminal application. The CMD shell on modern versions of Windows lacks many of the features necessary to make a good shell terminal, so Windows SSH clients are usually terminal emulators that offer a variety of access methods, such as telnet, rlogin, or even serial port access.

As a result, Windows SSH clients are usually graphical applications. They may offer additional command line utilities – typically for scripting – and file transfer utilities for SCP or SFTP. Let's examine several alternatives.

SSH Tectia

SSH Tectia (http://www.ssh.com/) is considered by many to be the gold standard of commercial SSH implementations. Their client package is sold separately from their server implementation but shares many of the same features, including an impressive amount of Windows integration. This native Windows application is shown in Figure 8.1.

Figure 8.1 The SSH Tectia Client

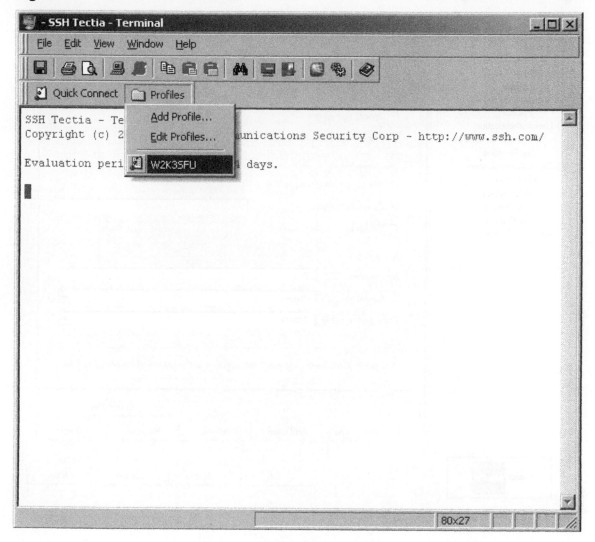

Installing the SSH Tectia client is a simple process with no tricks or complicated options. It offers a large amount of configuration (shown in Figure 8.2), including:

- Multiple connection profiles
- Per-profile control over ciphers and encryption protocols
- Configurable tunneling and proxy support
- Certificate-based authentication
- Integration with Windows Active Directory/Kerberos

Figure 8.2 Configuring the SSH Tectia Client

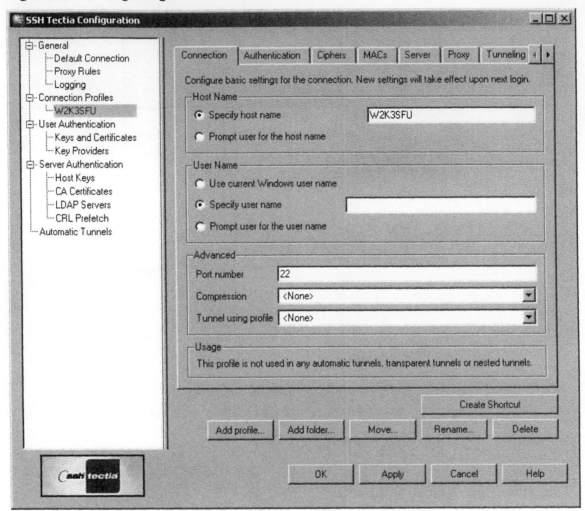

PuTTY

Moving into the realm of free software, PuTTY (http://www.chiark.greenend.org.uk/~sgtatham/putty/) is one of the most popular, simple, and friendly Windows SSH clients. It offers a number of deployment options, including the ability to download a single executable that can be run off of a removable drive or flash drive without first requiring installation. Figure 8.3 shows a typical PuTTY window.

Figure 8.3 The PuTTY SSH Connection

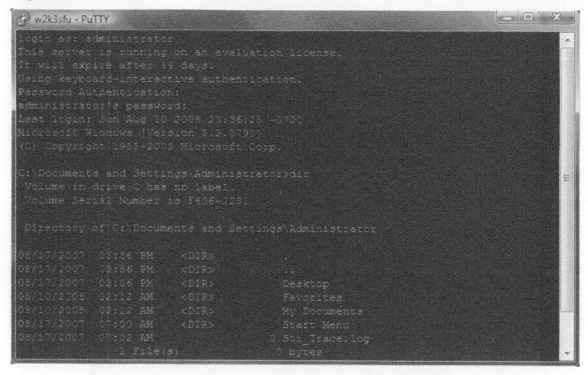

Like other clients, PuTTY offers the ability to create, save, and load a variety of connection profiles as shown in Figure 8.4. It also provides support for telnet and rlogin, as well as extensive control over the appearance of the terminal window and the terminal emulation options.

Figure 8.4 Configuring the PuTTY Connection Profile

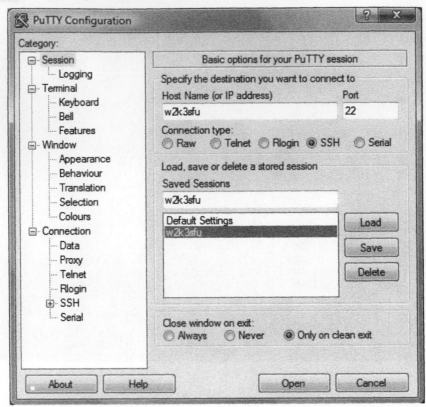

PuTTY also includes a number of command-line tools and utilities, including an SSH authentication agent, SCP, SFTP, and telnet.

TIP

While stock PuTTY doesn't offer many advanced options such as Kerberos or Active Directory support, the source code is freely available, which means that others have been able to modify it to add these features. One of the most intriguing variants, Quest PuTTY (http://rc.quest.com/topics/putty/), is provided by Quest Software and includes Active Directory and Kerberos integration.

WinSCP

If PuTTY is the king of free Windows SSH clients, then WinSCP (http://winscp.net/eng/index.php) is the king of free Windows graphical SCP/SFTP clients. WinSCP offers both a Windows Explorer-like interface (shown in Figure 8.5) as well as a Norton Commander-like interface.

Figure 8.5 The WinSCP Client

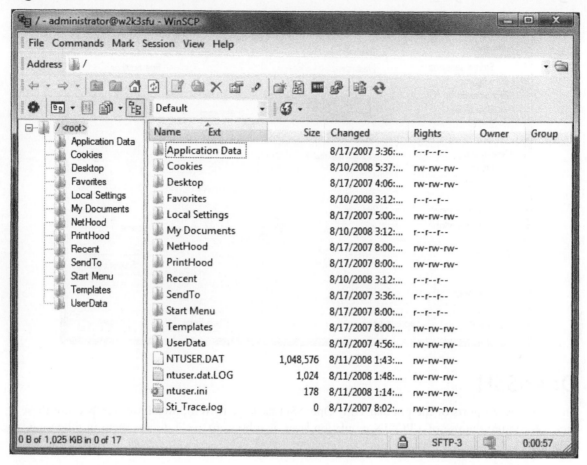

WinSCP offers a basic profile management capability, shown in Figure 8.6 Again, like PuTTY, it doesn't offer a lot of advanced features, but for basic secure file copying using passwords or certificates, it can't be beat.

Figure 8.6 Managing WinSCP Profiles

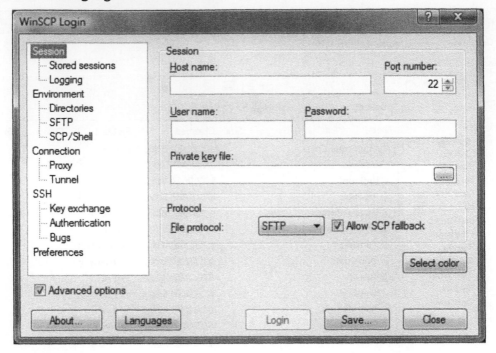

OpenSSH

There are several ports of the popular GPL OpenSSH package to Windows. However, because these packages require the use of a POSIX emulation layer or subsystem, we'll discuss them in following sections.

Selecting an SSH Server for Windows

In order to select the right SSH server for your Windows systems, you first need to choose which subsystem under which it will run. Because SSH server software was first developed for the Unix terminal architecture and networking model, initial implementations made heavy use of Unix-specific features for both security and scalability. As a result, porting SSH software to Windows typically presents interesting challengers that various developers have solved in three main ways.

Windows and POSIX

The Portable Operating System Interface (POSIX) was one of several attempts to develop a consistent set of standards for the large variety of Unix and Unix-like operating systems that were in existence. Although each variant shared many common characteristics, they also each had their own implementation quirks and peculiarities that made porting software between variants sometimes frustrating and difficult. POSIX was an attempt to hammer out some of these differences and allow developers to have a standard set of features in the Unix APIs on which they could count.

POSIX-compliant software was intended to be source-code compatible. In theory, POSIX-compliant software wouldn't need to be re-written or ported when moved between systems; the administrator would merely need to take the source code, compile it, and re-link it against the local system libraries. In reality, the standard was very ambiguous and allowed a surprising number of functions to be present only in skeleton format. As a result, a POSIX-compliant system could pass all of the tests simply by defining a stub version of functions, without doing much of the real work of implementing those functions usefully. While POSIX-compliant software would compile and link on these systems, it wouldn't actually do anything useful when executed.

However, POSIX had advantages that other standards didn't; so many entities (including the U.S. government) soon began requiring new operating systems to be POSIX-compliant. As a result, Microsoft made a crucial design choice when developing the native Win32 operating system, Windows NT. Instead of hard-wiring the Win32 APIs into the operating system, they would instead be presented as a separate sub-system on top of the Hardware Abstraction Layer and NT kernel. This design gave them a number of advantages, including the ability to provide a separate OS/2-compatible subsystem as well as a minimal POSIX subsystem in parallel with the Win32 subsystem. The Win32 subsystem, in turn, provided a 16-bit Windows emulation environment to run legacy 16-bit Windows software. As a result, Windows NT gave Microsoft a highly flexible, competitive offering for contracts that required POSIX compliance without actually requiring the use of POSIX-compliant software. The native Windows POSIX layer was extremely limited, couldn't easily share code or data with processes running in the other subsystems, and had no GUI support. It was mostly intended to provide support for useful filesystem semantics such as the Unix permission model and long file names.

Today, the original POSIX specification has been supplemented by additional POSIX extensions that define other useful types of behavior. Several commercial Unix variants support POSIX to one degree or other, while other operating systems such as OpenVMS also provide useful POSIX support through optional packages. Microsoft, however, dropped their limited native POSIX subsystem in Windows XP and Windows Server 2003, replacing it with the add-on Services for Unix (SFU).

Interix, SFU, and SUA

While the government may have been satisfied with a minimal POSIX subsystem in Windows, other developers were not. Once side effect of the Windows NT design was that third-party developers could write their own POSIX-compliant subsystems, and at least two software companies did just that. The MKS Toolkit (http://www.mkssoftware.com/products) was used by Microsoft for SFU 1.0 and SFU 2.0, which provided a full-featured POSIX subsystem for Windows NT 4.0 and Windows 2000, along with several useful precompiled utilities, a general Unix emulation environment, and several Windows services intended to help migration from and interoperability with NIS and NFS environments.

With SFU 3.0, Microsoft moved to the Interix subsystem, which they had acquired from Softway Systems in 1999. This version included support for Windows XP and included a full GNU SDK for the Interix subsystem. SFU 3.5 was distributed for free by Microsoft, dropping support for Windows NT 4.0 and adding Windows Server 3.0. It improved POSIX support by adding the POSIX threading extensions.

With Windows Server 2003 R2, Microsoft incorporated the SFU 3.5 features and added them to the R2 code base as native Windows components (installed from Disk 2). As a result, the various interoperability services were separated from the underlying Interix POSIX subsystem, which was renamed Subsystem for UNIX-based Applications (SUA). This was the same underlying codebase as SFU 3.5, however, and applications developed against one would run on the other.

In Windows Server 2008 and some versions of Windows Vista (Enterprise and Ultimate), Microsoft continues to provide SUA and Unix interoperability services. Unlike the SFU 3.5 codebase, however, the SDKs and Unix utilities are no longer included; they must be downloaded and installed separately.

SUA programs run in a parallel subsystem, but can share data and access to Win32 applications and APIs. As a result, typical Unix shells run under SUA can run Windows programs and scripts, such as VBScript and PowerShell. However, because it is a Unix-like environment, SUA requires a Unix-like set of system files and directories to be laid out on the filesystem, including a separate *passwd* and *group* file. The native authentication libraries do not directly tie in to the local machine accounts or to Active Directory, if the machine is joined to an Active Directory domain.

Cygwin

Rather than create their own POSIX subsystem, other developers took a different approach: write a Win32 emulation layer to provide the POSIX system calls, mapping them to native Win32 functionality when possible and providing any extra code necessary. Cygnus Solutions produced Cygwin (http://www.cygwin.com/), the most popular of these alternatives.

The modern Cygwin distribution provides the base emulation DLL along with a minimal tool chain. Administrators can then select from a wide variety of additional pre-compiled packages to be installed on the local system, or they can use the compiler and utilities to build existing software that has been ported to Cygwin. Many popular open source programs provide Windows compatibility by targeting the Cygwin environment.

The Cygwin system provides the extra POSIX compliance in a single DLL, allowing programs to mix POSIX, GNU C/C++, and Win32 code in the same application binary. Like Interix applications, shells run under Cygwin can access Win32 programs, and the Cygwin environment suffers from the same parallel structure that SUA does.

Cygwin is not the only emulation environment; AT&T Research develops and distributes the UWIN package, which accomplishes the same task. However, this chapter will not describe UWIN in any great detail; those interested are encouraged to go to the UWIN website (http://www.research.att.com/sw/tools/uwin/) for more details.

Win32

When porting or re-implementing complex network software such as SSH to Windows, the final option is to do the deep-level rewrites necessary to make the code native Win32 code. While this approach is obviously more work on the part of the developer, it potentially offers much greater advantages, especially when trying to get Windows administrators to use the software:

- The ability to create the SSH software as a native Windows service.

- Better integration with Windows operations and management features such as Group Policy, the Windows installer, the Windows Firewall, and the Windows event log system.

- The ability to leverage the existing Win32 interfaces to specific features such as Active Directory (Kerberos and LDAP), NTFS, or the Windows Management Instrumentation (WMI).

- Potential to use existing management and display frameworks such as the Microsoft Management Console (MMC), reducing the amount of code necessary to implement the product.

- The ability to take advantage of the Windows CyptoAPI, ensuring that a broad variety of security mechanisms can be supported, including one-time passwords and smart cards. In addition, the responsibility for implementing, testing, and maintaining the complex and sensitive cryptographic routines is delegated to developers who have special training and tools.

- A Microsoft-identified support and upgrade path for running and porting the software to 64-bit Windows environments.

For all these reasons, many Windows administrators prefer to run critical services as native Windows software.

Are You Owned?

Learning New Skills

Many Windows administrators have little or no experience with the intricacies of deploying and managing software that uses text configuration files. Unfortunately, by deploying any of the various OpenSSH variants for Windows (whether using the Cygwin or SUA subsystems), these administrators may be opening themselves up for trouble. Merely installing the software package isn't enough; you need to be willing and able to learn the following skills:

- **Deployment:** Each system must have the software installed and configured individually, or some other method must be found to distribute common configuration files to multiple computers. While you can include the base subsystem and SSH software as part of a system image, you'll need other methods to roll out updates. Because these systems aren't typical Windows applications, they don't have a familiar method for detecting updates. Administrators will need to have a routine or schedule to check for updates manually, download them, test them, and deploy them.

- **Configuration:** The default sshd_config and ssh_config files have many potentially useful features (such as Kerberos integration) turned off by default, which could make the SSH deployment significantly less safe than

Continued

it could be. At the very least, ensure that these configurations disable the use of the insecure SSH1 protocol. On the bright side, the configuration files are text files, so administrators with scripting skills can easily create a system for pushing out configuration files from a central source, such as such versioning repository such as SharePoint or even a source control package such as CVS or Subversion.

■ **Monitoring**: You can use native Windows monitoring tools to keep track of raw network traffic, but in order to get the specific details necessary to accurately monitor and troubleshoot your SSH sessions, you'll need to learn additional portions of the SUA or Cygwin environments in order to write monitoring scripts. You don't have the benefit of using standard Microsoft tools such as Operations Manager or protocols such as WMI, although you may be able to use SNMP to get at least some level of detail.

If you've got a mixed Windows/*nix environment, you probably have the skills in-house to handle these tasks. However, if you're running in a pure Windows shop, the continuing operational cost of these tasks may be sufficiently high to offset the initial savings you'll enjoy by using freely available software. For these environments, you may want to look into using native Windows software.

Using SUA SSH Servers

There's been a growing level of interest in the SUA system because it is offered and supported by Microsoft and has now been integrated into the latest versions of the Windows operating system. The fact that it runs as a separate subsystem, rather than as an emulation layer, has many Windows administrators convinced that it offers better performance than Cygwin.

The primary SUA SSH server is OpenSSH. This is a full native port of OpenSSH to the SUA subsystem, but it does not offer a native Windows control or configuration utility. Luckily, you can get a pre-compiled version of OpenSSH from the SUA Community (http://www.interopsystems.com/community/default.htm); you don't have to compile the software yourself.

Installing SUA/SFU

The first step is to activate the SUA subsystem. How you do this depends on which version of Windows you are running.

Windows 2000, Windows XP, or Windows Server 2003

On these systems, you must download SFU 3.5 from Microsoft (http://technet.microsoft.com/en-us/interopmigration/bb380242.aspx) and install it on your machine. Unless noted otherwise, you can accept the defaults:

1. Run the installer and accept the license.

2. Select **Custom Installation**.

3. When selecting the components, ensure that **Utilities** and **Interix GNU Components** are selected.

4. On the Security Settings screen, ensure that the **Enable setuid behavior for Interix programs** checkbox is selected.

5. On the User Name Mapping screen, you should select the **Remote User Name Mapping Server** radio button unless you know that you are going to install a local name mapping service. You can enter the name of the local host in the box if you don't plan on installing a name mapping service on your network; it's not required just to run OpenSSH.

6. Complete the rest of the installation and reboot.

You've now installed SFU and can move on to "Installing the Software" section of this chapter.

WARNING

On the Security Settings screen, there is an additional checkbox for enabling case-sensitivity behavior. Do not enable this checkbox unless you have thoroughly tested the behavior of each program that will be installed on this server! I once enabled this checkbox on a testing server and experienced problems installing native Windows applications whose developers were sloppy about how they referred to several mixed-case files.

However, you may need this function if you have to access files or directories with names that differ only by capitalization. Note that naming files in this fashion is considered risky practice, even on Unix systems, but sometimes it happens. If you fall into this situation, you may need to ensure that SFU and OpenSSH are installed on a stand-alone server reserved just for these applications.

Windows Server 2003 R2, Windows Vista (Enterprise or Ultimate), or Windows Server 2008

On Windows Server 2003 R2, you first have to continue the operating system installation from Disk 2 after the first disk is completed and you log on. If you don't perform this step, then the additional SUA components won't be placed into the Windows Setup program and you have what is effectively a Windows Server 2003 + SP1 system. In Windows Vista and Windows 2008, the SUA component is part of the regular build. Unless noted otherwise, you can accept the defaults:

1. Open the Control Panel, select **Add/Remove Programs**, and select **Add/Remove Windows Components**.

2. Select the **Subsystem for UNIX Applications** checkbox.

3. On Windows Server 2003 R2, complete the following steps:

    ■ Ensure that **Utilities** and **Interix GNU Components** are selected.

    ■ On the Security Settings screen, ensure that the **Enable setuid behavior for Interix programs** checkbox is selected.

    ■ On the User Name Mapping screen, you should select the **Remote User Name Mapping Server** radio button unless you know that you are going to install a local name mapping service. You can enter the name of the local host in the box if you don't plan on installing a name mapping service on your network; it's not required just to run OpenSSH.

4. Complete the rest of the installation and reboot.

You've now installed SUA and can move on to "Installing the SUA SDK and Utilities" section of this chapter.

WARNING

On the Security Settings screen, there is an additional checkbox for enabling case-sensitivity behavior. Do not enable this checkbox unless you have thoroughly tested the behavior of each program that will be installed on this server! I once enabled this checkbox on a testing server and experienced problems installing native Windows applications whose developers were sloppy about how they referred to several mixed-case files.

However, you may need this function if you have to access files or directories with names that differ only by capitalization. Note that naming files in this fashion is considered risky practice, even on Unix systems, but sometimes it happens. If you fall into this situation, you may need to ensure that SFU and OpenSSH are installed on a standalone server reserved just for these applications.

Installing the SUA SDK and Utilities

Now that you have the SUA subsystem in place, you must now install the SDK and various tools and utilities. While these utilities don't include the OpenSSH software, they do include various helper utilities and tools that SUA needs to actually function. If you're running Windows 2000, Windows XP, or Windows Server 2003, you can skip this step. Unless noted otherwise, you can accept the defaults:

1. Download the SUA SDK and utilities from http://go.microsoft.com/fwlink/?LinkID=59121.

2. Select **Custom Installation**.

3. When selecting the components, ensure that **Base Utilities, Base SDK, GNU Utilities**, and **GNU SDK** components are selected.

4. On the Security Settings screen, ensure that the **Enable SuToRoot behavior for SUA programs** and **Enable setuid behavior for SUA programs** checkboxes are selected.

5. Complete the rest of the installation and reboot.

With the SDK and utilities installed, you can move on to "Installing the Software" section of this chapter.

WARNING

On the Security Settings screen, there is an additional checkbox for enabling case-sensitivity behavior. Do not enable this checkbox unless you have thoroughly tested the behavior of each program that will be installed on this server! I once enabled this checkbox on a testing server and experienced problems installing native Windows applications whose developers were sloppy about how they referred to several mixed-case files.

However, you may need this function if you have to access files or directories with names that differ only by capitalization. Note that naming files in this fashion is considered risky practice, even on Unix systems, but sometimes it happens. If you fall into this situation, you may need to ensure that SFU and OpenSSH are installed on a standalone server reserved just for these applications.

Installing the Software

The final step is to download a software bundle from the SUA Community website. They offer four packaged bundles:

- The Power User bundle, which includes common software including OpenSSH.

- The Developer bundle, which includes the Power User bundle as well as all the utilities and GCC compilers necessary to allow you to build software from source code under SUA.

- The System Administrator bundle, which includes the Power User bundle as well as additional management utilities.

- The Complete Toolset bundle, which gives you everything in all three bundles.

Unless you're running short on disk space or have specific security concerns, you should just download and install the Complete Toolset bundle. This ensures that if you need to modify your version of OpenSSH (perhaps to include Kerberos support), you have the tools and libraries in place to do so.

Whichever bundle you download, the software comes as a standard Windows installer; simply execute it and run. There are no surprise options, so you can accept the defaults. When you're done, you now have a functional SUA installation, including OpenSSH. This is a standard OpenSSH installation, so we won't repeat the configuration instructions here; instead, refer to Chapter 9 for more instructions.

TIP

The SUA Community website also includes a lively set of forums and several helpful PDF documents that will help you get the most out of SUA, including instructions on how to get PowerShell to operate from an SSH session.

Using Cygwin SSH Servers

As is the case with SUA, OpenSSH is the primary SSH server under Cygwin. Again, it's a full native port of OpenSSH. However, there are versions that offer some additional native Windows functionality, such as a Windows-based control console or the ability to install SSH as a Windows service.

Installing Cygwin and OpenSSH

In order to install the Cygwin environment and OpenSSH, follow these steps:

1. Download the latest Cygwin installer from http://www.cygwin.com/.

2. Run the installer.

3. On the Choose a Download Source screen, you generally want to select the **Install from Internet** option.

4. On the Select Root Install Directory, provide the root directory; this directory forms the top of your Cygwin's Unix equivalency file system. Unless you have reasons to override them, keep the recommended defaults for the other settings.

5. On the Select Packages screen, select the following additional packages:

   ■ cygrun (provides the facility to control OpenSSH as a Windows service)

   ■ difftools (needed by the OpenSSH installation)

   ■ openssh (the OpenSSH package)

   ■ openssl (required for certificate handling)

6. Continue the installation. When it is complete, reboot the system.

You can access your new Cygwin environment from Start | All Programs | Cygwin | bash. This opens up a bash shell as your root user, allowing you to configure OpenSSH. This is a standard OpenSSH installation, so we won't repeat the configuration instructions here; instead, refer to Chapter 9 for more instructions.

Notes from the Underground...

SSH Tunnels and the Windows Administrator

SSH tunneling is just as compelling of a feature to Windows administrators as it is to Unix administrators. However, there's a definite right way and wrong way to do it, in part because of the nature of the Windows administrative tools and protocols. In particular, MS-RPC is particularly port-hungry and can be very difficult and port-intensive to configure through firewalls and SSH tunnels.

In order to do this, you should get in the habit of using a dedicated management console. This system can be Windows XP, Vista, Server 2003, or even Server 2008 (depending on application compatibilities), and it holds all of the management tools necessary. This system is then located anywhere on the network where you and your firewall administrators can agree; many firewall administrators don't like to allow MS-RPC between, say, your interior protected network and any perimeter networks. They, in turn, only have to open a single port – TCP 22 – for you to open up SSH to the management station. You then use port tunneling to allow an RDP session (TCP 33898) from your SSH client to the SSH server installed on the management station. Voila! Instant secure connection.

To tunnel RDP over SSH using Cygwin OpenSSH packages, you need to make a couple of configuration changes:

1. Install the Cygwin OpenSSH packages, but do not run the *ssh-host-config* command yet.

2. Edit the cygwin.bat file (normally found in C:\CYGWIN\) to contain the following line:set CYGWIN=binmode tty ntsec

3. Run the ssh-host-config command. Configure OpenSSH to use privilege separation and allow it to create the local privileged account. Allow it to install SSH as a service.

4. Configure the sshd_config file to allow other non-default options, such as permitting port tunnels or adding support for additional authentication mechanisms such as Kerberos or GSSAPI. (These methods may require you to install and configure other Cygwin packages.)

5. Start the SSH service.

6. Configure tunneling on your client.

Continued

So why not just use RDP? Well, that's a matter of taste and habit. In many environments, RDP is seen as insecure. Depending on the version of the server to which you're connecting, RDP may not support the encryption and hashing algorithms you need to use. Tunneling RDP over SSH solves this difficulty; it allows you to specify the authentication method, encryption algorithm, and hash strength used to protect the connection.

COPSSH

One of the big drawbacks to the default Cygwin OpenSSH package is that you have to duplicate your user management efforts; you not only must create users in Active Directory (or on the local Windows machine), but also you must create them in the Cygwin *passwd* and *group* files. For Windows administrators without Unix skills, or in a large environment, this can be an irritating level of work without specialized scripts to keep the accounts synchronized (and even then, password synchronization will be especially difficult).

The COPSSH package (http://www.itefix.no/copssh/) provides a Windows native management console, allowing you to work around this problem through a User Activation Wizard as shown in Figure 8.7.

Figure 8.7 The COPSSH User Activation Wizard

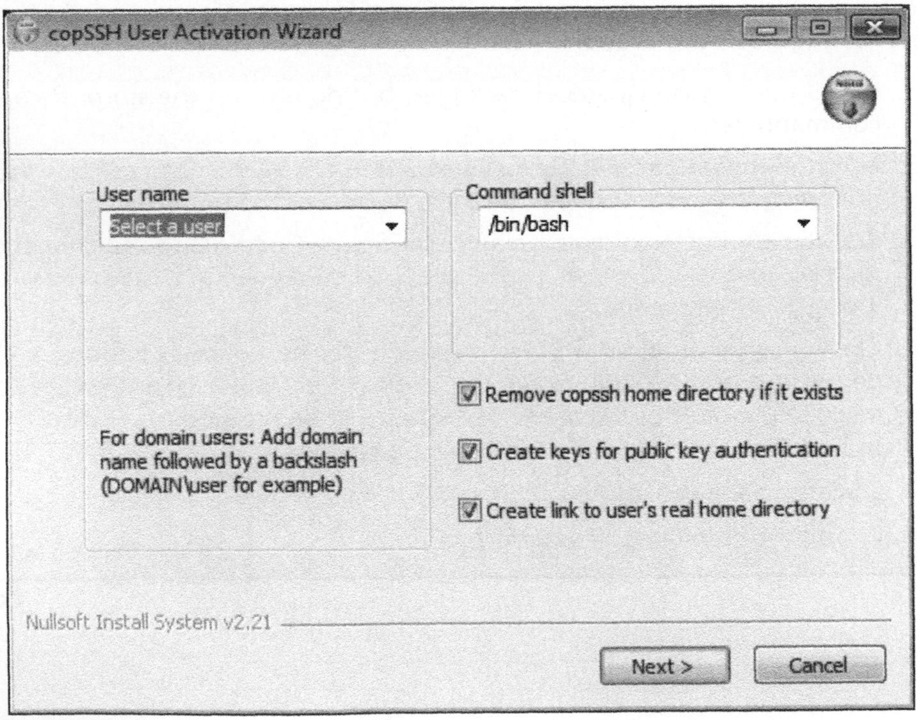

These console capabilities are provided as shortcuts in the Programs menu. Other than this functionality, COPSSH is a standard Cygwin OpenSSH package, so you sacrifice nothing by using it. In fact, the COPSSH package is a self-contained package; you don't need to have previously installed Cygwin to use it. If all you want is SSH, this is a good alternative.

Using Native Windows SSH Servers

After seeing some of the limitations you must work around for SUA or Cygwin-based OpenSSH, you may consider a native Windows SSH server to be a slam-dunk decision. Looking through the field, there would appear to be quite a selection. However, you will notice that almost all of the offerings are commercial; you have to pay money, sometimes quite a bit of money, in order to get them, and not all of these offerings are as fully featured as OpenSSH. We'll look at two Windows native SSH servers: the SSH Tectia server offering and freeSSHd.

SSH Tectia

SSH Tectia (http://www.ssh.com/) is considered by many to be the gold standard of commercial SSH implementations. Their server package is sold separately from their client implementation but shares many of the same features, including an impressive amount of Windows integration. This native Windows server application is shown in Figure 8.8.

Figure 8.8 SSH Tectia Server Console

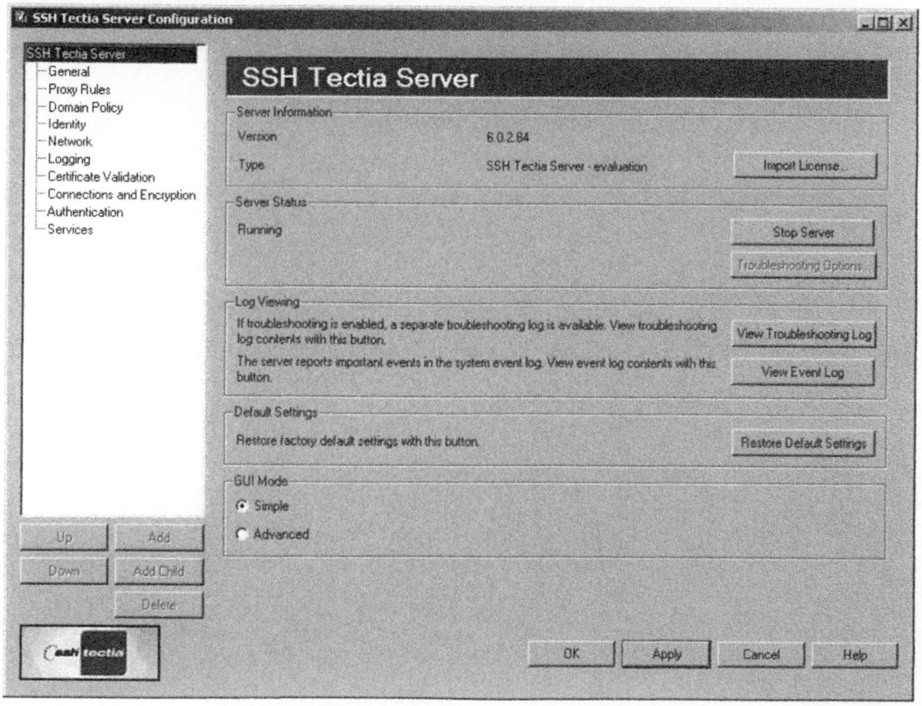

As with the SSH Tectia client, installing the server package is a simple process with no tricks or complicated options. Again, it offers a large number of configuration options and advanced functionality, including:

- The ability to view and monitor active connections
- Flexible control over ciphers and encryption protocols
- Configurable tunneling and proxy support
- Policy options
- Granular logging capabilities
- Certificate-based authentication
- Integration with Windows Active Directory/Kerberos

freeSSHd

The freeSSHd package is an impressive Windows-native SSH service (and, for those so inclined, a Telnet service as well), provided as free-as-in-beer software. While you don't get the source code, you do get a tidy little Windows service with full-featured graphical control console. The package can be quickly downloaded from the freeSSHd website (http://www.freesshd.com/index.php), and the author also makes available a user import tool.

Installing freeSSHd is easy, and when you're done, you have a console as shown in Figure 8.9.

Figure 8.9 The freeSSHd Console

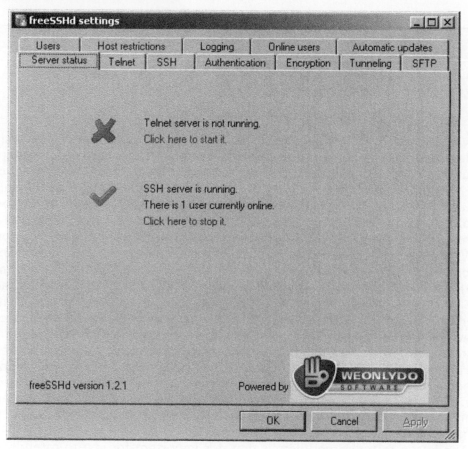

By clicking through the various tabs, you have the ability to add and remove users, control SSH/Telnet/tunnel access on a per-user basis, and control all the other attributes you would expect in an SSH server. While freeSSHd does not include Active Directory/Kerberos integration, it does include a built-in automatic update facility.

Tools & Traps…

SSH and the Windows Command Line

SSH was developed as a secure alternative to the native Unix remote shell facility; it was developed within the CLI-based, terminal-oriented technologies and assumptions that underlie the Unix operating systems. Because Unix systems (and later Linux and other variants) have developed from this command line modality, the management tools and interfaces work within these assumptions. While this makes SSH a good fit for both Unix administrators and users, it does mean that there can be some odd interactions with Windows that can catch Windows administrators and users by surprise.

While SSH seems to be a good fit, the fact that it has been adapted to the Windows environment, typically through some sort of POSIX emulation layer or interface, means that there will be the occasional glitch or incompatibility that pops up. For example, many of the 2007/2008 Microsoft applications include support for the Windows PowerShell 1.0 environment, a command line interactive interface based on the .NET framework. By using PowerShell, administrators can control Exchange Server 2007, Windows Server 2008, and many of the new applications using a consistent interface. Unfortunately, PowerShell 1.0 has no built-in remoting solution; because it expects to interact with a physical Windows terminal session and not the SSH pseudo-terminal, many SSH implementations do not correctly capture the output from PowerShell sessions. You can somewhat work around this by invoking PowerShell with an additional argument: **-command -**.

The lesson to be learned here is that it is important for you to carefully select your SSH server. You must be aware of not only which features it supports, but also whether it will be compatible with the applications you intend to use over SSH links. This means you must thoroughly test your SSH deployment before rolling it into production.

TIP

While future releases of PowerShell are supposed to include support for remote access, including over SSH, there's another alternative if you need it for PowerShell 1.0 (as is required by Exchange Server 2007 and other current Microsoft applications). /N Software's NetCmdlets v2.0, in beta at the time of this writing, includes support for PowerShell remoting over SSH. Check them out at:

http://www.nsoftware.com/powershell/netcmdlets/v2.aspx.

Summary

Because of the complexity of porting SSH server software over to Windows, you have many choices available. Utilities such as PuTTY and WinSCP provide Windows graphical clients for terminal sessions and file copying, or you can go with commercial clients such as SSH Tectia.

On the server side, you must first decide whether to use OpenSSH via the SUA POSIX subsystem, the Cygwin POSIX emulation layer, or select a Windows native server.

Solutions Fast Track

Using Windows SSH Clients

☑ Windows does not include a default, capable terminal emulation program.

☑ Most Windows SSH clients also include some multi-purpose terminal emulation.

☑ SCP/SFTP is typically provided with most SSH clients as command line tools.

☑ WinSCP is a graphical SCP/SFTP client that can be used with SSH clients.

Selecting an SSH Server for Windows

☑ SUA provides a complete POSIX compliance subsystem.

☑ Cygwin provides a POSIX emulation layer.

☑ Windows native applications usually offer greater integration.

Using SUA SSH Servers

☑ Install the SUA/SFU subsystem.

☑ Install the SDK and utilities.

☑ Install the OpenSSH software.

Using Cygwin SSH Servers

☑ Install the Cygwin subsystem.

☑ Install the OpenSSH software.

☑ Look at standalone Cygwin/OpenSSH bundles such as COPSSH.

Using Native Windows SSH Servers

☑ Offer the best degree of integration with Windows.

☑ Usually commercial software.

☑ Some free implementations available.

Frequently Asked Questions

Q: Why are Windows native implementations usually commercial offerings?

A: SSH is security software, and as such many of the common algorithms and ciphers used must be licensed by the developer.

Q: Why does OpenSSH need a POSIX subsystem or emulation layer?

A: Because it uses POSIX/Unix system calls, such as fork( ), that are not present in the Win32 APIs. These system calls allow a single listening process to quickly and easily spawn off new sshd processes for each incoming connection without having to employ compliated network listener logic. This helps improve security and performance.

Q: Why do I need a client? Can't I just use the ssh from a CMD.exe window?

A: You can, but if your SSH session uses any advanced terminal emulation features, the CMD.exe window will not be able to handle it. Most existing terminal emulation programs for Windows don't offer the ability to run commands from the command line.

Q: Which is better, SUA or Cygwin?

A: Each option has its advantages, depending on your needs. SUA is developed by Microsoft, which means that if you have problems with SUA and a Microsoft application, you can get support through standard channels. The SUA communit is active. However, most Open Software programs that offer Windows support do so through Cygwin.

Q: Which type of SSH server performs better, SUA, Cygwin or native Windows?

A: Again, this depends on your environment. If you're worried about performance, install all three and perform your own testing. See how they scale in your particular network with your expected usage.

Chapter 9

Linux SSH

Solutions in this chapter:

- **Installing OpenSSH Server**

- **Controlling Your SSH Server**

- **Configuring SSH to Ease Your Paranoia**

- **Using SSH**

- **Additional Avenues of Approach**

☑ Summary

☑ Solutions Fast Track

☑ Frequently Asked Questions

Introduction

In this chapter, we want to explore some of the aspects of using SSH on Linux. We want to look at how to install it, how to configure it, and what are some of the features that it provides. With its strong authentication and tight encryption, there are a wide variety of tasks that we can use it for when working with communication between machines.

With a number of products on the market, we want to pick one for our examples that is well known in the Open Source community. We also want to make sure that our configuration is one that will balance security, usability, and visibility. When we have SSH up and running, we then want to explore some of the ways that an administrator or enthusiast can use the tools that come with a standard SSH distribution. Along the way, we'll talk about some tips and tricks that we can use to help manage our Linux system.

Installing OpenSSH Server

OpenSSH is a package that is an offshoot of the original SSH implementation, which was started in 1995. Its widespread use makes it a good choice for our Secure Shell needs, and the first step is going to be actually installing the software package. There are several ways to do this in any given Linux distribution, but the choice comes down to a simple decision between installing the software using a package manager (like apt, yum, or YAST2) or installing the software from source (that is, building the required files from the source code using a compiler).

While this may seem like a simple choice, there are several points that we have to weigh when picking one over the other. Usually, when installing from source, you have a bit more control over the options that are installed and configured by default. When we want to do something non-standard with some software, such as using custom libraries or including optional functions, installing from source is the way to go. The only problem with this is that it requires build tools to be installed on the machine, and while they do not take up a lot of space, when working with a high security, low-profile server, the fewer packages that are installed, the more secure the server will be.

Another important aspect to look at when picking an install method is how you want to handle updates. When using a package manager, it is easy to roll all of a system's updates into a single set of actions. When installing from source, any updates will have to be manually applied, and often times, a rebuild of the entire software package is required. With the quick turn-around of patches and fixes that are made available by the Open Source community, installing OpenSSH using a package manager is an attractive solution.

Due to the large list of additional steps that installing from source requires, I'm going to recommend that we stick with the pre-packaged distribution that can be installed using the built-in package manager.

Installing OpenSSH Using a Package Manager

Even when using the package manager option to install our software, we still have a couple of choices to keep in mind and account for in our installation efforts. With a large number of different distributions available in the Linux community, simply providing a set of instructions for each distribution's package manager could take up a chapter for each distribution. Because almost all package managers follow the same type of instructions, I'll focus on using apt on Ubuntu. Based on Debian Linux, Ubuntu has earned a reputation for simplicity, stability, and security.

There are several graphical front ends that interact with apt (Ubuntu's base package management system), but when we install from the command line, we'll get a better feel for what we're installing and what it's doing in the background. To start, open a Terminal window (Applications | Accessories | Terminal), or log into the console on your server.

Once in the command line interface (CLI), it's time to start installing and hacking together a secure method for communication between machines. The first part of the install is to refresh apt's database of available packages by typing the following command at the prompt:

```
sudo apt-get update
```

If you have Internet connectivity, this command will have apt go out and touch all the repositories listed in apt's source configuration file to check for new or updated packages. Once the package list is updated (Figure 9.1), it's time to install.

Figure 9.1 Successful Update of Apt

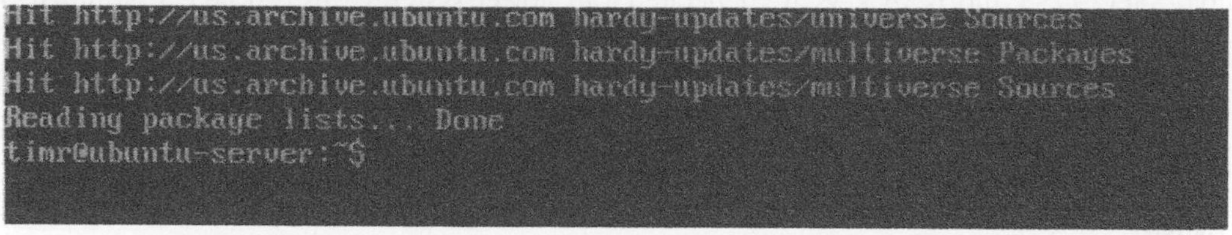

Tip

Updating the package list is not only a good idea, but also a requirement for a secure system. New exploits and holes are discovered every day, and the only way to keep someone from compromising your system is to keep up to date with all of the patches that are released for your system and software.

While it is not necessary to update the list on a daily basis, having apt go out and check for updated packages is a good way to see if it is time for some new installs.

Another one of the advantages of using a package manager is that most distributions will have a metapackage that contains all of the packages necessary for installing a complete software solution. To install everything we'll need for SSH, we just have to type the following at the prompt:

```
sudo apt-get install ssh
```

This should result in apt giving us a list (Figure 9.2) of several packages to be installed, and some that are recommended, but not required.

Figure 9.2 List of Packages to be Installed

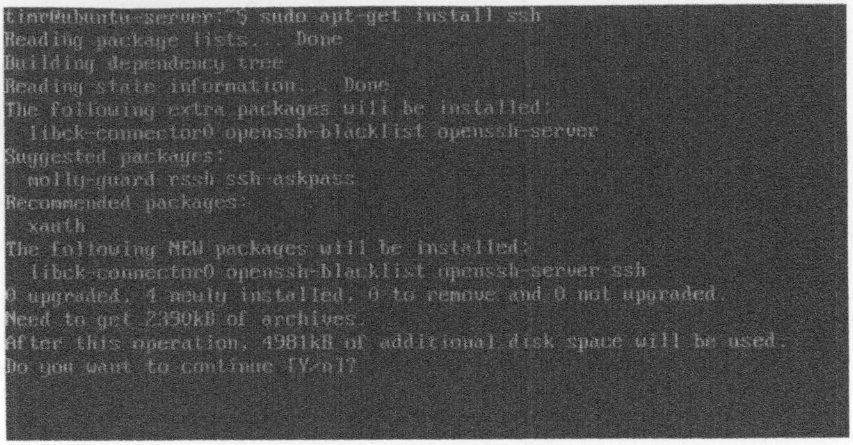

Once we chose to continue, apt heads out, downloads the required packages, installs them, and then starts the services. When installing openssh-server, it's important to note that during the install, the initial SSH2 DSA and RSA keys are generated. On slower systems, this can take a while. At the end of the install, your OpenSSH server should be running and you should have the ability to connect to other servers using ssh.

WARNING

When using an operating system that has built-in security features, it's important to know why they are in place and why you should use them. In many Linux systems, the root account is restricted and users are forced to elevate a normal user account to perform administrative tasks. There are ways around this (such as resetting the root password to allow local logins), but it is important to remember that in a production system, having a security flaw like that could mean a compromised system. Anything you can do as the root user, you can do with elevated privileges, and it's much easier to log and track what users do, rather than what root did.

When using systems that have restricted root accounts, it really is not all that hard to type an extra four characters at the start of a command. The peace of mind that you'll gain knowing that someone can't log into the system as root will far outweigh the extra keystrokes.

Controlling Your SSH server

Keeping tabs on a secure system requires that we know what is running, when it is running, and how to stop it or start it back up again. When using our SSH server, it's important to know that when we make a configuration change, we won't have to reboot the entire system to put those changes into effect.

Using the Start and Stop Commands

The simplest way to start and stop the SSH service is to pass a command to the script that controls the service. To do this, just enter the full path to the script and the command that you want the service to accomplish, such as restart (Figure 9.3), stop, or start:

```
/etc/init.d/ssh restart
```

Figure 9.3 Restarting the SSH Service

```
timr@ubuntu-server:~$ sudo /etc/init.d/ssh restart
 * Restarting OpenBSD Secure Shell server sshd                          [ OK ]
timr@ubuntu-server:~$
```

Tools & Traps...

Debian Helper Scripts

One of the advantages of using such a widely supported distribution of Linux is that there is a wide variety of tools out there that will help you administer and run your system. One of those sets of tools is a package of helper scripts that make managing services quick and simple. One of the tool collections that I install quite often is a package (debian-helper-scripts) that adds several useful commands.

With the helper scripts installed, instead of having to type the full path to a service, I can use just a command as a shortcut. A command like:

```
/etc/init.d/ssh reload
```

Can become:

```
service ssh reload
```

While it might not seem like much, when managing multiple Linux distributions, having a consistent way to control services and complete common activities can turn a long list of commands into one quick script that doesn't need to be ported from system to system.

The available functions of the sshd script are as follows:

■ Start: Starts the service if it is stopped.

■ Stop: Stops the service if it is running.

- Restart: Attempts to stop and then restart the service.

- Reload: Reloads the configuration file.

- Force-reload: Reloads the configuration file.

- Try-restart: Checks to make sure the service is stopped gracefully before trying to start it again.

Configuring SSH to Ease Your Paranoia

"Just because you're paranoid doesn't mean they aren't after you."[1]

— Joseph Heller

One of the facts of the computer industry is that there are people out there who mean you and your systems no good. They have been portrayed in movies and television shows as everything from super-villains to just misunderstood teens with hearts of gold. No matter what their true motivation, our job is to keep them out of our systems. While there can be no system that is "hacker-proof," we can minimize our exposure and our risk by configuring our systems in a sensible and secure manner. Because the entire goal of using SSH is to provide secure communication, it's essential that this aspect of our system be as tight as we can make it. All the encryption in the world won't help us if we leave the keys sitting in the back door.

While the actual risk of an attack isn't quite as high as the movies and television make them, it's important to keep in mind that we are configuring our systems to be as secure and low profile as we can reasonably make them. I want to stress "reasonably," because we *could* secure our servers to the point that they are expensive, electricity-hungry paperweights (they would be VERY secure, but you couldn't actually use them for anything). This would not suit our purposes of providing secure systems that people can actually use, so when looking at the configuration steps, remember that you have to strike a balance between usability and security.

Notes from the Underground...

Nothing to See Here; Move Along

When looking around for something to do, one of the tools that security administrators and crackers love to use is the famous nmap. Using it to scan ports for vulnerable servers can be a successful way for some people to work their nefarious purposes.

In the movie *The Matrix Reloaded*, geeks were excited to see an onscreen use of an SSH1 exploit. One of the main characters finds that a system is running an insecure

Continued

version of SSH and proceeds to hack in and gain control. While it is an exploit that was already fairly well known, the principle and method of the attack were still quite valid. If a cracker knows what you have running, it is easier to find an exploit.

While securing your environment through obfuscation is not really a good method of ensuring your data stays safe, it can't hurt to try to keep a low profile. Until every system in the world is totally secure and invulnerable, it helps not to be the low-hanging fruit that hangs right at eye level to everyone with a port scanner.

The best way to make sure that we are keeping our systems secure, usable, and low-visibility is to ensure that we have configured our services with these three goals in mind.

Editing the SSH Configuration File

In the interest of configuring SSH to hit those three goals, we have to dig into the default configuration file, /etc/ssh/sshd_config. This file is full of helpful settings and comments that control how the SSH service runs and what it is and isn't allowed to do.

Configuring SSH Protocols

The first thing to do when editing the sshd_config file is to make sure that the SSH1 protocol is turned off. The "Protocol" line in the file controls to which protocols sshd will listen and respond. It is possible to leave sshd listening for SSH1but specify that SSH2 be given precedence, but there is no compelling reason to leave something as insecure as SSH1 enabled.

In the sshd_config file, find the line:

```
Protocol 2,1
```

And change it to:

```
Protocol 2
```

A quick save of the file and a reload of the configuration by the service keep those pesky version 1 clients from connecting.

Restricting root Access

Another area where we will want to change the default setting is this line:

```
PermitRootLogin yes
```

Allowing the root user to log in via SSH is not a good idea in a system with the root user enabled. Even though a good, secure system will restrict the root account and require users to sudo, it still is a good idea to change the PermitRootLogin to "no."

Changing the Default Listening Port

In the interest of keeping a low profile, another option we need to set is moving SSH to a non-standard port. Generally speaking, the only people who would be connecting to your server with SSH will be administrators or other authorized users, so having SSH listen on a well-known port (so that anyone can find it) is not really a requirement.

To make this change, find the line that says:

```
Port 22
```

And change it to something in the range of unregistered port numbers (1024–65535).

Allowing and Denying Connections Using hosts Files

To further restrict access to our system, we can specify exactly who connects to our server and from where. We can accomplish these restrictions by using hosts.allow and hosts.deny. This solution is an extremely flexible way of configuring to whom and to what the SSH service will listen. The recommended way of using these files is to restrict access to only those network addresses that you are certain will need access. Like so many other security systems, the best way to do this is to use hosts.deny to deny all connections and then configure hosts.allow to allow only those few networks that you want to have access.

First we set the hosts.deny (Figure 9.4) file to deny access to everything:

Figure 9.4 Adding Restrictions to the hosts.deny File

Next, we want to set the hosts.allow (Figure 9.5) file to allow connections from the local networks that we will specify:

Figure 9.5 Adding Authorized Hosts to the hosts.allow File

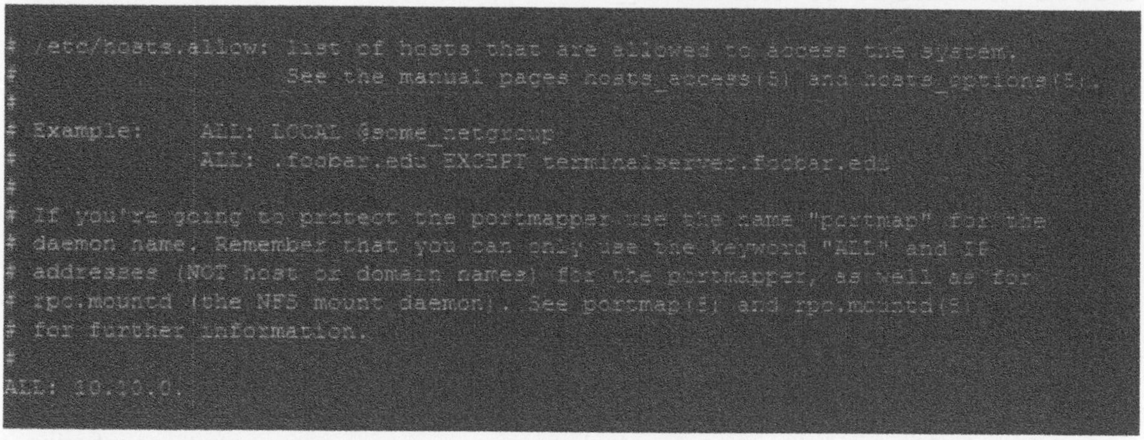

```
# /etc/hosts.allow: list of hosts that are allowed to access the system.
#                   See the manual pages hosts_access(5) and hosts_options(5).
#
# Example:    ALL: LOCAL @some_netgroup
#             ALL: .foobar.edu EXCEPT terminalserver.foobar.edu
#
# If you're going to protect the portmapper use the name "portmap" for the
# daemon name. Remember that you can only use the keyword "ALL" and IP
# addresses (NOT host or domain names) for the portmapper, as well as for
# rpc.mountd (the NFS mount daemon). See portmap(5) and rpc.mountd(8)
# for further information.
#
ALL: 10.10.0.
```

In this example, I am allowing everything that matches up to the last "." which will match everything on the 10.10.0.0/24 network (10.10.0.1-10.10.0.255). You can be more specific in what you allow and deny, but for most systems, this would be a good step on the path to a secure implementation of SSH.

Binding to a Specific Address

Most of the time, it is not necessary to specify a specific address to which SSH will bind; however, there are cases where you will want to restrict it to prevent spoofing attacks that look like they are coming from your internal network but are not.

To restrict the interface on which SSH will listen, look for this line in the sshd_config file:

```
#ListenAddress 0.0.0.0
```

To bind SSH to a specific IP, change the 0.0.0.0 to the correct address and remove the pound symbol. Once the configuration is saved, it's time to reload the sshd service.

WARNING

One thing to keep in mind when setting up SSH is that if you are making changes over SSH and make a mistake, it may be difficult to get back to a working order. Before you disconnect the session with which you are making changes, test the new configuration by opening a new SSH connection. If you are able to connect and log in, then you don't have to worry; however, if you are unsuccessful, it might be time to roll back some of those changes. No one likes having to go back to the console to fix a simple typo or mistake.

More Changes to the sshd_config File

While we have covered several settings that you can specify in the sshd_config file, there are many more. Each one can grant or limit the features that a user can use with SSH, but most of these other settings require consideration of the existing policies and infrastructure of a user's environment. Because each situation is different, we covered just some of the settings with broad applications. Just like each Linux distribution has a cult following, I'm sure that each setting in a config file has a group of vocal proponents, so there is a lot of material out there on what settings are good for specific situations. Don't hesitate to experiment and find the best balance for your own situation.

Using SSH

Now that we have SSH configured, it's time to start exploring some of the activities that you can actually do using SSH. Started in 1995 as a replacement for remote logins and TELNET, SSH has evolved. Now highly regarded as a secure method of connecting to a remote computer, transferring files, tunneling X11 and other applications, it has become a powerful tool for administration.

Logging into Remote Systems Securely

One primary use of SSH is to log into a remote system securely. The previous methods didn't provide strong authentication or encryption. Now that SSH is on the scene, it's easy to initiate a secure, encrypted connection to another machine and to do so with confidence that our communications will not be pried into. On most Linux desktop systems, once SSH is installed, all a user needs to do to connect is to open a terminal window and type in a quick command:

```
ssh 10.10.0.117
```

> **Tip**
>
> When you connect to a machine the first time via SSH, you will be prompted to either accept or reject the hostkey that is being offered by the remote machine. If you are connecting to a machine that you regularly administer and are prompted to accept a new hostkey, this prompt might be an indication that something is up and security might be compromised.

If we changed the port number to which SSH listens, then we have to change the way we connect as a client and specify the port:

```
ssh -p 22123 10.10.0.117
```

In both of these examples, we are assuming that we are connecting with an account that exists on the remote machine. If we wanted to specify a different user name, we have a couple of different options:

```
ssh -p 22123 -l timr 10.10.0.117
```

Or:

```
ssh -p 22123 timr@10.10.0.117
```

There are a number of ways you can use SSH to connect to a remote system, and almost all of them can be used to increase the security of our implementation. We do have to keep in mind that the more we secure our system, the more likely we will be increasing the difficulty of connecting to that system.

Tools & Traps…

Disconnected? Not a Problem!

One of the most frustrating things that can happen when working on a remote system with SSH is getting disconnected. When downloading a file or running a process that requires input, it's important to be able to see what's going on, but when you get disconnected, you're out of luck. Once you lose your connection to the SSH server, you can't reconnect to that same session. Because this is such a pain in the administrative area, I like to use a tool called screen.

Screen multiplexes a physical terminal session between several processes. These terminal sessions can be from the console or over SSH. You can log in, run screen, start your processes, and if you get disconnected, re-attach to that screen when you re-connect. This is a pretty powerful tool, so I recommend reading more about it.

File Transfer Using SSH

Once you have your connection set up and are logged in, sometimes it's necessary to bring some files over from another machine or push them out from the one on which you are currently working. We could use FTP or another protocol to copy the file around, but that would defeat the purpose of securing our server and files. To get around that **vulnerability**, there is a function of SSH that allows the secure transfer of files. This function is Secure Copy (scp). Using the same encryption and handshaking that SSH logins use, scp allows us to transfer files to and from systems in a secure manner.

To transfer files, we'll use many of the same switches that we use when we are connecting. To transfer a file using the standard ports and configurations, we would enter this command:

```
scp ~/example.file timr@10.10.0.117:~/done/example.file.moved
```

Once more, if we've made changes to the default settings, we will have to specify to what we're connecting:

```
scp -p 22123 ~/example.file timr@10.10.0.117:~/done/example.file.moved
```

In these two examples, we are seeing how to push a file from a local machine to a remote one. We can also use scp to pull files from a remote system or even cross-copy from one remote system to another, like so:

```
scp paulr@10.10.0.124:~/ example.file
timr@10.10.0.117:~/done/example.file2
```

This is a relatively simple way to copy files, but it doesn't handle some of the more advanced features that FTP would provide. If those are the types of transfers that are needed, then it is best to look beyond scp and find out more about other security protocols and technology, such as Secure File Transfer Protocol (SFTP).

Executing Secure Commands Remotely

SSH is secure. Because it is secure, we like to use it to perform tasks on remote systems. Most of what we've done so far have required logging into a system to accomplish our goals. SSH is smarter than that, though, and allows us to remotely execute commands in a secure manner. This simple little tidbit opens up a whole new range of uses for SSH by allowing us to include secure, remote commands in scripts.

To execute a remote command, all we have to do is follow the host address with the command that we want to run on the remote host. For example, to copy a backup of a file on a remote machine, we can type:

```
ssh -l timr -p 22123 10.10.0.117 cp ~/example.file ~/example.file.bak
```

This would copy the file on the remote system and return an error only if something went wrong, just as would happen in a normal file copy. If we wanted to do more with this, we could add some ssh commands to a script. Figure 9.6 is an example of a very short script that would return a list of all the running processes.

Figure 9.6 pscheck Script

While this little script is of limited use, we can embellish it and get it to do more. What if we wanted to have the script query a number of servers from the command line and list all the processes that have the letter "c" and then output the results of the remote command to a file for us to look at later? We could do this with a script (Figure 9.7).

Figure 9.7 pscheckv2 Script

```
#!/bin/bash
#Quick script to check ps on a remote machine over SSH
#looking for processes that have the letter .c.
#SSH Information
for x in $*
do
echo $1.':'.'\n' >> output.pscheckv2
ssh timr@$1 ps -A | grep -i 'c' >> output.pscheckv2
shift
done
```

To use this script, we would just have to invoke it from the command line, enter a list of servers to query, and then enter the password to authenticate.

Connecting to Your SSH Server from Windows

While you can manage multiple servers from another server machine, it is much simpler to administer them all from a desktop. While I like to think that there are administrators lurking in every server room who prefer Linux on the desktop, the reality of the situation is that Microsoft Windows is still the desktop operating system of choice. Fortunately, this doesn't limit the usefulness of SSH, as there are some fine tools out there for Windows. One of the best known is PuTTY (http://www.chiark. greenend.org.uk/~sgtatham/putty/), as shown in Figure 9.8.

Using this tool, it is quick and simple to connect to and manage multiple Linux servers from a Windows desktop.

Figure 9.8 Running PuTTY on Windows

Another great tool for Windows is WinSCP (http://winscp.net/eng/index.php). With this tool, you are able to securely copy files to and from a SSH server and never have to worry. It supports multiple encryption ciphers and protocols.

Additional Avenues of Approach

One idea that should be stressed is that there are several different ways that SSH can be used to secure communications between servers, clients, and the world in general. Some examples can include streaming X11 applications over a secure channel, installing personal keys on the server so that you don't have to use a password to log in, and compiling a set of binaries with custom configurations. In most cases, these other features and implementations require a lot of planning and detailed instructions that we just don't have room for here. To find out more on the subject, I recommend exploring the man pages that come with OpenSSH and some of the other technologies mentioned here.

One thing that I wanted to stress is that security is an evolving field in which there is always an effort to improve or break what is considered a secure setup. The settings and tricks mentioned here may change or not fit your particular situation. It never hurts to be on the lookout for more areas you can secure in your environment.

Through this chapter, we used the package OpenSSH, which is an Open Source distribution that is based on the original code. Other packages might be more to your liking. If you would like to find out more, I would recommend looking at a couple of products like these:

- Dropbear SSH (http://matt.ucc.asn.au/dropbear/dropbear.html)

- freeSSHd (http://www.freesshd.com/)

- SSH Tectia (http://www.ssh.com/products/client-server/)

While this is not an exhaustive list, it is a good place to start if you are looking for an alternative to OpenSSH.

Summary

In this chapter we've explored how to install SSH, how to configure it, and how to use it. In most Linux distributions, OpenSSH is a package that is easy to install. Installing from source is more complicated and requires specific instructions for each package or distribution, but it allows us a bit more freedom to pick and choose what our server is able to do.

In the configuration section, we went over some of the settings that can be used to help keep our SSH server as secure as possible. These methods can include restricting access from anyone not on the local network, limiting the protocols used to connect, and binding the service to a non-standard port. All of these various methods limit the attack surface that our server presents. Some of the options that we discussed are dependent on having the correct packages installed or the binaries compiled with those features in mind.

In the final section, we looked at some of the administration activities that you can do using SSH. Some of the more simple features like secure logins can build up to more advanced features, like running scripts with ssh commands inside them. There are many advanced features that require complex setups, but each person is going to have a different list of features and tasks that he or she wants to perform.

There are many people out there that make a living and take pleasure from attacking and cracking computer systems. Using tools like SSH can help us minimize the threat that people like that present. While security features like encryption and strong authentication are important, it is imperative that we keep up a vigilant front. Having the best software in the world won't help if we use weak passwords.

Solutions Fast Track

Installing OpenSSH Server

☑ Installing OpenSSH on most distributions is simple when using the distribution's package manager.

☑ Ubuntu uses apt as a package manager. To install OpenSSH, just type "sudo apt-get install ssh".

Controlling Your SSH Server

☑ Controlling the SSH daemon is done by using the sudo command in conjunction with the path to the init script in /etc/init.d/.

☑ The options for the service are Start, Stop, Reload, Force-Reload, Restart, and Try-Restart.

Configuring SSH to Ease Your Paranoia

☑ Configuration of the SSH service is controlled by the file sshd_config.

☑ SSH Protocol 1 is inherently insecure and its use should be prohibited by the config file.

☑ Root user access over SSH should be restricted in systems in which the root user has login privileges.

☑ Binding SSH to a non-standard port can make it more difficult for people of malicious intent to connect.

☑ Using the hosts.allow and hosts.deny files can give you granular control of the networks and hosts from which your server is accessed.

☑ Binding SSH to a specific address or interface can help reduce the attack surface of a server.

☑ There are many options in the sshd_config file and each administrator will have to find a balance of security, usability, and visibility.

Using SSH

☑ SSH was created as a replacement for Unix tools that did not have strong authentication and encryption.

☑ SSH can be used to log in to a remote system, transfer files, and run remote commands.

☑ SSH can be used in scripts to run remote commands on multiple systems.

☑ There are many tools for Windows that allow an administrator to manage a Linux server via SSH.

Additional Avenues of Approach

☑ There are many other features of SSH, such as X11 forwarding, using personal keys for authentication, and installing from source code.

☑ OpenSSH is just one package among many. There are several options for both SSH servers and clients.

Frequently Asked Questions

Q: What SSH package is best to use?

A: While OpenSSH is the most popular, there are several alternatives out there in the market. If you don't want to use Open Source software, there are options. If you want a package that is smaller or will run better on older hardware, there are options. Each situation will require a different set of criteria; you must judge which package will be best for that given situation.

Q: How do I install SSH on my particular distribution (RedHat, Gentoo, Suse etc.)?

A: Most distributions have good documentation on installing software packages and each package manager is different. The best way to install SSH is to find the package you want and then find out what the software maintainer recommends as a method of installation.

Q: How do I restore my sshd_config to its original state?

A: Most of the time you can find a copy of the original config files on the Internet. If you can't find it there, you also have the option of removing the package and re-installing it.

Q: What's the difference between SSH1 and SSH2?

A: SSH2 is a rewrite of SSH1 that incorporates better use of host keys for authentication, encrypts different parts of network packtets, and increases the speed, security and portabililty of the original protocol.

Q: Is it illegal to encrypt all that stuff?

A: The short of it is "no." The long of it is that while it is not illegal in the United States, it may be illegal in other countries to use it without a special permit. It may also be illegal to export the software when it is hosted on a U.S. server to countries under export restrictions.

Q: Will SSH work with other applications like firewalls and IMAP?

A: In some cases, yes. In others, no. Some applications have methods of secure communication built into them that supersede or make SSH extraneous. It is totally dependent on the application, however.

Note

1. Heller, Joseph. *Catch-22*. New York: Simon & Schuster, Inc., 1961.

Chapter 10

Mac SSH

Solutions in this chapter:

- Using SSH on a Mac
- Simplifying Key Management with the SSH Agent
- Scripting Securely with SSH

☑ Summary

☑ Solutions Fast Track

☑ Frequently Asked Questions

Introduction

The Mac OS X operating system brings together portions of the Mac and BSD kernels along with Nextstep's object-oriented design and graphical-user interface. Such a diverse group of ancestors makes for a superb experience in which an easy-to-use and beautifully designed graphical interface and a powerful command line with a distinct Unix feel are both available in the same box.

OS X has included OpenSSH in its standard distribution since version 10.1. Most of what you've learned in this book about SSH can be applied immediately to the Mac. This chapter will cover SSH-related capabilities and characteristics that are either specific to the Mac or used differently due to the idiosyncrasies of the operating system.

Using SSH on a Mac

The familiar command line **ssh** utility can be run via OS X's **Terminal** application. To do so, launch the **Terminal** application, located within the **Applications/Utilities** folder, and type **ssh**, as seen in Figure 10.1 (command output is from OS X Version 10.5.3).

Figure 10.1 Using SSH in Terminal

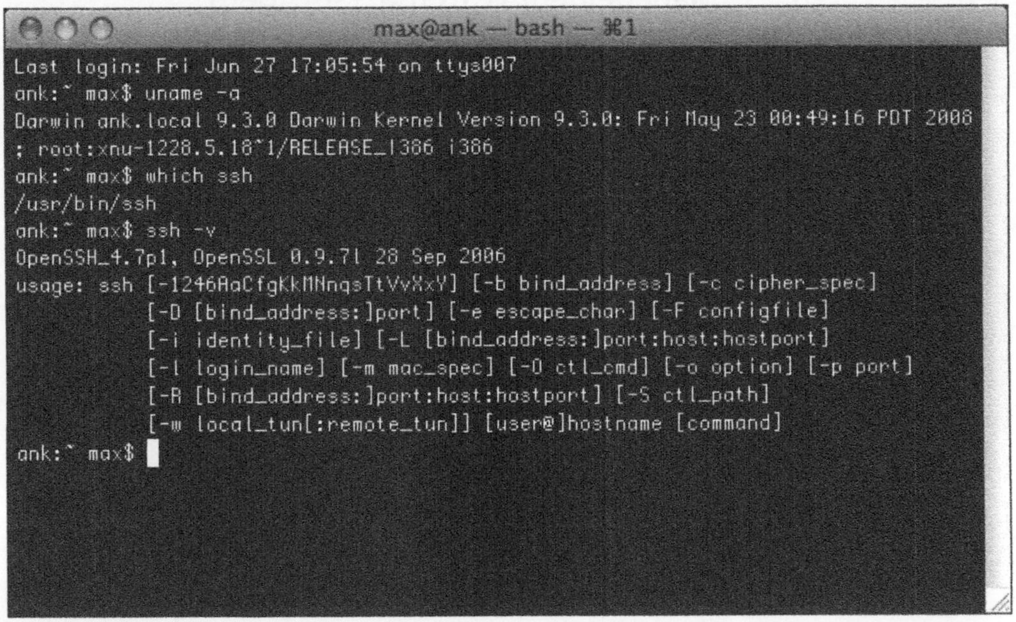

```
Last login: Fri Jun 27 17:05:54 on ttys007
ank:~ max$ uname -a
Darwin ank.local 9.3.0 Darwin Kernel Version 9.3.0: Fri May 23 00:49:16 PDT 2008
; root:xnu-1228.5.18~1/RELEASE_I386 i386
ank:~ max$ which ssh
/usr/bin/ssh
ank:~ max$ ssh -v
OpenSSH_4.7p1, OpenSSL 0.9.7l 28 Sep 2006
usage: ssh [-1246AaCfgKkMNnqsTtVvXxY] [-b bind_address] [-c cipher_spec]
           [-D [bind_address:]port] [-e escape_char] [-F configfile]
           [-i identity_file] [-L [bind_address:]port:host:hostport]
           [-l login_name] [-m mac_spec] [-O ctl_cmd] [-o option] [-p port]
           [-R [bind_address:]port:host:hostport] [-S ctl_path]
           [-w local_tun[:remote_tun]] [user@]hostname [command]
ank:~ max$
```

Connecting Securely to a Remote Server

Initiating a secure terminal session to a remote server with the bundled SSH is no different than what you would do in other systems. To initiate a remote SSH session via the Terminal type:

```
ank:~ max$ ssh royale -l max
max@royale's password:
Linux royale 2.6.20-15-generic #2 SMP Sun Apr 15 07:36:31 UTC 2007 i686
Last login: Mon Jun 30 14:20:52 2008 from ank.local
max@royale:~$ hostname
royale
```

All OpenSSH features available in the version bundled with your version of OS X are available to you when using the Terminal. Refer to Chapter 6 for a more comprehensive description of the standard SSH client.

Transferring Files Securely with SCP and SFTP

OS X 10.5 includes all the SSH-related tools you would expect, including SCP (secure copy) and SFTP (secure file transfer program). To copy a file securely with SCP via the Terminal type:

```
ank:Pictures max$ scp tessarlo-1920x1200.jpg max@royale:pics
max@royale's password:
tessarlo-1920x1200.jpg               100%   2165KB   2.1MB/s   00:01
ank:Pictures max$
```

Similarly, for SFTP:

```
ank:Pictures max$ sftp max@royale
Connecting to royale...
max@royale's password:
sftp> ls
Desktop pics
sftp> put *.jpg
Uploading dan-funderburgh-1680x1050.jpg to /home/ubuntu/dan-funderburgh-1680x1050.jpg
dan-funderburgh-1680x1050.jpg        100%   317KB   317.1KB/s   00:00
Uploading jeanjullien-1280x1024.jpg to /home/ubuntu/jeanjullien-1280x1024.jpg
jeanjullien-1280x1024.jpg            100%   609KB   609.4KB/s   000:01
Uploading mcbess-1920x1200.jpg to /home/ubuntu/mcbess-1920x1200.jpg
mcbess-1920x1200.jpg                 100%   1780KB   1.7MB/s   00:00
Uploading reyortega-1920x1200.jpg to /home/ubuntu/reyortega-1920x1200.jpg
reyortega-1920x1200.jpg              100%   2446KB   2.4MB/s   00:00
Uploading tessarlo-1920x1200.jpg to /home/ubuntu/tessarlo-1920x1200.jpg
tessarlo-1920x1200.jpg               100%   2165KB   2.1MB/s   00:00
sftp> quit
ank:Pictures max$
```

Tools & Traps...

When Dangerous Fish Come to the Rescue

Depending on your (or your users') comfort level with the **Terminal**, you may find that using SCP and SFTP is a perfectly valid solution for transferring files securely across your network. However, if **Terminal** is a no-go, or if you'd rather keep your users as far away from it as possible, there are some additional options for you.

Fugu is a quite a pricey fish and potentially lethal. Fortunately the fine folks at University of Michigan have made such a remarkable fish available for free at http://rsug.itd.umich.edu/software/fugu/under a BSD license.

In the authors' own words:

"Fugu is a graphical frontend to the commandline Secure File Transfer application (SFTP). SFTP is similar to FTP, but unlike FTP, the entire session is encrypted, meaning no passwords are sent in cleartext form, and is thus much less vulnerable to third-party interception. Fugu allows you to take advantage of SFTP's security without having to sacrifice the ease of use found in a GUI."

Fugu provides a familiar side-by-side UI, not unlike OS X's Finder, to easily navigate local and remote file systems. Transferring single or multiple files is drag-and-drop simple, ideal for letting your designers upload content to your website in a secure manner without requiring them to drop to the **Terminal** (see Figure 10.2).

Additionally, **Transmit** from Panic (at http://www.panic.com/transmit/) can also do SFTP file transfers with an intuitive UI, among other things such as WebDAV and traditional FTP transfers. **Transmit** isn't free but you won't risk death by eating it (although you could get run by it), so consume at your own peril.

Figure 10.2 Transferring Files Using Fugu

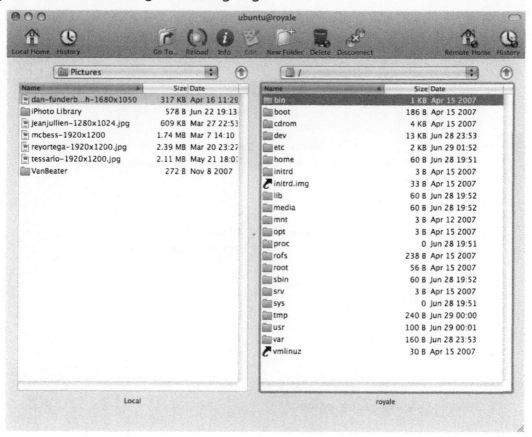

Configuring Your Mac for Remote Access

OS X comes bundled not only with a standard SSH client, but also with a server. Starting the server and ensuring the built-in firewall allows incoming connections to TCP port 22 is as simple as enabling **Remote Login** in your **Sharing** preferences. To do so open **System Preferences** (via its icon on the **Dock**, or by launching it from the **Applications** folder in the **Finder**), select **Sharing**, and ensure the checkbox next to **Remote Login** is checked. You should see a message on the panel to the right of the service list displaying "*Remote Login: On*," along with the user and IP address to use to log into your computer remotely, as shown in Figure 10.3.

Through **System Preferences** it is also possible to restrict which users can log in remotely to your computer via SSH.

Figure 10.3 Enabling Remote Login via System Preferences

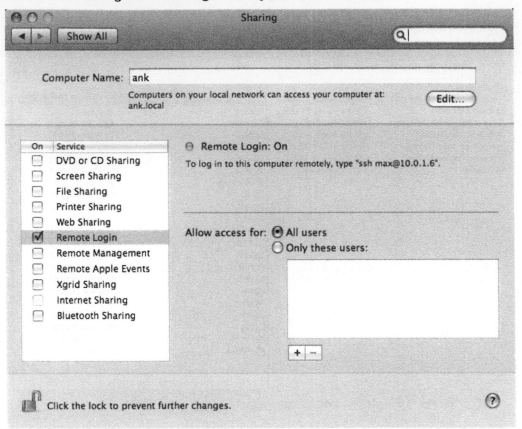

> The standard configuration file for the SSH daemon is located at /etc/sshd_config in OS X.

X11 Forwarding

Your Mac can also interoperate with other computers as an X11 display client or server, using X11 forwarding. Although not a requirement, it is highly recommended that you tunnel X11 sessions through SSH, as they do not offer much security by themselves and you probably do not want other people to look at your screen or to record every one of your keystrokes and mouse movements.

Even though X11 comes standard with OS X, the package is not installed in a default OS install. To install X11 insert your OS X Install DVD (or CD #1), open **Optional Installs**, and check the **X11** box within **Applications**, as shown in Figure 10.4.

Figure 10.4 Installing X11

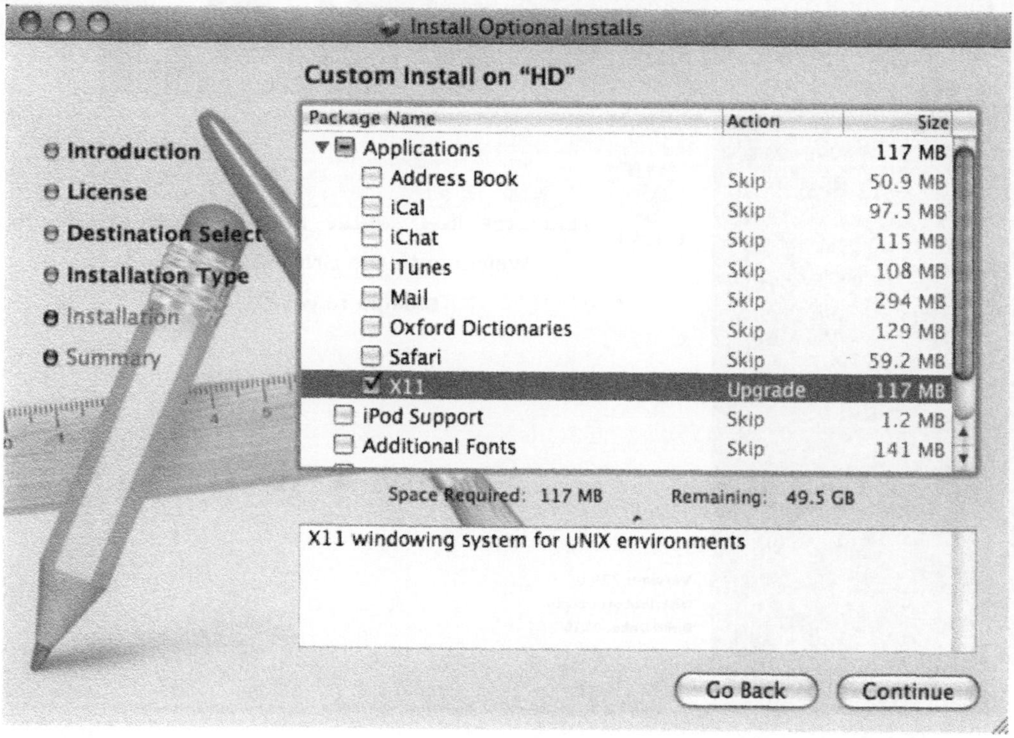

Establishing an X11 Forwarding Session with a Remote Computer

With the optional X11 package installed and assuming the remote computer is configured to allow X11 forwarding via SSH (has X11Forwarding yes in its sshd_config), establishing a new forwarding session is as easy as adding the $-X$ or $-Y$ argument (the actual argument depends on the security settings of the computer to which you are connecting) to your regular ssh **Terminal** invocation. The X11 application is run automatically by the SSH command if it is not already running. X11 forwarding and the DISPLAY environment variable are set up automatically for you by the **ssh** command so that any X application launched within the SSH session will automatically use your Mac's display, as show in Figure 10.5.

Figure 10.5 Forwarding Linux X Display to a Mac via SSH

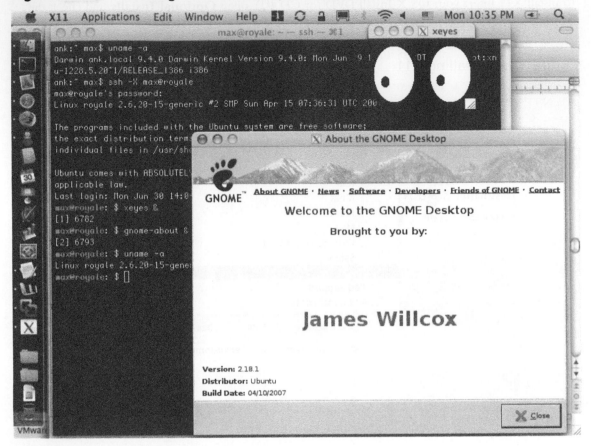

X11 Forwarding from a Mac to a Remote X Server

Although less common, it is equally simple to forward the X display of a Mac to a remote server. To do so follow these steps:

1. Ensure that **Remote Login** is enabled in your **Sharing** preferences to allow incoming SSH connections.

2. Enable X11 forwarding for SSHD, which is not enabled by default, by adding a line to /etc/sshd_config that reads X11Forwarding yes.

3. SSH to the Mac from the X server with the −X argument to enable X11 forwarding.

Simplifying Key Management with the SSH Agent

If you routinely SSH into multiple hosts, you may find it difficult to remember all the different username and password combinations or tedious to enter them over and over again. A simple solution to this problem is to use SSH with RSA or DSA authentication keys. Authentication key pairs are generated with the **ssh-keygen** utility, and after the appropriate public keys are distributed to the remote hosts, it is possible to SSH into them without having to supply a username and password. See Chapter 11 for a more in-depth look into SSH keys.

When using authentication keys your private keys are the proverbial "keys to the kingdom." If you lose them or if they become compromised, all the systems where those keys are trusted could be compromised as well. To prevent this from happening, every private key must be protected with a strong pass-phrase, which also can be set with the **ssh-keygen** utility. Once a pass-phrase is configured, you will have to supply it every time SSH needs to use the private key to authenticate to a trusted system.

We have alleviated the problem of having to remember multiple usernames and passwords. We now have to remember only a limited number of pass-phrases, one for each set of authentication keys in use. However, we still have to keep entering them all the time. Fortunately there is a better way to manage these pass-phrases: the SSH agent. The **ssh-agent** tool is a standard component of the OpenSSH distribution. The aim of this tool is to keep recently used pass-phrases in memory for the duration of a login session, so that we do not have to re-enter them multiple times. Starting with OS X 10.5 (Leopard), the standard **ssh-agent** tool is modified to start automatically via **launchd** and to leverage OS X's wonderful **Keychain** utility so that we do not have to even remember pass-phrases anymore. Once a pass-phrase for a key is stored in the **Keychain**, you won't have to enter it ever again.

⚠ WARNING

Using RSA or DSA keys for authentication is a powerful method to log in to multiple systems, but it can be very dangerous if used incorrectly. Every time you copy your public key to a new host, you are creating a new trust relationship that could be abused by a malicious attacker with access to a system with a trusted private key. Protecting this private key then becomes more important as more systems trust it. Always protect all your private keys with strong pass-phrases and leverage the **Keychain** to ensure they are loaded only when you are sitting at the keyboard.

If you are at the console, the first time you attempt to SSH to a remote system using an authentication key protected by a pass-phrase, Leopard will display a dialog for you to enter it, as shown in Figure 10.6. Checking **Remember password in my keychain** will instruct Leopard to store your pass-phrase in your **Keychain**. This pass-phrase will then be automatically recovered every-time SSH requires it without any intervention from you, assuming the **Keychain** is unlocked. If the **Keychain** is locked, you will be required to unlock it by entering your **Keychain** password.

Figure 10.6 Leopard's SSH Password Dialog

If you are not at the console (for instance, if you are connected via SSH to this Mac), you still can manage your keys with the **ssh-add** command-line utility. To store the pass-phrase for a key in the Keychain, run the following command in the **Terminal**:

```
ssh-add -K path-to-keyfile
```

To store the pass-phrase for the default key in the Keychain:

```
ssh-add -K
```

To list all the keys currently managed by the agent:

```
ssh-add -l
```

Tools & Traps...

Keeping the Big Fish Under Control

If you are not yet running Leopard, or if you are a bit more paranoid than most, you still can get the benefits of an integrated SSH agent and the **Keychain** with the help of the free **SSHKeychain** utility.

In addition to remembering your pass-phrases and providing a visual interface to the SSH agent **SSHKeychain** can be configured to unload keys from the agent upon certain important events, such as when the screensaver kicks in, a timer expires, or when the computer goes to sleep. These settings can be very valuable for laptops and desktops in shared offices, where you may want to be extra-careful about how long your SSH keys are loaded in the agent.

The tool can also be used to easily configure, establish, and tear down SSH tunnels from within its menu in the Menu Bar, which makes it an even more valuable addition to your Mac desktop if you rely on SSH tunneling.

SSHKeychain is available at http://www.sshkeychain.org.

Scripting Securely with SSH

As we've mentioned before, the Mac, and more specifically OS X, is a unique environment in that an operating system created around the premise of providing a rich graphical environment to the user is now built on top of a solid Unix foundation. In the Unix world the command line is king (first there was a command line and then there were windows); thus, an SSH session into a Unix system gives you as much flexibility as you would ever want. Even if you run a modern graphical desktop environment, such as GNOME or KDE, avoiding the command line would be quite difficult. However, this is not the case for OS X. You can accomplish pretty much all you would ever want on a Mac without ever dropping into the Terminal. This is not inherently a bad thing, but it does mean that most Mac users will be less familiar with the capabilities of the command line. It also means that some simple activities traditionally executed with the aid of graphical applications (such as checking somebody's phone number on the Address Book or finding a file with Spotlight) may not have simple or straightforward counterparts within the command line.

This is not a book about the OS X command line, but a book about SSH. However, to effectively take advantage of SSH on a Mac environment, it is important to gain an understanding of how some of these GUI-oriented tasks can be accomplished via the command line and, in turn, through an SSH connection.

This section will cover some recipes for dealing with ailments common to working with a remote SSH connection into a Mac. We hope these recipes will come to the rescue when you most need them.

NOTE

Mac OS X comes bundled with a multitude of familiar command line tools you can use within an SSH session. These tools include *curl, grep, gzip, lpr, lpq, nc, openssl, rsync, tar, vi,* and *zip* among hundreds of others. To keep this section short and on topic, only OS X-specific commands will be covered here. Information about these other tools can be found easily online and via the built-in manual pages.

Using Spotlight

Max OS X version 10.4 introduced Spotlight, a powerful desktop search capability that dramatically simplifies and speeds up the task of finding a specific piece of content in the sea of documents that are on our computers.

Spotlight is typically used by clicking on the magnifying glass icon on the Menu Bar, or by pressing **Command-Space**. The **mdfind** utility can be used to accomplish the same task via the command line.

Searching for Documents that Include the Words SSH, Mac, and Book

```
ank:~ max$ mdfind "ssh mac book"
/Users/max/Documents/ssh/ch10au.doc
```

Searching for Documents with the Word fish or the Word Chips

```
ank:~ max$ mdfind "(fish_chips)"
```

The **mdfind** tool supports specifying more complex queries via the command line. Consult its manual page to learn more about all its arguments.

TIP

The **mdfind** tool, as well as all the other tools discussed in this section, often have additional knobs and switches accessible via command line arguments that allow you to tailor its operation to your needs. To learn more about a tool's arguments, consult the tool's *man page* using the **man**. For example, to open the *man page* for **mdfind**, type the following command in the Terminal:

```
man mdfind
```

Working with Disk Images

It is not uncommon for Mac software to be distributed in disk images with the .dmg extension. Working with DMG files on a Mac is often done through the **Finder**, which can automatically mount and unmount them. The **hdiutil** utility can be used to accomplish the same through the command line. Here are a couple of examples:

Mounting a DMG Disk Image

```
ank:~ max$ hdiutil attach ~/Downloads/WebKit-SVN-r34824.dmg
expected CRC32 $E255EA9E
/dev/disk1      Apple_partition_scheme
/dev/disk1s1    Apple_partition_map
/dev/disk1s2    Apple_HFS
  /Volumes/WebKit
ank:~ max$ ls -l /Volumes
total 8
lrwxr-xr-x    1 root    admin    1     Jul 1    00:11 HD@ -> /
drwxr-xr-x    4 max     max      204   Jun 27   00:55 WebKit/
```

Ejecting a Mounted Disk Image

```
ank:~ max$ hdiutil detach /Volumes/WebKit
"disk1" unmounted.
"disk1" ejected.
ank:~ max$      ls -l /Volumes
total 8
lrwxr-xr-x       1 root    admin    1 Jul    1       00:11    HD@ -> /
ank:~ max$
```

The **hdiutil** tool has many additional capabilities, such as creating encrypted images, breaking existing images into smaller chunks, converting images between different formats, and burning images to CD.

Managing Local Disks

Computers often have a way of misbehaving when we are away from a console. A disk may fail, or a bad application install may wreck file permissions on our system. The **Disk Utility** application (within the **Application/Utilities** folder) is used to perform disk management tasks on a Mac from a graphical console, while the **diskutil** utility can be used to do the same from the command line.

diskutil can obtain details about all your disks, verify and repair the integrity of a file system, repair file permissions, format disks, and manage RAID sets. Refer to **diskutil**'s manual page (man diskutil) for more details. Here's a quick sample of some of **diskutil**'s commands in action.

Enumerating Available Disks and Their Partitions

```
ank:~ max$ diskutil list
/dev/disk0
#:      TYPE NAME                 SIZE          IDENTIFIER
0:      GUID_partition_scheme    *149.1 Gi     disk0
1:      EFI                       200.0 Mi     disk0s1
2:      Apple_HFS HD              148.7 Gi     disk0s2
```

Obtaining Disk Details

```
ank:scripts max$ diskutil info /
    Device Identifier:        disk0s2
    Device Node:              /dev/disk0s2
    Part Of Whole:            disk0
    Device / Media Name:      Apple_HFS_Untitled_1

    Volume Name:              HD
    Mount Point:              /
    File System:              Journaled HFS+
                              Journal size 16384 KB at offset 0x4a8000
    Owners:                   Enabled

    Partition Type:           Apple_HFS
    Bootable:                 Is bootable
    Media Type:               Generic
    Protocol:                 SATA
    SMART Status:             Verified
    Volume UUID:              E8EB94B9-C4F9-3737-8822-9B54DF93D96D

    Total Size:               148.7 Gi (159697911808 B) (311909984 512-byte blocks)
    Free Space:               49.5 Gi (53162356736 B) (103832728 512-byte blocks)

    Read Only:                No
    Ejectable:                No
    Whole:                    No
    Internal:                 Yes
```

Verifying Permissions

```
ank:~ max$ diskutil verifyPermissions /
Started verify/repair permissions on disk disk0s2 HD
Permissions differ on "private/var/log/secure.log", should be -rw------- ,
they are -rw-r-----
Permissions differ on "Applications/Utilities/AirPort Utility.app/Contents/
Resources/lanArrow.png", should be -rwxrwxr-x , they are -rw-rw-r--
Permissions differ on "Applications/Utilities/AirPort Utility.app/Contents/
Resources/lanCheck.png", should be -rwxrwxr-x , they are -rw-rw-r—
```

```
[output shortened for brevity]
Group differs on "private/etc/cups", should be 0, group is 26
[ + 0%..10%..20%..30%..40%..50%..60%..70%..80%..90%..100% ]
Finished verify/repair permissions on disk disk0s2 HD
```

Accessing System Configuration

The **systemsetup** command-line utility provides access to some of the most important system settings available via the **System Preferences** dialog. The tool can be used to set date/time and time zone, configure various inactivity timers, and even control whether remote login (SSH access) is allowed.

> **WARNING**
>
> As with some of the other tools discussed in this section, it is very well possible to lock yourself out of a system by issuing the wrong command (such as `systemsetup -setremotelogin -f off`). Always review the syntax of risky administrative commands twice before issuing them over a remote SSH session.

The **sw_vers** command line utility displays the OS X system version in format that is complementary to the more standard and POSIX **uname** utility, which also is available.

Controlling the Computer's Sleep Timer

```
ank:~ max$ systemsetup -getcomputersleep
Computer Sleep: Never
ank:~ max$ systemsetup -setcomputersleep 10
setcomputersleep: 10
ank:~ max$ systemsetup -getcomputersleep
Computer Sleep: after 10 minutes
```

Enabling Wake on Network Access

```
ank:~ max$ systemsetup -getwakeonnetworkaccess
Wake On Network Access: Off
ank:~ max$ systemsetup -setwakeonnetworkaccess on
setwakeonnetworkaccess: On
ank:~ max$ systemsetup -getwakeonnetworkaccess
Wake On Network Access: On
```

Printing Mac OS X Version Information

```
ank:          ~ max$ sw_vers
ProductName:    Mac OS X
ProductVersion: 10.5.4
BuildVersion:   9E17
```

For Everything Else, There Is AppleScript

If there is a task you currently perform via a graphical application for which you cannot find a command line equivalent, it is very likely you can carry it out using AppleScript.

AppleScript is a scripting language built into OS X that can be used to control applications and automate common tasks. In the context of SSH sessions, the **osascript** utility can be used to execute AppleScripts from the command line. Here are a couple of examples to give you a taste of the kinds of activities you can perform with AppleScript in the command line.

Accessing Your Personal Information

OS X's built-in **Address Book** is a fantastic tool to store all your contacts, until that day when you've forgotten to synchronize your laptop with your home computer before your business trip. Here's how you can use AppleScript to recover information from your **Address Book** from within an SSH session:

Recovering Phone Numbers

```
$ osascript <<EOI
> tell app "Address Book"
> set aPerson to first person whose organization is "Apple Inc."
> value of phones of aPerson
> end tell
> EOI
1-800-MY-APPLE
```

Recovering Addresses

```
$ osascript <<EOI
> tell app "Address Book"
> set aPerson to first person whose organization is "Apple Inc."
> set answer to (street of address of aPerson) & (city of address of aPerson)
& (state of address of aPerson)
> end tell
> EOI
1  Infinite Loop, Cupertino, CA
```

Having Fun with Multimedia

OS X has great audio and video capabilities, a relatively sophisticated voice synthesizer, and most modern Macs have built-in cameras. All these capabilities can be used via the command line through OS X's powerful scripting engine.

Recording Video Remotely (or Checking in on the Kids)

```
$ osascript <<EOI
> tell app "QuickTime Player"
> new movie recording
> start recording true
> delay 5
> stop recording true
> set aMovie to last document
> save aMovie
> path of aMovie
> end tell
> EOI
/Users/max/Desktop/Movie 4.mov
```

Recording Audio Remotely (or Bugging the Living Room)

```
$ osascript <<EOI
> tell app "QuickTime Player"
> new audio recording
> start recording true
> delay 5
> stop recording true
> set aClip to last document
> save aClip
> path of aClip
> end tell
> EOI
/Users/max/Desktop/Audio.mov
```

Spooking Your In-Laws

```
$ osascript -e 'say "Hello, Professor Falken. Would you like to play a game?"
using "Bruce""
```

Tools & Traps...

Using Script Editor to Browse Application Dictionaries

It is up to each application's developers to decide which capabilities to make available to scripting and in what capacity. Thus, even though the AppleScript language is well specified, there are few common sets of actions or properties used to communicate with a given application.

In order to make specific capabilities available for scripting, each application embeds a *Scripting Dictionary*. You can use the built-in **Script Editor** utility to browse an application's scripting dictionary. **Script Editor** can be found within the **Applications/ AppleScript** folder.

Select **File/Open Dictionary** in **Script Editor**'s main menu to see a list of installed scriptable applications. Select an application and click **OK** to open the application's scripting dictionary on a new window (see Figure 10.7.).

Script Editor also can be used as a simple editor to develop and troubleshoot AppleScripts.

Figure 10.7 Browsing Address Book's Scripting Dictionary Using Script Editor

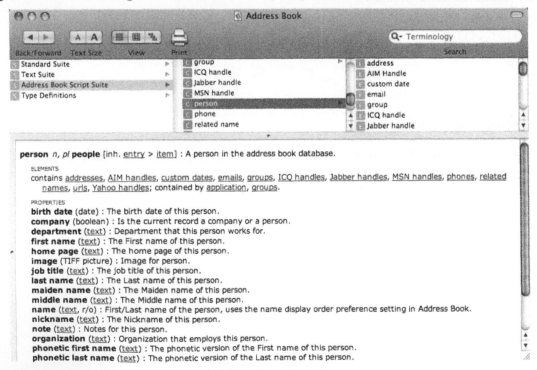

Summary

In this chapter, we've learned how to use SSH on a Mac, as well as how to take advantage of Mac-specific capabilities available in OS X, such as X11 forwarding and integration with the **Keychain**. Familiar SSH and Mac-specific capabilities come together to provide a powerful environment to manage multiple systems remotely in a secure manner. Furthermore, OS X's scripting capabilities using the AppleScript programming language can be an invaluable addition to your SSH bag of tricks.

Solutions Fast Track

Using SSH on a Mac

- ☑ Mac OS X includes its own build of the OpenSSH distribution.

- ☑ Standard SSH tools are ready to be used via the **Terminal**.

- ☑ Any Mac can be configured as an SSH server by enabling **Remote Login** via **Sharing** preferences.

- ☑ X11 traffic to and from a Mac can be forwarded easily through SSH for traversing firewalls and improved security.

Simplifying Key Management with the SSH Agent

- ☑ Using SSH keys for authentication can dramatically reduce the number of passwords that need to be remembered and enables simple automation via SSH.

- ☑ Leopard's **ssh-agent** can keep unlocked SSH keys in memory so that you have to enter their pass-phrases only once for every new session.

- ☑ Integration with OS X's **Keychain** allows **ssh-agent** to recover pass-phrases automatically, and without user intervention, while still preserving security.

Scripting Securely with SSH

- ☑ OS X capabilities typically available via the graphical console (such as **Spotlight**, **Disk Utility,** and **System Preferences**) often have command-line equivalents that can be used via SSH.

- ☑ Standard Unix tools are supplemented with OS X-specific ones to create a powerful scripting environment.

- ☑ AppleScript and the **osascript** tool can be used to automate applications via the command line.

Frequently Asked Questions

Q: What do I need to install to use SSH on my Mac?

A: Nothing. Mac OS X includes its own distribution of OpenSSH.

Q: How do I access an SFTP server?

A: The **sftp** utility can be used to access SFTP servers. The free **Fugu** and the commercial **Transmit** tools offer graphical SFTP clients.

Q: How do I enable SSH access to my Mac?

A: Enable **Remote Login** within the **Sharing** section of **System Preferences.**

Q: How can I use X Windows on a remote computer from the Mac?

A: Connect to the remote computer using SSH with either the −*X* or −*Y* arguments to enable X11 forwarding. SSH will automatically launch the X11 server, if installed, and set up your environment so that any X Windows application that you launch afterward will display on your Mac's display.

Q: How can I set up SSH key authentication with a remote host?

A: Use the **ssh-keygen** utility to generate a new key, and then copy ~**/.ssh/id_dsa.pub** to the remote system at ~**/.ssh/authorized_keys2** with **scp.** Always protect your SSH keys with a strong pass-phrase.

Q: Is it possible not to have to keep re-entering the pass-phrase for my SSH key every time I SSH to a server?

A: In Leopard just check **Remember password in my keychain** when the **Password** dialog pops up.

Q: How can I cache a key in the SSH agent from the command-line?

A: `ssh-add` stores the key in the agent; `ssh-add -K` also stores the pass-phrase in your keychain.

Q: How can I get the benefits of the SSH agent if I am not running Leopard?

A: You can use the **SSHKeychain** utility, available for download from http://sshkeychain.org.

Q: How can I search the file system using **Spotlight** when connected to a remote Mac via SSH?

A: The **mdfind** utility lets you interface with **Spotlight** via the command line.

Q: How can I mount image files in the DMG format from the command line?

A: You can mount DMG images from the command line using the **hdiutil** tool with the *attach* argument.

Q: Is there a way to run AppleScripts from the command line?

A: Yes. The **osascript** utility allows you to execute AppleScripts from the command line and in remote SSH sessions.

Q: Where can I find documentation about which commands are available to script a given application?

A: The **Script Editor** utility lets you browse scripting dictionaries for all your scriptable applications.

Q: Why is my AppleScript failing when running it with **osascript**?

A: If you are passing your script via the command line using the −*e* argument, make sure you are escaping quotes correctly; **osascript** expects your complete script to be contained in the argument right after −*e*. If your script is relatively complex, you may get better mileage using a *here document* (see http://en.wikipedia.org/wiki/Heredoc). Additionally, not all AppleScript commands are available from the command line.

## Chapter 11

SSH Command Line and Advanced Client Use

Solutions in this chapter:

- **Client Configuration**
- **Verbose Medium**
- **Secure Copy**

☑ **Summary**

☑ **Solutions Fast Track**

☑ **Frequently Asked Questions**

Introduction

In previous chapters we have looked at a variety of SSH features, usages, servers and applications. In this chapter we will explore the command line features of PuTTY as well as other aspects of CLI (Command Line Interface) usages and advanced SSH client topics.

Our major focus will be on PuTTY, but we will look at a couple of other command line clients as well.

Client Configuration

PuTTY is an open source SSH utility; it also supports rlogin, telnet, serial, and raw data connectivity. There are versions for both Linux and Windows. It is a freely available utility that can be downloaded in executable or installable format. The installable format supports a command line as well as a GUI option.

NOTE

The binary, installable and source code for PuTTY is available at www.chiark. greenend.org.uk/~sgtatham/putty/download.html. If you download the binary putty. exe, it will be GUI only. If you download putty-*x.xx*-installer.exe where *x.xx* is the current version of the program, you will get both GUI and command line. This site also contains all the source code for PuTTY for both UNIX and Windows.

This section will focus on the installation procedure for PuTTY from the installer file.

Once the PuTTY installer is downloaded to the system, you can invoke the installation by clicking the icon, as shown in Figure 11.1.

Figure 11.1 PuTTY Installer Icon

Figure 11.2 appears and asks for the following information:

Figure 11.2 Security Warning for PuTTY Installer

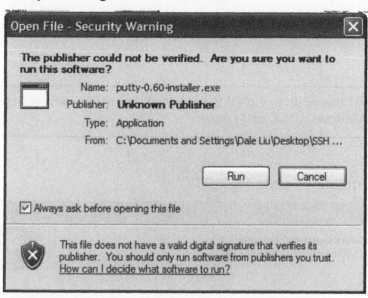

This security warning gives you the chance to verify the validity of the file and make sure it the file you want to execute. Putty-0.60-installer.exe is the filename we selected, and it is ready to install. Click Run to continue the process.

Figure 11.3 Welcome Wizard for PuTTY

This screen confirms you wish to install PuTTY on your system and verifies the version again. It then prompts you to click Next to move to the next step. Please see Figure 11.3.

NOTE

At the time of this writing, PuTTY Version 0.60 was the current release across all platforms (Windows, UNIX, and Linux).

Figure 11.4 Destination Folder for PuTTY

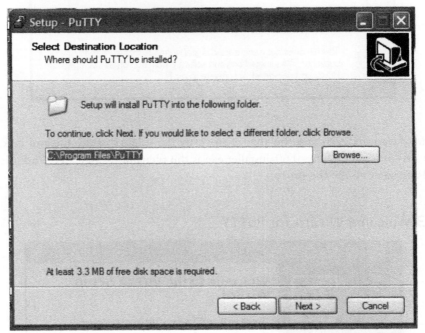

This dialog box (Figure 11.4) gives you the opportunity to relocate where PuTTY is installed on your computer. Some users have a separate hard drive just for applications, and this will allow you to install this application in that location. The Browse feature will display the following tree structure of the computer. Please see Figure 11.5. From this screen, you can select the drive, the folder, and subfolder into which you want to install PuTTY. Once you have selected the destination in the tree, if you chose the Browse button, click OK on the tree, and then click Next after you have set the location.

Figure 11.5 Folder Tree from Browse Button

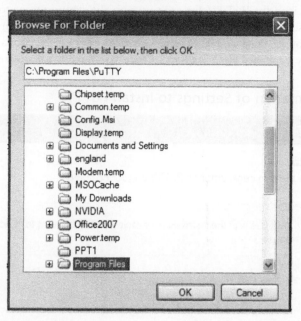

Figure 11.6 Customizing the Install of PuTTY

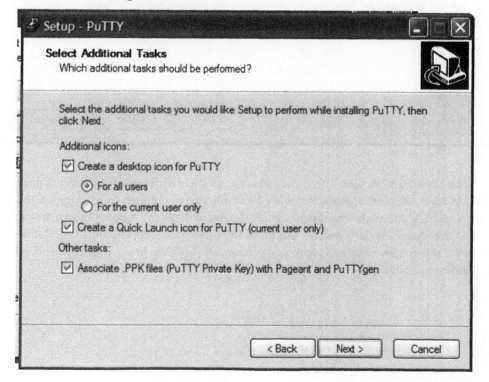

The next screen (Figure 11.6) allows you to customize some of the installation activities. You can select to have a desktop icon for PuTTY, for each user on the computer, or for just the account that is logged on. You can also put a quick launch icon in the area next to the Start icon on the taskbar. In addition, you can associate the PuTTY Private keys from previous versions with the new PuTTY and PuTTYgen (the key generator for SSH keys). Once you have made your selections, click Next.

Figure 11.7 Confirmation of Settings to Install PuTTY

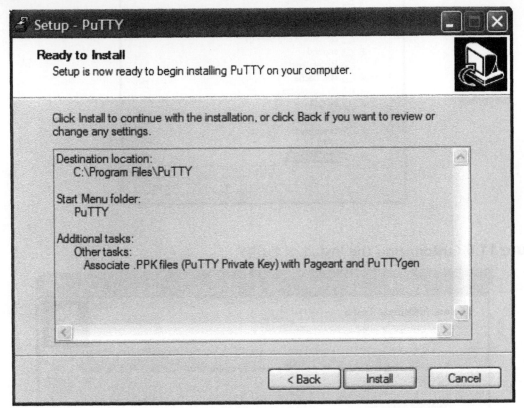

Once you have made all your selections and are at this screen (Figure 11.7), it will display all the selections you have made throughout this wizard and ask you to confirm by clicking on the Install button or to go back and make changes or cancel the install. If all the options shown are correct, click the Install button. You then will see the following progress screen (Figure 11.8). Because this progress screen shows how near you are to completion, all you have to do is sit back and wait for the PuTTY Installer to complete.

Figure 11.8 Installation Progress Screen

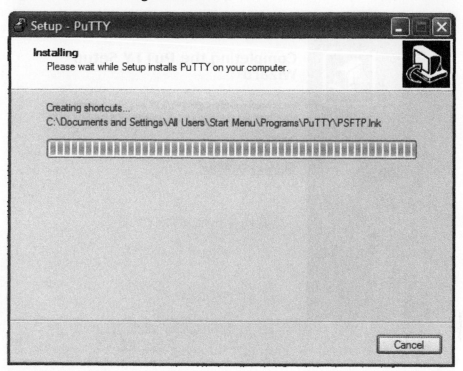

Once the progress screen completes, it will change to the completion screen. Please see Figure 11.9. Once the completion screen is displayed, you have the option of reading the readme file or not reading the readme file.

If you leave the checkbox in the default state and click the Finish button, the readme file will be displayed. There is important information for users wanting to use the command line interface.

After you have read the readme and closed the file, it is time to prepare Windows for using the command line version of PuTTY.

Figure 11.9 Completion of PuTTY

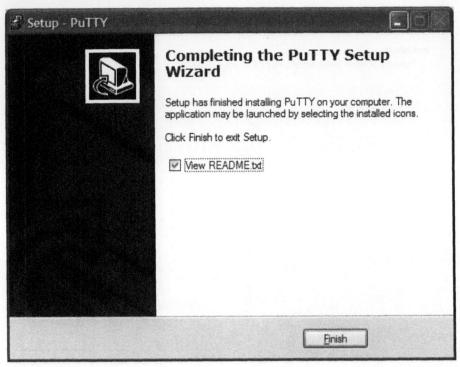

Now that you have completed the installation of the software, it is time to follow the readme and add to the Windows system path statement the folder into which you chose to install PuTTY. By adding this directory to the path, you will be able to access the PuTTY command line utilities in the directories where the files and documents to copy are located. If you do not do this, you will have to be in the PuTTY folder to access the command line utilities. In the currently supported versions of Windows (Windows XP and Vista), you need to first open the Control Panel. Please see Figure 11.10.

Figure 11.10 Windows XP Control Panel (w/ Service Pack 2) Classic View

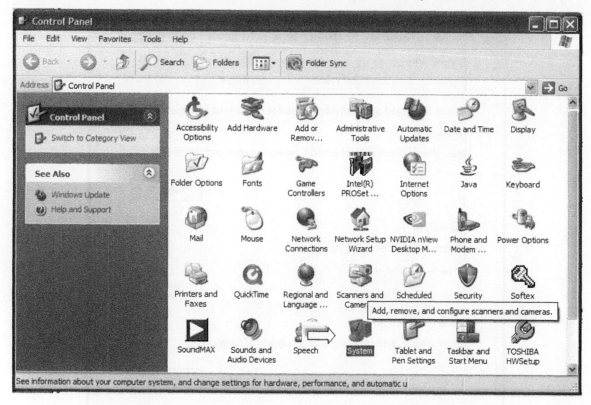

Once you have opened the Control Panel, you need to locate the System icon and double-click it.

After opening the System icon, you need to locate the Advanced tab (Figure 11.11.)

Figure 11.11 Advanced Tab of System Control Panel Tool

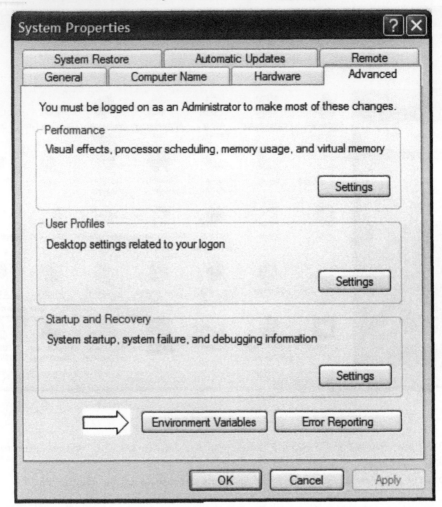

Once you have selected the Advanced tab, find the button labeled Environment Variables. Click this to bring up the screen that allows you to change the system path. Please see Figure 11.12.

Figure 11.12 Environment Variable Screen

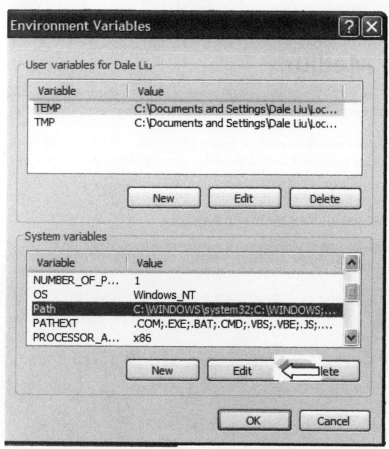

Highlight the path variable and click Edit. Once you do this, scroll to the end of the current path and add the directory path for PuTTY (the destination folder from above). If you selected the default location, you would add C:\Program Files\PuTTY\ to the path (Figure 11.13).

Figure 11.13 Edit Path Variable

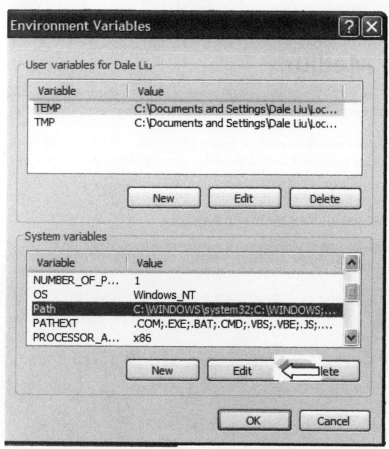

Once you have completed this, you can click OK here and close the other Control Panel windows. Now you will have access to the "Command Line" version of PuTTY, as well as the GUI version from the desktop icon.

Verbose Medium

Most people who use PuTTY probably would never need the command line options. However, for those who do use scripting and other automated features, the command line features are there for their use.

From any Windows command prompt (Figure 11.14), you can execute any of the PuTTY commands, if you have correctly followed the above steps in adding the PuTTY path to your system variables.

Figure 11.14 Windows XP Command Prompt

The first command will initiate a standard SSH session between a client and a server from the command prompt. The command is: **putty –method** (where method can be SSH, Telnet, Rlogin, or Raw) user@host where user is optional, (see example below). For example, if I wanted to connect to my server talesfromtheterminal.com using SSH, I could type the following from the command line:

Putty –ssh **u35764221@talesfromtheterminal.com** (Figure 11.15).

Figure 11.15 PuTTY Command Line to Call Up Session with SSH

Once I enter the password, I have my SSH connection and can do anything I could have done had I started with the GUI.

If you do not include the username in the command, you will be prompted for both username and password once the connection to the SSH server is made.

You can also use the command line to open PuTTY with other clear text protocols like Telnet, SMTP, and others: t protocols:

putty –telnet host port

For example to connect to the mail server for company XYZ (mail.companyxzy.com), you would enter the following command:

putty –telnet mail.companyxyz.com 25

This would take you to a PuTTY window with an open session to the mail server.

Tools & Traps…

Accessing Port 25 via Telnet over the Internet

Port 25 is the Simple Mail Transport Protocol (SMTP). You can use PuTTY to connect directly to this port and create e-mails directly on the server. These e-mails can appear to come from any location. Due to increases in security and firewall protection, this may not always work over the Internet. However, this command will always work on the internal network of the e-mail server because there is not a physical separation between the flat network and the e-mail server.

PuTTY can be used to connect to a POP3 email server from a command prompt to read email directly. You would do this when you don't have access to an email client. You could type the following:

putty –telnet host 110 (Figure 11.16)

You then could use the POP3 commands from the PuTTY window.
Some of the POP3 commands are as follows:

User: Syntax user *username*

Pass: Syntax pass *password*

List: Syntax list <cr> shows list of current emails

Retr #: Syntax retr # (where # is the number of the message to retrieve)

Dele #: Syntax dele # (where # is the number of the message to delete)

Figure 11.16 Output of PuTTY Session from POP3

```
+OK POP3 server ready <7e93c70b-28c8-4660-9aaf-32841cc72809>

-ERR Invalid command
user myname@mydomain.com  ⇐
+OK User:'user@mydomain.com' ok
pass mysecretpassword  ⇐
+OK Password ok
list       ⇐
+OK 6 messages (1827506 octets)
1 22965
2 1762800
3 7789
4 16953
5 7880
6 9119

retr 3   ⇐
+OK 7789 octets
Return-Path: <jamieken4@legwork.com.ng>
Received: from ag-out-0708.google.com [72.14.246.241] by maila3.mydomain.com with SMTP;
   Mon, 14 Jul 2008 11:50:40 -0700
Received: by ag-out-0708.google.com with SMTP id 8so8644101agc.0
   for <user@mydomain.com>; Mon, 14 Jul 2008 11:50:40 -0700 (PDT)
Received: by 10.100.210.9 with SMTP id i9mr10518446ang.133.1216061440145;
   Mon, 14 Jul 2008 11:50:40 -0700 (PDT)
Received: by 10.100.125.9 with HTTP; Mon, 14 Jul 2008 11:50:40 -0700 (PDT)
Message-ID: <ff4c6ce30807141150q30c19c14w5f4014e1193f1813@mail.gmail.com>
Date: Mon, 14 Jul 2008 20:50:40 +0200
From: "jamie ken" <jamieken4@legwork.com.ng>
Subject: This has a low chance of being Spam CONTACT ROYAL SECURITY COMPANY FOR YOUR FUND IN PACKAGE BOX.
MIME-Version: 1.0
Content-Type: multipart/alternative;
   boundary="----=_Part_65338_28599139.1216061440118"
X-Rcpt-To: <daleliu@computer-revolution-ent.com>
X-SmarterMail-Spam: SpamAssassin 16.4 [raw: 8.2], SPF_None
```

As the arrows above indicate, you can enter your username and password in clear text. This lists all your messages and command "**retr**", retrieves individual messages. With the "dele" command, you can delete specific messages. This works with most emails. If the e-mail is digitally signed (encrypted), you will not be able to read with this method.

The PuTTY option **–v** (for verbose) in some cases you can have PuTTY give you more information on the session for debugging purposes. In opening a simple session, there is no extra available information. This option will help you more with debugging PuTTY problems.

The **–l** option will let you specify a login name, and the **–pw** option will let you specify a password for the session. Please see Figure 11.17. This becomes handy if you are scripting PuTTY sessions to use in recurring batch jobs. The other option that is useful with scripting is the **–m** option; it allows you to read a remote command or script from a file.

Figure 11.17 PuTTY Command Line with Username and Password

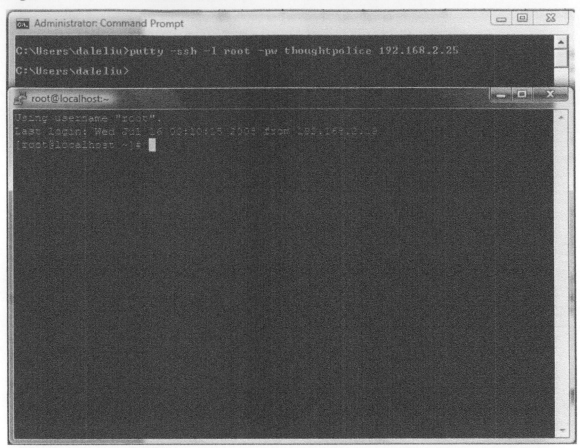

For example, if you entered the command PuTTY –ssh mysshserver –l myusername –pw secretpassword –m startupfile, it would connect to the server sshserver using your username and password. It then would execute the file named startup in the home directory of the user. This is useful when you have automated tasks that have to happen at the same time every day but that do not need to be monitored.

As demonstrated in Chapter 13, PuTTY also has the capabilities of setting up port forwarding. The options **–L** and **–R** are used in the same manner as the options in OpenSSH.

NOTE

At the time of this writing, this feature works only if the server is OpenSSH because ssh.com uses a proprietary protocol at this time and is not compatible with PuTTY. Until SSH.com's protocol is published or adheres to the current standards, it will remain incompatible.

The **–A** and **–a** options are used with agent forwarding. This is a process that allows applications on the SSH server to access the SSH client. The **–A** option turns on this feature, and the **–a** option turns it off. This feature is primarily used with PKI authentication and storage of the keys in a local repository so that the server can access them as you open other applications through your PuTTY SSH session.

To open a PuTTY SSH session with compression, you can use the **–c** option. To specify a specific release of SSH, version 1 or 2, you can use the **-1** or **-2** options (Figure 11.18), respectively. In addition, to specify a private key, you would use the **–i** command.

Figure 11.18 PuTTY SSH Session Forcing SSH Version 1 with the -1 Option

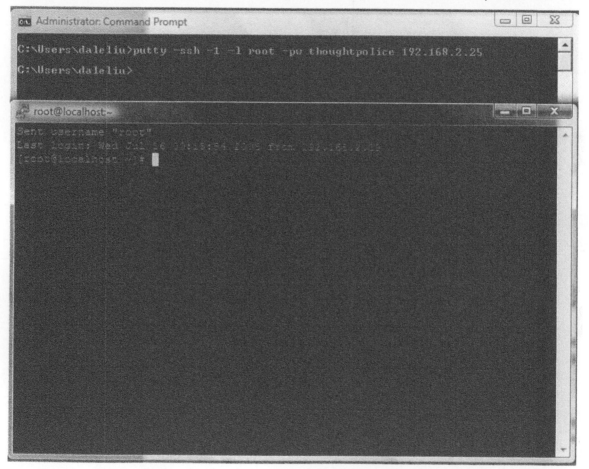

Secure Copy

PuTTY comes with a few other command line utilities, including pageant, plink, pftp, and pscp.

plink Command Line Link Utility

The plink utility is a command line SSH connector that will open the SSH session in the command prompt window (see figure below). This allows you to directly enter into an SSH session and enter commands without having to open a separate window. This is a convenient tool; however, the display is less than visually friendly.

As you can see in Figure 11.19, using plink in Windows Vista and Windows XP displays all the command codes.

Figure 11.19 plink Command Example

PuTTY Pageant Key Management Utility

Pageant is a utility that manages the SSH keys for PuTTY. This tool gives you control of the keys used with all the different SSH servers (see figure below). Pageant is a useful utility for managing public keys for multiple SSH servers. By storing the keys in Pageant, you can easily open many sessions quickly without having to type the password or passphrase for each session. The Pageant utility will also streamline batch file programming and automated tasks with the command line options for PuTTY.

Figure 11.20 Pageant Key Utility for PuTTY

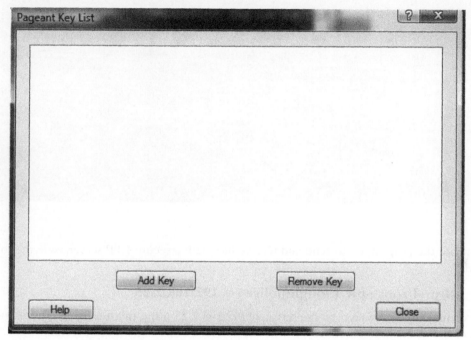

With the Pageant utility you can store, remove, and clear all the RSA key pairs out of the registry. Please see Figure 11.20.

PuTTY psftp Secure FTP Utility

The next utility included with PuTTY is psftp. This is a SSH-encrypted FTP (File Transfer Protocol); it gives you the ability to send files to and using a secure protocol, like the FTP protocol, without sending your credentials in clear text. The psftp program works much like FTP, but with more security. It uses a lot of the same options as plink and PuTTY, including the **-1** and **-2** options to force the SSH version.

Below (Figure 11.21) is a screen showing the options for psftp; the figure shows how you how you can initiate these transfers.

Figure 11.21 psftp Options Screen (PuTTY Secure FTP)

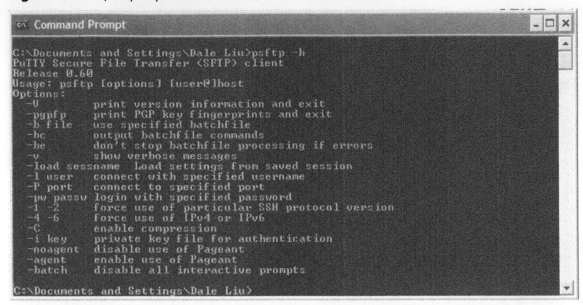

To initiate the psftp utility to send and receive files with a secure FTP server, issue the following command:

psftp −l root −pw thoughtpolice −v 192.168.2.25

This command will connect to the server at 192.168.2.25 using the username of root and the password of thoughtpolice; in addition, it will display verbose messages (Figure 11.22):

Figure 11.22 psftp Session Initialized to Show Key Exchange

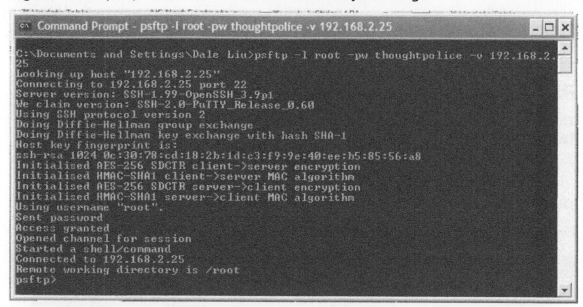

Once you have initiated the session, you have the following commands within the session. Please see Figure 11.23.

Figure 11.23 psftp Commands

```
psftp> help
!        run a local command
bye      finish your SFTP session
cd       change your remote working directory
chmod    change file permissions and modes
close    finish your SFTP session but do not quit PSFTP
del      delete files on the remote server
dir      list remote files
exit     finish your SFTP session
get      download a file from the server to your local machine
help     give help
lcd      change local working directory
lpwd     print local working directory
ls       list remote files
mget     download multiple files at once
mkdir    create directories on the remote server
mput     upload multiple files at once
mv       move or rename file(s) on the remote server
open     connect to a host
put      upload a file from your local machine to the server
pwd      print your remote working directory
quit     finish your SFTP session
reget    continue downloading files
ren      move or rename file(s) on the remote server
reput    continue uploading files
rm       delete files on the remote server
rmdir    remove directories on the remote server
psftp> _
```

Note these commands are the same as those used with FTP. The biggest difference is that when using psftp your data is secured. It is encrypted using PuTTY, as shown above, the AES-256 encryption block cipher protocol (see Chapter 4 for list of protocols). Thus, if this session were captured using a program like Wireshark™, it would not compromise the username and password used to initiate this session.

PuTTY pscp Secure Copy Utility

The pscp command is a secure copy command that is run from the Windows command prompt. This command runs in two modes: Push and Pull. In Push mode you copy files from local machine to remote machine from the command line; in Pull mode you pull files from the server to the local machine from the command line. Below (Figure 11.24) is a screen shot showing the pscp options.

Figure 11.24 pscp (PuTTY Secure Copy) Command Line Options

```
Command Prompt
C:\Documents and Settings\Dale Liu>pscp
PuTTY Secure Copy client
Release 0.60
Usage: pscp [options] [user@]host:source target
       pscp [options] source [source...] [user@]host:target
       pscp [options] -ls [user@]host:filespec
Options:
  -V        print version information and exit
  -pgpfp    print PGP key fingerprints and exit
  -p        preserve file attributes
  -q        quiet, don't show statistics
  -r        copy directories recursively
  -v        show verbose messages
  -load sessname  Load settings from saved session
  -P port   connect to specified port
  -l user   connect with specified username
  -pw passw login with specified password
  -1 -2     force use of particular SSH protocol version
  -4 -6     force use of IPv4 or IPv6
  -C        enable compression
  -i key    private key file for authentication
  -noagent  disable use of Pageant
  -agent    enable use of Pageant
  -batch    disable all interactive prompts
  -unsafe   allow server-side wildcards (DANGEROUS)
  -sftp     force use of SFTP protocol
  -scp      force use of SCP protocol

C:\Documents and Settings\Dale Liu>_
```

Like PuTTY and plink, a lot of the options are the same; however, there are a few more, including the **–psftp** and **–scp** options. They allow you to determine what secure copy protocol to use with this command.

To push a file from a local computer, you could use the following example:

    pscp –pw thoughtpolice myipconfig.bat root@192.168.2.25:myipconfig.bat

Below (Figure 11.25) the output from the above command.

Figure 11.25 PuTTY pscp Push from
the Local Computer to the Remote Computer

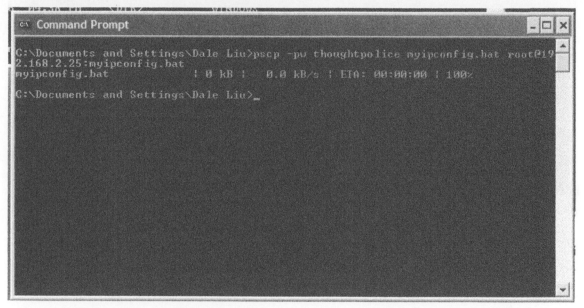

To pull a file from the remote computer, use the following command.

    pscp –pw thoughtpolice root@192.168.2.25:install.log linuxinstall.log

Below (Figure 11.26) is the output from this example.

Figure 11.26 PuTTY pscp Pull from the
Remote Computer to the Local Computer

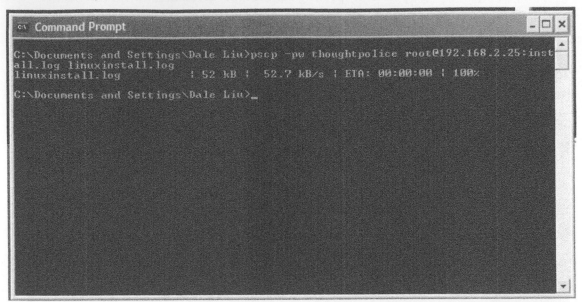

The command utilities that are included in the PuTTY suite extend the functionality of the Secure Shell (SSH) protocol. These utilities give you the utilities to move, copy, and transfer files in an encrypted method and a way to manage the PuTTY keys used for encryption.

Summary

In this chapter we looked at how to install the PuTTY client onto a Windows box. The options available during the installation and how to add the PuTTY features to the command line, by adding the PuTTY folder to the system path make both the PuTTY GUI and the command line utilities available.

We then looked at the command line features of PuTTY that allow us to control how PuTTY is started. We also looked at some of the features. We saw options that will allow us to log into a PuTTY SSH session and run a scripted file to automate repetitive tasks; this is very useful in batch file scripting in a Windows environment to control a Linux/UNIX environment. We also saw that the commands covered in Chapter 13 with OpenSSH can be used with PuTTY for SSH port forwarding. These commands extend the GUI application.

In the final section we looked at plink, psftp, pscp, and pageant. These tools offer a PuTTY link within a command prompt, a secure FTP service, a secure copy service, and a key management tool for the SSH keys. These tools offer services that extend the PuTTY application, allowing other services that are normally not encrypted a secure channel in which to operate.

Solutions Fast Track

Client Configuration

☑ Download the PuTTY installer putty-*x.xx*-installer.exe at http://www.chiark.greenend .org.uk/~sgtatham/putty/download.html.

☑ During the installation you will have the option to place the PuTTY folder in an alternative location.

☑ During the installation you have the option to have a desktop icon created and allow all users on the PC to use the PuTTY software.

☑ Adding the location of the PuTTY folder to the system path variable gives you command-line access to the command line utilities.

Verbose Medium

☑ PuTTY from the command line can be controlled by various options that control how the program is started.

☑ The command line options help you use PuTTY in batch file scripting.

☑ The command line options allow PuTTY to do port forwarding similar to OpenSSH.

Secure Copy

☑ The following utilities are included in the PuTTY suite: plink, pageant, pscp, and pftp.

☑ plink is a command line PuTTY link within a command window.

☑ pageant is a key management utility.

☑ pscp is a command-line secure copy program that can push or pull files from a remote SSH server.

☑ pftp is a command-line secure FTP program that can create an encrypted channel for working with FTP between a PuTTY client and an SSH server.

Frequently Asked Questions

Q: Are there any SSH clients other than PuTTY?

A: Yes. As discussed in Chapter 4, there are other clients. PuTTY is just the most commonly used in Windows environments. It is an open source free utility with robust features.

Q: Are there different versions of PuTTY?

A: Yes, you can download the source and modify it, as long as you could leave the required license and copyright information.

Q: Why do I need to add the PuTTY directory to the system path variable to use the command line options and tools?

A: You don't. If you do not add the directory to the path, you then have to cdo the folder to use the utilities and options. This is inconvenient, but possible. If you add the directory to the path, you can call the commands from any directory.

Q: Do all the command line options work with all the utilities?

A: No. Some are specific to the utility; however, most are the same across all utilities.

Q: If I don't have an SSHv2-capable server, can I force the utilities to use SSHv1?

A: Yes: The **–1** and **–2** command line options will let you force the version used.

Q: Why would I need the option to push or pull files with the pscp command?

A: If you run a service that creates a log file or data file in Windows that needs to be sent to a server, the push feature is best. If you have a log file or data file created on a Linux/UNIX box that has to be copied to a Windows box, the pull feature would be the best option.

Chapter 12

SSH Server
Advanced Use

Solutions in this chapter:

- **Allowing SSH Connections**
- **Maintaining System Time**
- **Configuring the Warning Banner**
- **Securing User Home Directories**
- **Controlling Session Timeouts**
- **Logging Options**
- **Additional SSH Server Options**
- **Debugging SSH**

☑ **Summary**

☑ **Solutions Fast Track**

☑ **Frequently Asked Questions**

Introduction

Some people fail to realize the real power that SSH brings to the table. Sure you can connect to a remote system, manage that system, and perform other administrative tasks. There is no doubt these abilities are handy to have. The fact that you can do so securely, unlike with telnet or with an unencrypted VNC session, makes it all the more valuable. In all likelihood, many tasks are easier through the GUI. In most cases if you want to perform some administrative task on a system, unless it is very trivial, you will probably connect to a virtual desktop such as VNC or Xwindows. The real strength of SSH is in the ability to perform tasks remotely and in a secure fashion. Some devices, particularly networking gear, might not have a GUI at all, leaving SSH as the only *secure* way to manage them. By implementing SSH with two-factor authentication, you add a powerful tool to your administrative toolbox, allowing you to get the job done on a large number of systems quickly and securely.

At this point you presumably have a working SSH implementation. You should have been able to test both the SSH client and server components and made test connections. Perhaps you would like to further customize your SSH server and explore some of the more advanced features that are available. Alternatively, if you are having problems with a particular SSH implementation, the debugging section of this chapter can help. In that case, you might want to skip to the debugging section of this chapter first and then come back to the remainder of the chapter at your convenience In most cases you will be able to sort out the problem armed with this additional information.

However you arrived here – whether in the normal course of digesting this text or as a last ditch act of frustration –you are in the right place. This chapter focuses on exactly the type of advanced options that can help. Key considerations are covered with special attention towards restricting who is allowed to connect to the SSH server. Given the sensitive nature of offering a remote session, securing the SSH sessions should be a top priority. Other topics include session timeouts, key management, logging options, debugging failing session, and more.

Allowing SSH Connections

Arguably, securing your SSH server is the most important part of getting the server up and running. After all having a non-working SSH implementation will not usually result in a compromised system, while having an *insecure* implementation of the SSH server running almost certainly will. What follows is an in depth look at the various methods that can be used to secure your SSH server. The general approach is to discuss access control methods starting with the most generic (meaning not sshd specific) such as firewalls and ending with the controls available specifically within sshd itself. It is recommended that at least some minimal security measures be employed before the system is ever connected to an uncontrolled network. An unsecured system is usually a compromised system in short order.

Controlling Access Using ACLs

The first line of defense is at the network level. In most networks this will mean a firewall, in the form of either an appliance or a local firewall on the SSH server itself. By implementing access control lists (ACLs), you can restrict access to not only the SSH process but also to the entire host. Both the Windows Firewall and the netfilter firewall on Linux allow you to restrict access based on the server port number and to a lesser degree, the process executable.

Configuring the Windows Firewall

Because it is enabled by default (after Windows XP SP2), an SSH server process running on a modern Windows operating system probably has some firewall protection in place already. The Windows Firewall is relatively simple in its capabilities, and overall is not very robust. Filtering options are limited to basic source and destination IP address and port combinations. Despite the limitations of the Windows Firewall, it is easy to configure and can play a part in a defense-in-depth strategy. Assuming the firewall is already enabled, you would have to open up access for the SSH server anyway, so you might as well do it right.

You can access your Windows Firewall through the GUI by navigating to **Start | Settings | Control Panel | Windows Firewall**. There is an easier way, which is to use the command line. There is nothing wrong with using the GUI, but in most cases, I find it is far quicker to accomplish the same thing using the command line tool. Configuration of the Windows Firewall via the command line is accomplished via the netsh tool. Microsoft added Netsh firewall support to Windows XP as of Service Pack 2. Netsh can be used in an interactive mode or by entering the entire command on one line. To use Netsh in interactive mode, simply enter **netsh** at the command prompt. Your command prompt will change to **netsh>**. From there you can get guided help at each level of the system by entering a question mark followed by pressing Enter.

If you wish to simply enter the command you need all on a single line, interactive mode is not needed. This method is also quicker assuming you know what command you need. The entire command for opening port 22 is as follows:

```
netsh firewall add portopening TCP 22 "SSH Server"
```

The Windows firewall provides some limited ability to restrict access based on the source address. To limit access to a port to only a particular subnet, in this example 192.168.1.0, you would add the custom scope command, followed by a list of source addresses:

```
netsh firewall add portopening TCP 22 "SSH Server" CUSTOM 192.168.1.0/24
```

One nice feature of the Windows Firewall is the ability to permit access based on the program that is running instead of on the port number. For the standard services, you probably know what port is needed, but sometimes a single application might need a large number of ports, or it may use a custom port and you're not sure which port it needs. In these cases, you can permit the application to open a listening port, and the firewall will allow inbound connections. To allow sshd.exe to listen on any port for connections sourced from the local subnet, use the following command:

```
netsh firewall add allowedprogram C:\sshd.exe "SSH Servr" CUSTOM LocalSubnet
```

WARNING

Depending on how your Internet connection is configured, the Internet router may NAT inbound traffic to an internal address. If this is the case, the external address would appear as an internal address and a Windows Firewall scope of LocalSubnet would still grant them access. In short, remember that NAT'ed addresses can sometimes lead to undesirable access through ACLs.

Other useful commands are **netsh firewall show portopening** and **netsh firewall show allowedprogram**, which will allow you to quickly see which ports and programs have been granted access on a particular system, including verifying that the access you just enabled was entered properly. This is a handy command to know in general. Failure to grant access on the Windows Firewall has been the bane of many user-based services. Sample output is shown in Figure 12.1.

Figure 12.1 Windows Firewall netsh Output

```
C:\Users\Eric>netsh firewall show portopening

Port configuration for Domain profile:
Port    Protocol    Mode    Traffic direction    Name
-----------------------------------------------------------------

Port configuration for Standard profile:
Port    Protocol    Mode    Traffic direction    Name
-----------------------------------------------------------------
22      TCP         Enable  Inbound              SSH Server
```

Tools & Traps…

What's in a Name?

The ability to specify access through the Windows Firewall based on the program name is pretty handy. You won't need to figure out which port it needs or whether the program needs to listen on a lot of ports. This ease is not without its pitfalls, however. The access is based on the program name and nothing else. This means if the Windows Firewall is configured to allow inbound connections to *helpdesk.exe*, and a user renames *badapp.exe* to *helpdesk.exe*, connections to *badapp will* be permitted through the firewall. This is why renaming an executable of the user's choosing is a popular method of bypassing Windows Firewall restrictions.

Configuring the Linux Firewall

The Linux firewall functionality is provided by Netfilter. Netfilter is far more sophisticated than the Windows Firewall. A firewall worthy of protecting an enterprise can be crafted using a hardened Linux computer and the netfilter firewall, while the Windows Firewall is suitable only for protecting the host on which it resides. The utility that is used to manage the firewall rules and otherwise manipulate the firewall is iptables. Assuming you are using a default policy action of DROP for your INPUT chain, you can use the following command to add a rule to allow inbound connections to port 22 from the 192.168.1.0 subnet:

```
iptables -A INPUT -p tcp -s 192.168.1.0/24 --dport 22 -j ACCEPT
```

In the example above, –A tells iptables you want to add a rule. The –p options specifies the protocol to match, while the –s option specifies the sources to match. The --dport option is for the destination port and –j tells netfilter what action to perform when this rule is matched. You can verify the rules that are currently configured by entering **iptables –L**; your output should include the following rule:

```
#iptables -L
Chain INPUT (policy DROP)
Target      prot  opt  source            destination
ACCEPT      tcp   --   192.168.1.0/24    anywhere    tcp dpt:ssh
```

Using TCP Wrappers

In the Linux utility TCP Wrappers, you can find functionality similar to the Windows Firewall's capability to permit access based on a program name. TCP Wrappers filters access to services (by name) on the host on which the service is running. Only services that are compiled against the libwrap.a library can use TCP Wrappers. With TCP Wrappers enabled, attempts to access a given service will be compared against the /etc/hosts.allow file and then the /etc/hosts.deny file (in that order). Rules are checked sequentially and processing of the rules files stop when a match is found. If a match is not found in either file, access will be granted. As an example, if you wanted to allow connections only from 192.168.1.0 to sshd while rejecting all other connection attempts to sshd, you would have the following two lines in your hosts.allow and hosts.deny files:

```
/etc/hosts.allow
sshd : 192.168.1.
```

```
/etc/hosts.deny
sshd : ALL
```

A default deny policy can easily be implemented by placing ALL : ALL within the hosts.deny file. From that point you can add any access you wish to allow in the hosts.allow file. While you would not want to rely on TCP Wrappers as your only means of protection, it does have the advantage that the access is not dependent on the listening port as it is with netfilter. The two filter files accept several wildcards and follow the basic format of *<daemon>*: *<client(s)>* :*<option>* :*<option>*. Wildcards include *ALL, LOCAL, KNOWN, UNKNOWN,* and *PARANOID*. The KNOWN wildcard matches on any host when the hostname or host address is known or when the user in known. The UNKNOWN similarly matches when the hostname, host address, or user name is unknown. The PARANOID option should be used with care as it matches whenever the hostname and host address do not match. This is dependant on DNS to function; thus, if DNS is unavailable or not working, all hosts resolved through DNS will be a match.

With TCP Wrappers' limited functionality and syntax, you might wonder why you would ever use it over simply using netfilter. Because iptables works at the packet level, if you want to deny access to a particular process, such as HTTP, you must do it based on port number. Thus, if you use netfilter to explicitly block connection attempts to port 80, and the user starts up the Web server and tells it to listen on port 8080, the connection will be allowed. With TCP Wrappers, you permit or deny access to a *process* instead of a *port*. In this way, you can ensure that a given process will work regardless of the port it is using.

This distinction could prove invaluable if you have a service that uses a large number of listening ports. Some services want you to open up a very large range of ports, rendering your local firewall nearly useless. Some services use an incrementing port with each instance that is spawned, again requiring a large range of ports to be opened. Finally, perhaps an even more common scenario that renders packet level port filtering useless is when the session is tunneled within another protocol. For example, if you are tunneling FTP within SSH, a packet filter will see it as port 22 encrypted traffic, but TCP Wrapper can see it as ftpd and block based on the hosts.allow and hosts.deny files accordingly.

TIP

If the line is too long in the hosts.allow or hosts.deny file, you will generate an error. You must \
    separate lines that wrap to the next line with a slash at the end of the line to prevent an \
    error from occurring.

Using sshd_config Options

The /etc/ssh/sshd_config file is the key mechanism for controlling how the SSH daemon behaves. The configuration file has several options that can be used to restrict who has access to the sshd process. The most applicable options include the AllowGroups, AllowUsers, DenyGroups, and DenyUsers keywords. These keywords accept user or group names and pretty much do exactly what it sounds like they would. The keywords are processed in the following order: DenyUsers, AllowUsers, DenyGroups, and AllowGroups, regardless of the order in which they appear inside the sshd_config file. This means the more granular user-based permissions override the group-based permissions.

The sshd_config file lists default values for various options, but they are all commented out. To change a value from the default, you must first uncomment a line and then configure the desired value. The AllowUsers and other options in which we are interested are not listed in the configuration file by default and must be added. To permit connections from the users "test" and "test1," you would add the following anywhere in the /etc/ssh/sshd_config file:

```
AllowUsers test test1
```

Multiple entries for these keywords are all made on one line with a space between values. After making changes to the sshd_conf file, you will need to restart the sshd process for them to take effect. This can be done by entering:

```
sh /etc/rc.d/rc.sshd restart
```

or

```
sh /etc/init.d/sshd restart
```

The ListenAddress keyword is another way to tighten security for the SSH server. By default the ListenAddress value is 0.0.0.0, which means sshd will listen for inbound connections on any and all local addresses. If your SSH server contains multiple interfaces, this can be a good way to limit access to only an internal interface (in addition to using netfilter, of course). While listening on all addresses might not always pose a problem, it is one more way you can restrict and control who connects to the SSH server, as follows:

```
ListenAddress 192.168.1.99
```

The above entry in the sshd_config file would limit sshd to listen for inbound connections only on the 192.168.1.99 local address.

Using Host Keys for Authentication

Another way you can restrict who can connect via SSH is to use public keys for user authentication instead of password authentication. There are two common reasons for doing this. The first is because you can generate a user key pair without a password for the key. When you configure the SSH server with that key, the user can connect and will not be prompted for a password. Being able to connect without a password may sound appealing but it is really not the most secure method to use. Connecting in this manner is typically most appropriate when the public key file is considered well secured, such as on a server in a secured data center.

> **TIP**
>
> You cannot use the same system as both the SSH client and SSH server for public key encryption; it won't work. While you *can* connect to yourself for testing *password* authenticated SSH, you need a different system to test public key authentication. Knowing this little tip might save you a lot of time and frustration.

An even better reason to use public key authentication is to increase security. By placing a password on the keyfile, you still will be prompted for a password when making a connection. Doing this allows you to implement two-factor authentication, requiring both something you have (the keyfile) and something you know (the keyfile password) in order to authenticate. This is the most secure way to authenticate SSH connections out of the box. To enable public key authentication, follow these steps:

1. Create a keypair for the *client* if one does not already exist. Enter **ssh-keygen –t dsa** for example. Follow the prompts and enter a password for the keypair if you want to use two-factor authentication. The default dsa keypair will be id_dsa and id_dsa.pub.

2. Copy the .pub key from the host to the authorized keys file on the SSH server. Note that the AuthorizedKeysFile keyword in /etc/ssh/sshd_config specifies a *file*, not a directory path. The default .ssh/authorized_keys value tells sshd to look in the file named authorized_keys for the public key. You can copy the contents of the host's public key by entering **cat id_dsa.pub >> authorized_keys**.

3. At this point you should be able to log on using the public key for authentication. If you created the key without a password, you will be connected without being prompted for one. The SSH server will still accept a password for authentication, however. This can be a useful fallback in case a client attempts to connect for whom no key has been copied to authorized_keys. To prevent this behavior edit the sshd_config file and change the **PasswordAuthentication** keyword value to **no**.

4. Restart sshd (sh /etc/rc.d/rc.sshd restart) for the change to sshd_confg to take effect.

If everything went well you should be able to log on using the public key, with or without a password depending on which type of keyfile you generated. You can verify that everything is working properly by connecting with the –v (or –vv) option. A sample connection using a keyfile without a password and –v is shown in Figure 12.2 with some output omitted to conserve space.

Figure 12.2 SSH Client Public Key Authentication

```
C:\Pers\Apps\_Network\Netcat>ssh -v test@192.168.1.70
OpenSSH_3.8.1p1, OpenSSL 0.9.7d 17 Mar 2004
debug1: Reading configuration data /etc/ssh_config
debug1: Connecting to 192.168.1.70 [192.168.1.70] port 22.
debug1: Connection established.
<output omitted>
This is the warning banner from banner.txt
debug1: Authentications that can continue: publickey,keyboard-interactive
debug1: Next authentication method: publickey
debug1: Trying private key: /home/eseagren/.ssh/identity
debug1: Trying private key: /home/eseagren/.ssh/id_rsa
debug1: Offering public key: /home/eseagren/.ssh/id_dsa
debug1: Server accepts key: pkalg ssh-dss blen 433
debug1: read PEM private key done: type DSA
debug1: Authentication succeeded (publickey).
debug1: channel 0: new [client-session]
debug1: Entering interactive session.
Last login: Sat Jul 19 10:40:08 2008 from stsic21358
Linux 2.6.21.5.
bt ~  $
```

Using public key encryption to authenticate SSH sessions adds a whole new level of security. Even if you choose to use keyfiles without passwords, there are legitimate uses for doing so. If you have servers in the data center that need to run automated processes over an SSH session, it might be a perfect use for public key authentication without a password. The alternative is to allow password-based authentication and to permit a blank password for the account, which is very insecure. SSH is a powerful tool, and like all powerful tools, access to it should be carefully guarded. With all of the security controls in place for establishing connections to the SSH server, we can move on to looking at other server settings.

Maintaining System Time

Another important consideration for the SSH server is the system time. You might think that having inaccurate time is a trivial thing. Without an accurate system time, all system logs become less valuable for forensics. This is especially true when it comes to pursuing legal action. If you cannot state with certainty when an action occurred, prosecution will be that much more difficult. If you are performing centralized log collection, it will make sorting through them all that much more difficult when events on different systems cannot be correlated to a common clock.

Configuring your SSH server to use NTP (Network Time Protocol) to keep the system clock accurate is very easy. If NTP is not already installed, you will need to install it. On most Linux distributions, NTP comes pre-installed though it may or may not be enabled. On a Redhat-based system, you can check the run levels of installed services by entering the following:

```
#chkconfig –list | grep ntp
ntpd   0:off   1:off    2:on    3:on    4:on    5:on     6:off
```

If ntpd is not enabled, you can enable it for runlevels 2-5 by entering:

```
chkconfig –level 2345 ntpd on
```

The NTP process can be started by entering ntpd in a terminal window. Once ntpd is enabled, it is controlled through the /etc/ntpd.conf or /etc/ntp.conf configuration file, depending on your distribution.

The configuration file needs two lines at a minimum to get things working. The following line tells NTP which server to use as a time source, in this case clock.redhat.com:

```
server clock.redhat.com
```

The next line will ensure that NTP will receive time from clock.redhat.com but will not allow that time server to modify your server's configuration (nomodify) or pull time from your server (noquery):

```
restrict clock.redhat.com mask 255.255.255.255 nomodify notrap noquery.
```

You can verify that NTP is synching with the time server by running **ntpq –p**. Initially the time may be off by a large margin. If this is the case, you can use ntpdate *<timeserver>* to set the time before letting ntpd manage the smaller adjustments. You may need to run ntpdate multiple times before it will adjust the time completely. This entire process is shown in Figure 12.3.

NOTE

Ntpdate will not set the time if ntpd is currently running. In order to make the large adjustments using ntpdate, stop ntpd first using **service ntpd stop** for example.

Figure 12.3 Adjusting the System Time

```
[root@centos etc]# ntpq -p
remote              refid    st  t  when  poll  reach  delay   offset   jitter
==============================================================================
clock1.redhat.c .CDMA.      1   u  51    64    377    26.936  633125.  289200.
# service ntpd stop
Shutting down ntpd:                                          [ OK ]
#
# ntpdate clock.redhat.com
19 Jul 15:49:51 ntpdate[4882]: step time server 66.187.233.4 offset 795.005159 sec
# ntpdate clock.redhat.com
19 Jul 15:49:58 ntpdate[4883]: step time server 66.187.224.4 offset 3.927370 sec
# ntpdate clock.redhat.com
19 Jul 15:50:00 ntpdate[4884]: step time server 66.187.233.4 offset 0.96149 sec
# service ntpd start
ntpd: Synchronizing with time server:                       [ OK ]
Starting ntpd:                                              [ OK ]
# ntpq -p
remote              refid    st  t  when  poll  reach  delay   offset   jitter
==============================================================================
clock1.redhat.c .CDMA.      1   u  1     64    1      34.249  1410.89  0.001
```

The most critical value for the ntpq output is the offset, which is the difference between the system clock and the referenced time source; it is expressed in milliseconds. You should configure more than one time server if possible so that ntpd can use all of them to select the best time. This also helps ensure that any single faulty time source cannot misadjust all your devices to the wrong time.

Configuring the Warning Banner

In many locations a warning banner is considered part of due diligence. Although a warning banner, no matter how hostile sounding it may be, is not likely to *stop* a hacker, it at least establishes beyond a shadow of a doubt that the hacker was not welcome or authorized to access the system. Changing the warning banner is simple and requires editing the sshd_config file. Locate the line containing #Banner and uncomment it. Set the path to a banner file of your choosing, such as the following:

```
Banner /etc/banner.txt
```

This would set the banner to display whatever is contained in the /etc/banner.txt file. This warning banner will be displayed *before* the user is authenticated. For password authentication the banner message will be displayed before the user is prompted for a password. If you are using public key authentication without a password, the banner will be displayed right before the user is logged in and given a command prompt. In all cases, any banner you choose to use should be reviewed by your organization's legal advisors. If you would like some ideas on where to start, refer to http://csrc.nist.gov/groups/SMA/fasp/archive.htmlfor several good banners in the document titled "Decision paper on use of screen warning banner."

If the banner option is not enough warning for your taste, or if you merely want to be able to display some additional information after the user has authenticated, the message of the day (motd) provides a good way to accomplish this. By default the motd will be displayed right *after* authenticating but before the shell is spawned. This behavior can be disabled by changing the **PrintMotd** keyword value in the sshd_config file from the default of **yes** to a value of **no**. Restart the sshd service for changes to take effect.

Securing User Home Directories

By default ssh will place a new connection in that user's home directory. The home directory then can be used to limit the user's access as desired. If there is no home directory matching the user's name (in this example, the username is test) you will see an error similar to the following:

```
Could not chdir to home directory /home/test: No such file or directory.
```

When this occurs the user will be placed at the root on Linux. The windows SSH server will place the user in the same directory in which sshd was installed (at least with OpenSSH at the time of this writing). The key to remember here is that you want to maintain control of where the user is being deposited. Without this it becomes very difficult to properly secure the file level permissions. Even if security is not a concern, the default location for the SSH client files is /home/test/.ssh, so it could create problems if you did not have a home directory and wanted to SSH back out to another host. The directory structure you should see is /home/username/.ssh on Linux and C:\documents and settings\username\.ssh on Windows.

The sshd_config file also contains a keyword to control how secure the user's home directories must be. The StrictModes keyword is set to "yes" by default. This tells sshd to check the permissions on the user's home directory, the .ssh directory, and the Authorized_keys file. Typically the user's home directory should have permissions set to 700 and the folder containing the authorized_keys file should be 755 (these were these defaults on the test distributions). There may be some variance between different distributions and SSH implementations. If the authorized_keys file or folder is world-writeable, sshd will ignore the keys and fall back to password authentication. If the home directory is world-writeable, the connection will be refused with an error similar to this one:

```
Authentication refused: bad ownership or modes for directory /home/test
```

Controlling Session Timeouts

SSH offers several mechanisms to control how and when sessions will time out. This flexibility is useful to allow administrators control over the SSH server resources. Each session consumes memory, processor time, and bandwidth on the SSH server. Idle sessions need some form of timeout so that the resources can be recovered and security can be increased. If you allow an unauthenticated session to wait indefinitely, you are setting yourself up to be the victim of a denial-of-service attack. Another reason to have effective timeouts is that if you walk away from your desk without logging out of your session, someone could come in behind you and take over the session from your session. They could then, using your rights and permissions, cause damage to the system or steal files. Thus, controlling the session timeouts and keeping them short will prevent this type of situation.

Fortunately sshd provides some options for controlling various session timeout values. The first timer starts before the user has even logged in; this is the login grace time. This is configured in the sshd_confg file with the keyword LoginGraceTime. This determines how long the user has to complete authentication before the session is disconnected. The default timer is 120 seconds. A value of zero will disable the timer completely. Setting this to zero is not recommended for the reasons mentioned above.

The next three keywords – ClientAliveCountMax, ClientAliveInterval, and TCPKeepAlive – all deal with the active SSH session. TCPKeepAlive is the most basic counter with only "yes" or "no" as acceptable values. The default is "yes," which tells sshd that if the TCP keepalive messages cannot reach their destination, the session will be terminated. These keep alive messages are standard TCP packets that are *not* sent over the encrypted tunnel. This could be an important distinction as these keepalive packets can be spoofed, sniffed, and so on. The value of this type of keepalives it to close a session for which the communication path has been lost due to, for example, a down circuit or a bad route.

The ClientAliveCountMax and ClientAliveInterval values work together in much the same way as the TCP keep alive messages, except these are sent over the encrypted tunnel. The ClientAliveInterval is the time in seconds in which there has been no client activity before a message is sent to the client. The ClientAliveCountMax value determines how many of these messages can be unanswered before the session is terminated. As an example, let us suppose the client alive interval is 10 seconds. After 10 seconds of inactivity, a keepalive message will be sent over the encrypted tunnel to the client. If the client does not respond, another one will be sent after 10 more seconds, and a third 10 seconds after that. If the client alive count max is set to the default of 3, the SSH client would be disconnected after the third keepalive was sent.

Using either type of keepalive message may be required. Often an inactive session will timeout on the session table of a firewall between the SSH server and SSH client. This is sometimes the cause for sessions that seem to drop when left idle. By setting one or both of the keepalive options, you can prevent this behavior and help ensure that sessions close only when you want them to.

Logging Options

Linux and the SSH process offer many options for logging. Based on the configuration options covered in this chapter, you can generate log entries from the netfilter firewall, from TCP Wrappers, and of course from sshd itself. Each of these options has its value. It is worth pointing out that more is not always better. Sometimes the first inclination is to log as much information as possible. Besides consuming storage space and processor cycles needlessly, it may decrease security. This is due to the fact that an administrator can sift through only so many log entries at a time. Too much information can cause the really important entries to get lost in the clutter. Determining what level of logging is appropriate will depend on your log parsing mechanisms, storage space, processor capabilities, and of course your organization's security policy.

Logging Using sshd

The sshd_config file contains the SyslogFacility and LoggingLevel keywords. The logging level keyword determines the amount of information sshd will generate when logging. By default the facility is AUTH and the default logging level is INFO. You can easily set up a separate log file exclusively for your sshd logs. To do so, edit your /etc/ssh/sshd_confg file as follows:

```
SyslogFacility LOCAL0
LogLevel VERBOSE
```

This tells sshd to provide verbose logging information and to use the local0 facility for the logs. You could use another facility if that is more appropriate for you. In this example local0 makes filtering the sshd log entries into their own log file simpler in the syslog.conf configuration. Edit the /etc/syslog.conf next and create a separate rule to handle all local0 log entries generated by sshd. Add the following line to the /etc/syslog.conf file:

```
local0.* /var/log/sshd
```

After doing this, restart both sshd and syslog for the changes to take effect. You can monitor the sshd log file using **tail –f /var/log/sshd** to verify that you are logging everything from sshd to the new logfile. You can send a test message using logger. The –p option allow you to specify the facility and severity. For example you could use:

```
logger -p local0.info testmessagetolocal0
```

If syslog is parsing properly, you should see the payload of "testmessagetolocal0" in /var/log/sshd, similar to the example in Figure 12.4. The first three syslog entries were created by sshd after a test connection was made. The last entry was made manually using the logger utility.

Figure 12.4 Sample Syslog Entries from sshd with LogLevel Verbose

```
Jul 31 21:48:25 bt sshd[5915]: Connection from 192.168.1.99 port 63661
Jul 31 21:48:27 bt sshd[5915]: Failed none for test from 192.168.1.99
port 63661 ssh2
Jul 31 21:48:30 bt sshd[5915]: Accepted password for test from
192.168.1.99 port 63661 ssh2
Jul 31 21:49:36 bt root: testmessagetolocal0
```

Logging Using TCP Wrappers

TCP Wrappers also offers some logging capability via the hosts.allow and hosts.deny files. For the logging options to work, –DPROCESS_OPTIONS must have been enabled at program build time. You can test for these options by adding a test rule with the DENY option in the hosts.allow file. If the DENY causes the session to be blocked, you know the DPROCESS_OPTIONS were enabled. An example command to do this would be as follows:

```
ALL : 192.168.1.44 : DENY
```

If the DENY option does not result in the session being blocked, your implementation does not have the process options enabled. Note this is a DENY rule in the hosts.allow file. Only by using the process options can this type of command be enabled. Some prefer to place this type of DENY entries in the hosts.allow file, or vice versa, but it also tends to make both files harder to read and follow, increasing the odds of an error being made.

TCP Wrappers does very little in the way of logging on its own. The logging it does provide can be manipulated by using the severity option. This option allows you to specify the severity (and optionally the facility) to which TCP Wrappers should log. For example to log all SSH connections to local0 with a severity of informational, use the following line in the hosts.allow or hosts.deny file:

```
sshd : 192.168.1. : severity local0.info
```

You can also perform the logging by writing straight to the log file directly using the spawn option. This is useful for daemons that do not support TCP Wrappers, or if you want to add your own custom logging information. The following commands both do the same thing, which is write "some_message" to the /var/log/sshd file. The first example writes to the log file directly using echo, while the second example spawns logger to send the message via syslog. Of course, to use logger this way, your syslog configuration would need to be set up to process local0.info messages to /var/log/sshd, as was the case with previous examples.

```
sshd : 192.168.1. : spawn /bin/echo some_message >> /var/log/sshd
sshd : 192.168.1. : spawn logger -p local0.info some_message
```

Logging Using Netfilter

Your host-based firewall is yet another means to provide logging information. If you are permitting connections from any IP source logging, these may not be useful. If on the other hand you are blocking outside connections or limiting the SSH connections to only an administrative subnet, logging the connection *attempts* that the firewall blocks may be valuable.

Recall from the previous example that the following command would permit connections to TCP port 22 from the 192.168.1.0 subnet:

```
iptables -A INPUT -p tcp -s 192.168.1.0/24 --dport 22 -j ACCEPT
```

If you wanted to deny and log all other connection attempts to port 22, you would use the following two additional rules. The LOG target does not stop processing the rules like other targets, so you need to basically create a two-rule pair, one to LOG and another rule to DROP the traffic.

```
iptables -A INPUT -p tcp --dport 22 -j LOG --log-level 4
iptables -A INPUT -p tcp --dport 22 -j DROP
```

The --log–level options are used to set the severity for the netfilter syslog messages. The log messages will be routed based on a kernel facility, the severity you have configured (in this example severity 4 for "warning"), and your syslog configuration. If you do not specify a log level, the default is "warning." The --log-prefix <*prefix*> option will allow you to add a small snippet of text of your own choosing to the beginning of all log messages generated by that rule. This can be especially useful for noting the rule from which the log entry was generated:

```
iptables -A INPUT -p tcp --dport 22 -j LOG --log-prefix "[Blocked SSH]"
iptables -A INPUT -p tcp --dport 22 -j DROP
```

Once this is done, you can search through the logs quickly using grep. To find all occurrences of "SSH" in the /var/log/firewall log file, simply enter **grep "SSH" /var/log/firewall**. With careful use of the log prefix option, you can make it very easy to find the log entries for which you are looking. A sample log entry from netfilter looks like the following:

```
Jul 31 22:31:21 bt kernel: [Blocked SSH]IN=eth0 OUT= MAC=00:01:02:03:04:05:06:07:
08:09:10:11:12:13 SRC=192.168.1.99 DST=192.168.1.70 LEN=40 TOS=0x00 PREC=0x00
TTL=128 ID=6601 DF PROTO=TCP SPT=63733 DPT=22 WINDOW=251 RES=0x00 ACK URGP=0
```

On a Microsoft Windows system, the find utility will perform the same function, though the number of parsing options is far less. Entering **find "SSH" C:\firewall.log** will generate the same results as the grep example, assuming you were using the same log file as input.

Security Considerations of Logging

With all of these logs being generated and analyzed, you might stop and ask, "What are the security implications of sending syslog messages every which way on my network?" Because syslog messages are sent in cleartext, and because a centralized syslog server offers many advantages, this is a very legitimate question. The answer is not as straight forward as you might have hoped for, however.

The first step, of course, is to understand exactly what data will be sent in your syslog messages. If your syslog messages do not contain any confidential information, security may be a non-issue. If they do, however, you will need some way to keep the easily sniffed syslog traffic away from prying eyes. Some organizations accomplish this by using an entirely different network and physical interface dedicated to logging. While secure, the additional hardware and administrative overhead involved with this solution places it out of reach of many organizations.

The other option is to encrypt the syslog messages. Syslog will send its messages over UDP by default. While this is efficient and provides for a low-overhead means of sending messages, it is inconvenient for encryption. Many encryption protocols will not work with UDP-based traffic. While most clients have no problems sending traffic over TCP, some servers will not. In the case of Windows based syslog servers, there are no free syslog servers that will receive TCP-based messages (at least none that I am aware of). This means your options are to encrypt the UDP-based traffic over IPSEC or to use a TCP-based syslog.

If you are able to use a TCP based syslog, you have many options for encryption. These include IPSEC or other lighter encryption mechanisms, such as tunneling the syslog over SSH, SSL, or any of a number of available VPN type solutions. If you already have working SSH implementations on all your systems for administration, SSH might be the easiest way to go. If not, SSL offers a fairly easy setup and simple port tunneling and redirection via popular tools such as stunnel.

Additional SSH Server Options

Many of the option keywords available to control sshd have been covered so far. There are still a few that are noteworthy, however. The **KeyRegenerationInterval** determines how often the server key is regenerated. This value is the number of seconds before a new key is used. A lower value will mean that if an attacker captures and decodes a portion of traffic, that portion will be smaller as new keys are generated more frequently. The default value is 3600 seconds, which is one hour. Setting the value to zero will disable key regeneration and is not recommended, though this could be useful for troubleshooting purposes.

The **MaxStartups** value determines how many concurrent *unauthenticated* sessions can be opened to the SSH daemon. The primary purpose of this setting is to mitigate a DOS attack intended to consume server resources. It would also prevent a rogue process or script from killing the SSH server by accidentally spawning an unlimited number of sessions. Newer sshds also support a feature called "random early drop," which allows you to specify a start point at which unauthenticated connections are randomly dropped. You also can specify the starting drop rate. This drop rate is increased linearly until it reaches a 100% drop rate at the full value.

The format of these setting is *start:rate:full*, where *start* is the point at which connections begin being dropped, *rate* is the percent of connections that will be dropped, and *full* is the number at which all connections are dropped. As an example, take **MaxStartups 20:50:80**. Once there are 20 unauthenticated connections, sshd will begin dropping 50% of them. If the number of unauthenticated connections still continues to climb, the percent that are dropped will increase linearly until 100% of the connections are being dropped at 80 concurrent unauthenticated connections.

Debugging SSH

When you cannot complete a connection via SSH, there are several troubleshooting and debugging steps you can use to find the problem. The first and foremost are the debugging options within SSH itself. Both the client and server offer a debugging mode. The client can be spawned with a **–v** option to see what is happening behind the scenes. This type of debugging is almost always enough to tell you what is happening, but if you want even more detail, you can use –v again (–v –v or –vv) for more information or –vvv for even more detailed debugging. Refer back to Figure 12.2 to see a sample of client output with debug level 1.

The SSH server offers similar functionality. If you spawn the server using sshd –d, it will place the server in debug mode. While in this mode, the server does not go to the background and it will process only a single connection. This makes debug mode suitable only for troubleshooting a specific issue. If you want to see a great deal of logging data on a day-to-day basis, this can be configured within the sshd_config file. The LogLevel keyword tells sshd how verbose to be when logging via syslog. Valid values are QUIET, FATAL, ERROR, INFO, VERBOSE, DEBUG, DEBUG1, DEBUG2, and DEBUG3. DEBUG and DEBUG1 are really the same setting and result in the same logging output.

TIP

If you are trying to troubleshoot a connection to a heavily used SSH server, placing the server in debug mode may have its own problems. Other users who are not having any problems may connect before you have a chance to connect with the user account you are trying to test. In these cases, it may be simpler to start sshd on a different port. You can do this by entering **sshd –d –p 2222**, which allows you to troubleshoot without someone else being able to connect to the port before you.

If there are permission problems, it will probably be obvious in the logs. You can temporarily disable the permission checking by setting StrictModes to "no" in the sshd_config file. This is often an easier test than manually verifying the permissions on the user directories and files. If you are doing heavy duty testing, starting sshd manually can be a good approach and the **–f** *<configuration file>* option allows you to specify a configuration file other than the default /etc/ssh/sshd_config. You could then use a troubleshooting configuration file, which turns logging to DEBUG3, changes the logging facility to something more noticeable, and disables strict permissions mode.

Summary

SSH can provide a valuable tool for secure remote access. There are many tools provided by the operating system for securing your SSH server. Between a local firewall, TCP Wrappers, and customizing your syslog configuration, your SSH server can be well protected. Except for these OS-level access control mechanisms, the SSH server itself offers an impressive array of customization and security options. The theme throughout the chapter has been that SSH is, at its heart, a remote access mechanism and it should be guarded as such.

With this in mind, logging can prove to be the most valuable method to detect trends, identify intrusion attempts, and generally keep your finger on the pulse of what your SSH implementation is doing. A little attention up front to such details as log parsing, log security, log rotation, and log analysis can pay for itself later on. Such decisions as whether to log to a syslog server over TCP or UDP can have a major impact on the choices available to you. If an attacker does manage to compromise a system despite your defenses, system logs may be the only thing left to provide clues as to what happened and how. Analyzing this evidence after a breach is critical to ensuring that the event does not repeat itself.

A scary sounding logon banner will not actually prevent an attacker from connecting to the service if he or she can. It can, however, serve as a deterrent and cause some of the more casual hackers to find softer targets elsewhere. Given the choice between some private SSH server and a corporate-sounding warning banner that threatens legal action, some hackers may steer clear. A logon banner should not be viewed as a measure that will make you safe from attackers; rather it is simply part of a defense-in-depth strategy and another task that is part of doing your due diligence.

Solutions Fast Track

Allowing SSH Connections

- ☑ Control connectivity to the SSH server process via firewall ACLs and stop traffic before the SSH server even sees it.

- ☑ Control access based on the process name (in this case sshd) independently of the port numbers in use using TCP Wrappers.

- ☑ Take advantage of several sshd_config options to restrict access to the SSH server.

- ☑ Provide two-factor authentication to the SSH server for increased security.

Maintaining System Time

- ☑ Ensure proper system time via ntpd and ntpdate.

- ☑ Accurate system time is critical for event log correlation, to establish a reliable timeline for forensic purposes, and to pursue legal action.

Configuring the Warning Banner

☑ Warning banners provide a first line of defense and establish beyond a doubt that a hacker does not have authorization to connect. Seek the advice of legal counsel to ensure that the warning banner meets local requirements.

☑ The SSH server can be configured to display a banner of your choosing *prior* to authentication.

☑ The SSH server can display the message of the day *after* the user is authenticated.

Securing User Home Directories

☑ If sshd cannot find a user directory with the same name as the user, the user will be placed in the system root upon logon.

☑ User directory access rights are checked by default and world-readable folders may prevent a successful logon.

☑ The StrictModes option in the sshd_config file can disable permission checking if desired.

Controlling Session Timeouts

☑ Managing session timeouts is necessary to protect the SSH server resources and to prevent a DOS attack.

☑ TCP keepalive messages will allow the SSH server to efficiently drop sessions that have lost the communication path, conserving system resources.

☑ SSH client keepalive messages can prevent intervening firewalls from dropping inactive sessions.

Logging Options

☑ Logging can provide insight into the inner workings of your SSH servers and clients. This insight can be invaluable for everything from spotting hackers to troubleshooting issues.

☑ SSH provides the ability to customize the facility and severity to which sshd messages are logged. Combined with a custom syslog configuration, you can route all sshd messages to their own log file for analysis.

☑ TCP Wrappers provides limited logging capabilities. There are several vehicles to accomplish this via the hosts.allow or hosts.deny file.

☑ Firewall logs (via netfilter) also offer a limited ability to perform logging relative to SSH server connections, including a custom field that can be inserted at the beginning of all netfilter log entries on a per-rule basis.

☑ Extensive logs combined with automated parsing capabilities will leave you well positioned to react proactively to security incidents and configuration errors.

Additional SSH Server Options

☑ The MaxStartups setting restricts the number of allowed concurrent *unauthenticated* sessions; the configuration file allows you to configure random early drops to begin pruning unauthenticated sessions after a preconfigured threshold had been reached.

Debugging SSH

☑ Three different levels of debug output are available on the SSH client, providing very detailed information on each step of session establishment and shutdown.

☑ The sshd can be run in "debug mode" this is a special mode exclusively for troubleshooting connectivity issues.

☑ Using a custom configuration file for the SSH server can provide a quick and easy way to configure many troubleshooting parameters.

Frequently Asked Questions

Q: If you advise to set a password on the keyfiles for public key encryption, what is the point of using public key encryption? Wouldn't it be easier to just use a password for authentication?

A: Even if the process does not become any easier and you have to enter a password in both scenarios, the second scenario if far more secure. Two-factor authentication is far more secure and the benefits are something an auditing group can really appreciate. While not really SSH-server related, keys could be managed on the client-side with something like ssh-agent; thus, you have to enter only a single password to use all your password protected keys.

Q: Your instructions don't work with my version of SSH. What is wrong?

A: Different distributions tend to do things their own way. File locations can change and even file names are sometimes different. My suggestion would be to experiment with a non-production system until you are comfortable with the SSH client and server component. This way you know what things *should* look like and what to expect. If you do not have a spare system handy, something like vmware and a bootable Linux ISO can prove invaluable. Just for comparison, I was using a combination of Backtrack3, CentOS 4.4 live, and Ubuntu 7.10 Desktop Live for testing.

Q: What should my warning banner look include?

A: Although the basic message is the same and usually boils down to "unauthorized users are not welcome," the devil is in the details. In some jurisdictions, the requirements may vary. For example, it may be legally advisable to warn the intruder that they will have no privacy and all actions will be monitored and recorded. In other areas such as warning may not be needed. Notifying the user that connecting represents consent to such monitoring may be required as well. Some systems warn the user that he or she is connecting to a government computer while others give away no information about who owns the system. It is precisely because of these considerations that it is always advisable for your legal counsel to review and approve the warning banner before implemting it.

Q: All this logging is eating up all my drive space; what can I do to remedy this without losing my logs?

A: Logging to a centralized syslog server is not only the most secure option, but also one that provides a one-stop shop for log file parsing, review, and analysis. If centralized logging is not an option, most systems include a few utilities to make handling log files easier. Something like logrotate can be configured to periodically compress, delete, and/or email log files.

Q: Should I use a Windows server or a *nux server as my centralized syslog server?

A: While there are several very robust syslog servers available for Windows, the level of support, utilities, and the options does not approach that which is available on *nix systems. All of the tools you need are also free on a *nix platform, while the best Windows utilities are not free. Even the well known Kiwi syslog server, while very powerful, has many features that are not available with the free version. Personally I would use a Linux server as my centralized syslog server.

Q: If I use a *nix server as my centralized syslog server, how can I integrate my Windows event logs into that syslog server?

A: There are a host of free utilities for exporting Windows event logs into syslog format or for generating syslog events manually from a Windows host. Try any of these free tools for exporting Windows event logs to a syslog server:

■ Eventlog to Syslog Utility is available from https://engineering.purdue.edu/ECN/Resources/Documents/UNIX/evtsys/.

■ NTsyslog is available from http://sourceforge.net/projects/ntsyslog/.

■ SNARE is available fromwww.intersectalliance.com/projects/SnareWindows/.

## Chapter 13

SSH Port Forwarding

Solutions in this chapter:

- **SSH Port Forwarding Commands**

- **Securing Email with SSH Local –L Port Forwarding**

- **Bypassing Firewalls with SSH Remote –R Port Forwarding**

- **Using SSH SOCKS Proxy –D to Tunnel Your HTTP/DNS Traffic**

☑ **Summary**

☑ **Solutions Fast Track**

☑ **Frequently Asked Questions**

Introduction

As discussed in previous chapters, SSH is a secure network protocol which allows for data to be exchanged securely between two or more computers. SSH has been mainly used by system administrators to securely manage devices such as network routers and UNIX servers as well as securely transferring files. SSH provides a secure tunnel in which all communication is encrypted.

SSH port forwarding or tunneling allows you to forward otherwise unsecure TCP traffic inside a secure SSH tunnel. Protocols such as FTP, POP3, SMTP, HTTP, TELNET, and others can all be forwarded inside this SSH tunnel providing increased security features such as encryption and authentication that may not otherwise be supported, as shown in Figure 13.1. Tunneling unsecure protocols via SSH secures data exchange between devices.

Figure 13.1 Port Forwarding Unsecured Protocols via SSH Tunnel

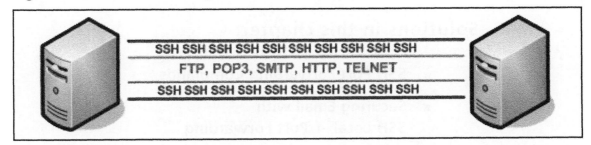

SSH Port Forwarding Commands

It is time that we introduce some core SSH Port Forwarding commands and go over their options. Within this chapter we will be using OpenSSH_4.3p2 version of SSH to demonstrate all of our commands and our examples. OpenSSH is a very popular SSH server and client among administrators. Figure 13.2 displays the help output from SSH command along with the −R and −L options which we will cover shortly.

Figure 13.2 Output From SSH −H Command Displaying Available Options

```
root@SERVER_1:~
[root@SERVER_1 ~]# ssh -H
ssh: illegal option -- H
usage: ssh [-1246AaCfgkMNnqsTtVvXxY] [-b bind_address] [-c cipher_spec]
           [-D [bind_address:]port] [-e escape_char] [-F configfile]
           [-i identity_file] [-L [bind_address:]port:host:hostport]
           [-l login_name] [-m mac_spec] [-O ctl_cmd] [-o option] [-p port]
           [-R [bind_address:]port:host:hostport] [-S ctl_path]
           [-w tunnel:tunnel] [user@]hostname [command]
[root@SERVER_1 ~]#
```

The two "-L" and "-R" highlighted commands are your most important commands within OpenSSH when it comes to port forwarding.

There are two types of port forwarding mechanisms: Local port forwarding "-L" and Remote port forwarding "-R." These two types of forwarding mechanisms are also commonly referred to as Outgoing tunnel and Incoming tunnel.

The -L [bind_address:]port:host:hostport] command specifies that a given port on the local (client) host is to be forwarded to the given host and port on the remote side. For example: command ssh –L 4444:localhost:23 username@host will forward all client traffic coming into port 4444 to port 23 on the server.

The –R [bind_address:]port:host:hostport] command specifies that a given port on the remote (server) host is to be forwarded to the given host and port on the local side. For example: command ssh –R 4444:localhost:23 username@host will forward all server traffic coming into port 4444 to port 23 on the client. Figures 13.3 and 13.4 display OpenSSH help pages and its full detail explanation between the R and L options.

Figure 13.3 OpenSSH Main Page on "-L" Option

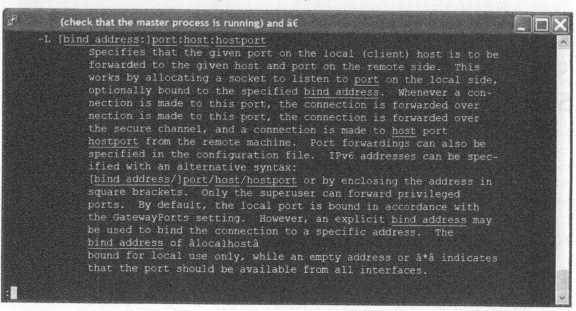

Figure 13.4 OpenSSH Main Page on "-R" Option

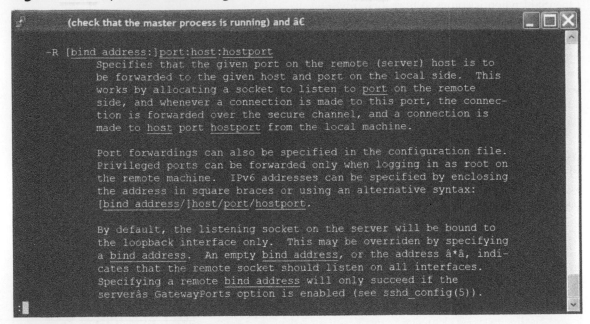

Securing E-mail with
SSH Local –*L* Port Forwarding

Let us get down and dirty and perform some hands-on, real-world examples by securing our
e-mail traffic between two servers across the Internet. Figure 13.5 represents our current unsecure
environment where our contracted e-mail filtering Company XYZ is currently accepting all of our
mail for spam and virus detection and then forwards clean mail to our corporate mail server.
Company XYZ sends all of our mail via SMTP to our mail server.

Figure 13.5 Unsecured SMTP Environment without SSH Port Forwarding

As you see, our current environment sends mail from our contract Company XYZ into our corporate MailServer via unsecured clear text SMTP. SMTP is a mail protocol. It is a carrier of mail that delivers mail in clear text via the Internet. Because SMTP sends mail in clear text, it provides a great opportunity for hackers to tap in between the communication and sniff out this data for important and confidential information. Figure 13.6 shows the hacker's view of a sniffer trace captured while mail was traveling between Company XYZ and the Corporate Mailserver. As you can see, this mail is in clear text, revealing all of its content to the hacker without any protection.

Figure 13.6 Reading Mail in Clear Text

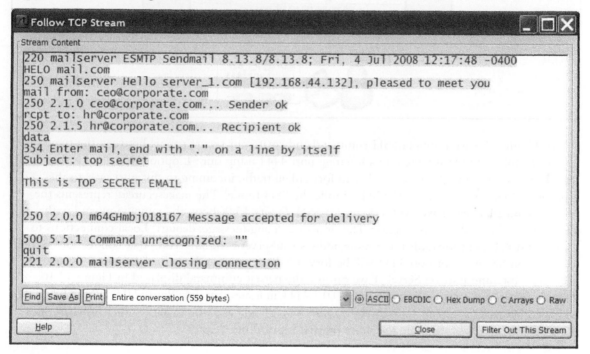

NOTE

Wireshark™ is a network analyzer program that can be freely downloaded at http://www.wireshark.org. Wireshark™ came from the original Ethereal open source project and is used by network administrators and in the examples in this chapter, most importantly in Figure 13.6 with its TCP Stream capability.

Let us now take a look at how we can use SSH Port Forwarding in order to create a secure tunnel between Company XYZ and our Corporate MailServer. First, we must make sure that TCP port 22 for SSH is open in the direction of our SSH flow. In this case scenario, we will first allow

Company XYZ SSH in to our MailServer and create a secure SSH tunnel which will be used over SMTP traffic. Second, we will push SMTP-Port 25 inside the secured SSH tunnel. Figure 13.7 provides a visual of what we're trying to accomplish.

Figure 13.7 End Result for Securing SMTP Traffic Inside SSH Tunnel

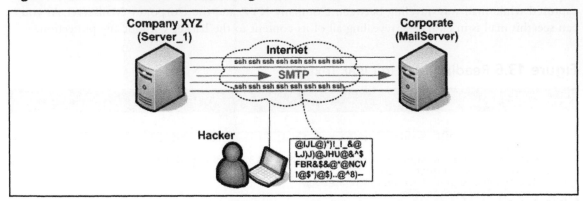

In Figure 13.8 we issue our SSH command and create our secure tunnel between the two servers. In this example we open up a listening port 4444 using our –L option described earlier in this chapter on the localhost (server_1) and forward all traffic incoming to this port over to the Corporate MailServer on port 25 SMTP inside the SSH tunnel. The makesecure@ represents the username on MailServer we used to login via SSH. Figure 13.9 shows the same command with added –v (verbose) debugging option. The displayed debug message: debug1: Local connections to LOCALHOST:4444 forwarded to remote address mailserver.com:25 verifies that connections to our localhost on Server_1 for port 4444 will be forwarded out on port 25 to the mailserver. To further verify our listening port on Server_1 we can use the netstat command displayed in Figure 13.10. The output from the netstat command, 127.0.0.1:4444, indicates that only the 127.0.0.1 (local loopback) address is allowed to initiate connectivity to port 4444. There is a way to allow other hosts, not just the localhost, to access this port, but more on that later in this chapter.

NOTE

Ports that are less than 1024 are considered to be privileged ports and require root/administrative rights in order to be created (open in LISTEN mode) on any machine. Ports over 1023 can be opened by regular users.

Figure 13.8 SSH Forwarding Command from Server_1 to MailServer

```
makesecure@MAILSERVER:~
[root@SERVER_1 ~]# ssh -L 4444:mailserver.com:25 makesecure@mailserver.com
makesecure@mailserver.com's password:
Last login: Fri Jul  4 23:58:30 2008 from server_1.com
[makesecure@MAILSERVER ~]$
[makesecure@MAILSERVER ~]$
```

Figure 13.9 SSH Forwarding Command from Server_1 to MailServer with –v Option for Verbose (debug)

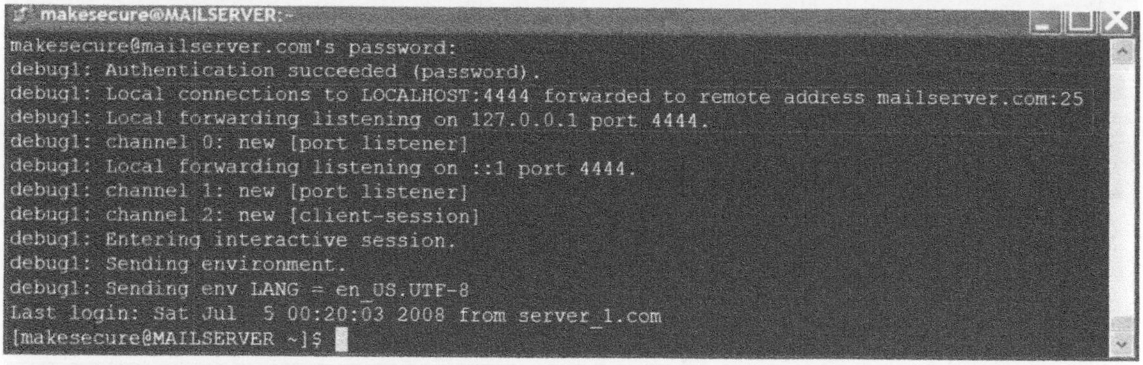

```
makesecure@MAILSERVER:~
makesecure@mailserver.com's password:
debug1: Authentication succeeded (password).
debug1: Local connections to LOCALHOST:4444 forwarded to remote address mailserver.com:25
debug1: Local forwarding listening on 127.0.0.1 port 4444.
debug1: channel 0: new [port listener]
debug1: Local forwarding listening on ::1 port 4444.
debug1: channel 1: new [port listener]
debug1: channel 2: new [client-session]
debug1: Entering interactive session.
debug1: Sending environment.
debug1: Sending env LANG = en_US.UTF-8
Last login: Sat Jul  5 00:20:03 2008 from server_1.com
[makesecure@MAILSERVER ~]$
```

Figure 13.10 Netstat Command Showing Port 4444 is Open on Server_1 and in LISTEN Mode

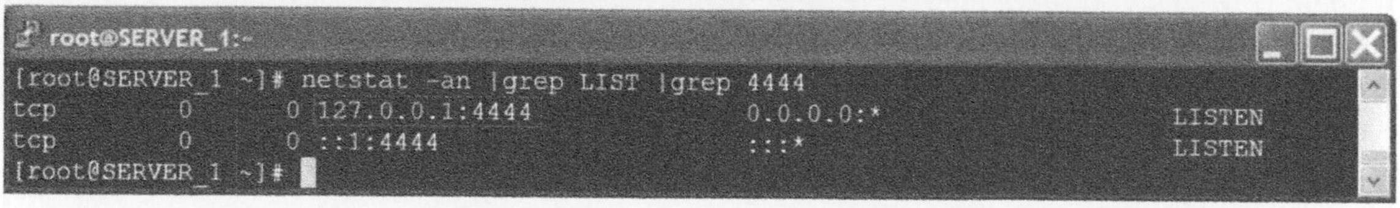

```
root@SERVER_1:~
[root@SERVER_1 ~]# netstat -an |grep LIST |grep 4444
tcp        0        0 127.0.0.1:4444          0.0.0.0:*               LISTEN
tcp        0        0 ::1:4444                :::*                    LISTEN
[root@SERVER_1 ~]#
```

We have successfully configured a secure SSH Port Forwarding tunnel between our Company XYZ and Corporate Mailserver. The last thing to do is to configure Company XYZ server_1 mail application to forward all of our mail to its localhost on port 4444 where it will be packaged and put inside the SSH tunnel and come out at the other end on port 25. Configuring the mail application is outside the scope of this book, but you get the idea of what needs to be done. As a proof of this concept, let us telnet from Server_1 in to its port 4444 and see if we come out at SMTP port 25 on the other side. In Figure 13.11, notice that we've connected to port 25 on MailServer! Now as our last proof—let's take another look at our sniffer trace using Wireshark™ that we did earlier and verify that all of our mail is now secured and we no longer have the ability to read its content. Figure 13.12 displays TCP flow—notice that all we see is gibberish as all SMTP(25) is securely tunneled inside SSH(22) and it's all encrypted. It is important to note that SMTP will only be encrypted between the two servers and not anywhere else. Users out on the Internet sending e-mail via SMTP to Server_1 will be unencrypted.

This whole process can be repeated to secure other protocols such as your IMAP or POP3 protocols which are used to retrieve e-mail from your mail server and make them secured. All you really need to do is change the ports around in our examples above to match your desired protocol.

Figure 13.11 Telneting into Port 4444 Tunnels to MailServer Port 25

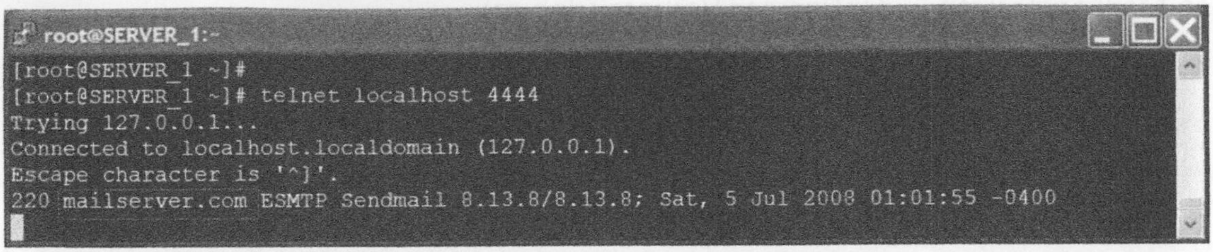

```
root@SERVER_1:~
[root@SERVER_1 ~]#
[root@SERVER_1 ~]# telnet localhost 4444
Trying 127.0.0.1...
Connected to localhost.localdomain (127.0.0.1).
Escape character is '^]'.
220 mailserver.com ESMTP Sendmail 8.13.8/8.13.8; Sat, 5 Jul 2008 01:01:55 -0400
```

Figure 13.12 Sniffer Trace After SMTP Is Protected by SSH

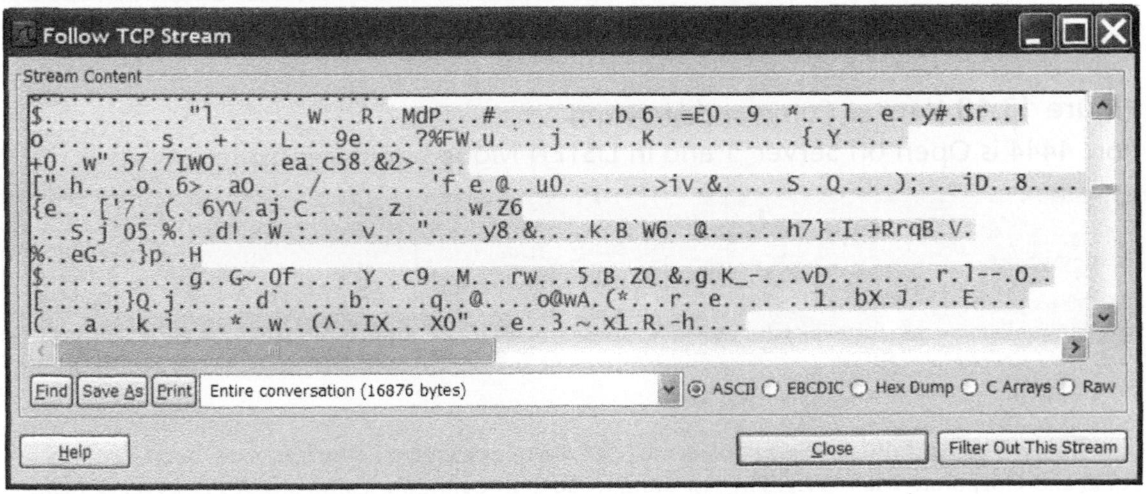

```
Follow TCP Stream
Stream Content
$...........".1.....W...R..MdP...#..... `...b.6..=E0..9..*...1..e..y#.$r..!
o........s..+....L..9e....?%FW.u. `..j.....K.........{.Y.....
+0..w".57.7IWO.....ea.c58.&2>....
[".h....o..6>..a0..../........'f.e.@..u0.......>iv.&.....S..Q....);.._iD..8....
{e...['7..(..6YV.aj.C......z.....w.Z6
...S.j`05.%...d!..W.:....v....."....y8.&....k.B`W6..@.....h7}.I.+RrqB.V.
%..eG...}p..H
$.............g..G~.0f....Y..c9..M...rw...5.B.ZQ.&.g.K_-..vD.........r.1--.0..
[.....;}Q.j......d`.....b.....q..@....o@wA.(*...r..e.... ..1..bX.J....E....
(...a...k.i....*..w..(^..IX...X0"...e..3.~.x1.R.-h....

Find  Save As  Print   Entire conversation (16876 bytes)          ⊙ ASCII ○ EBCDIC ○ Hex Dump ○ C Arrays ○ Raw

Help                                                        Close        Filter Out This Stream
```

Bypassing Firewalls with SSH Remote –R Port Forwarding

Up until now we have reviewed the –L Local port forwarding within SSH. In this section we'll discuss the –R Remote port forwarding feature within SSH. Let us review that the –L Local port forwarding is a listening port on the client and initiated by the client waiting for the connection to be tunneled out to the server. The –R Remote port forwarding is just the opposite—the tunnel is initiated from the server-host back to the client and the listening port lives on the client that is forwarded back to the server.

Let us look at an example of how this –R Remote port forwarding feature can come in handy in the real world. Figure 13.13 displays a typical corporate office sitting behind a firewall. This firewall for security reasons is configured to block all traffic initiated from the Internet and to only allow a handful of protocols such as HTTP and SSH out to the Internet from corporate servers.

Figure 13.13 Bypassing a Firewall with –R Port Forwarding Scenario

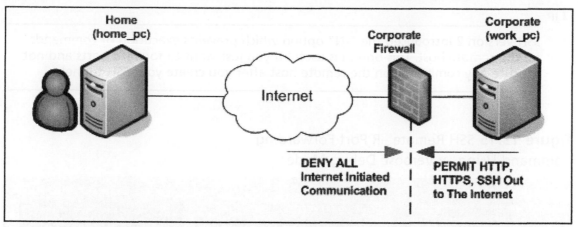

The security department does not allow you to connect to your corporate location (work_pc) from your home (home_pc) as it will be blocked by the corporate firewall. SSH port forwarding to the rescue! As long as you are allowed to SSH out from your corporate server to your home server, you have the ability to tunnel and connect back to your work_pc from home!

WARNING

You should always follow your corporate security policy and make sure that you're not breaking any rules. If you're not sure, always check with your security department. Just because you can bypass security's firewall doesn't mean that it is allowed.

Our first step is to initiate SSH connection from our work_pc to our home_pc and chose the right options to tunnel back to the work_pc from our home_pc over SSH. Figure 13.14 shows us just that. In this figure we are using the –R Remote forwarding command initiated from our work_pc: ssh –R 7777:localhost:22 makesecure@home_pc which will open up a 7777 TCP port on our home_pc and forward all connections to it back to our work_pc on port 22(ssh). Figure 13.15 displays the same command with the added –v option for verbose debug mode—notice that we have successfully initiated our Remote port forwarding remote forward success for: listen 7777, connect localhost:22.

Figure 13.14 SSH Remote –R Port Forwarding Command

```
makesecure@home_pc:~
[root@work_pc ~]#
[root@work_pc ~]# ssh -R 7777:localhost:22 makesecure@home_pc
makesecure@home_pc's password:
Last login: Sat Jul  5 15:35:21 2008 from mailserver.com
[makesecure@home_pc ~]$
[makesecure@home_pc ~]$
```

TIP

SSH version 2 introduced the "-N" option which prevents execution of commands on the remote host. This option is useful if you just want to forward ports and not execute any commands on the remote host after you create your SSH tunnel.

Figure 13.15 SSH Remote –R Port Forwarding
Command Using –v Verbose Debug Mode

```
makesecure@home_pc:~
debug1: Next authentication method: password
makesecure@home_pc's password:
debug1: Authentication succeeded (password).
debug1: Remote connections from LOCALHOST:7777 forwarded to local address localhost:22
debug1: channel 0: new [client-session]
debug1: Entering interactive session.
debug1: remote forward success for: listen 7777, connect localhost:22
debug1: Sending environment.
debug1: Sending env LANG = en_US.UTF-8
Last login: Sat Jul  5 16:05:46 2008 from mailserver.com
[makesecure@home_pc ~]$
[makesecure@home_pc ~]$
```

We now have an SSH tunnel created between our work_pc and home_pc and all that is left for us to do is to go home to our home_pc and connect back to our work_pc, which would normally be blocked by corporate firewall. Let's get on our home_pc and verify this. Figure 13.16 shows a netstat command verifying that port 7777 is still up and listening for a connection coming only from our localloopback IP address. Figure 13.17 shows us our home_pc initiating a connection back to work_pc on port 7777. And we are in! We have successfully SSH back to our work machine from home.

TIP

Most firewalls will close down sessions that are idle too long for security measures. If it takes you a long time to get home from work your session between your work_pc and home_pc could idle out and close. To bypass this and keep your session active simply ping on the other side of the tunnel.

The *[makesecure@home_pc ~]$ ping -i 10 127.0.0.1* command is issued on home_pc after creating your SSH tunnel from work_pc. It will ping every 10 seconds and keep your SSH tunnel active.

Figure 13.16 Using netstat Command on home_pc to Verify that Port 7777 is Listening

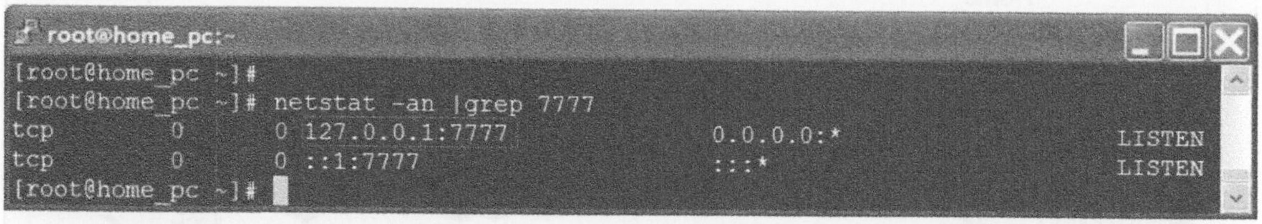

```
 root@home_pc:~                                                    _ □ X
[root@home_pc ~]#
[root@home_pc ~]# netstat -an |grep 7777
tcp       0        0 127.0.0.1:7777            0.0.0.0:*          LISTEN
tcp       0        0 ::1:7777                  :::*               LISTEN
[root@home_pc ~]#
```

Figure 13.17 Connecting Back to Work via SSH

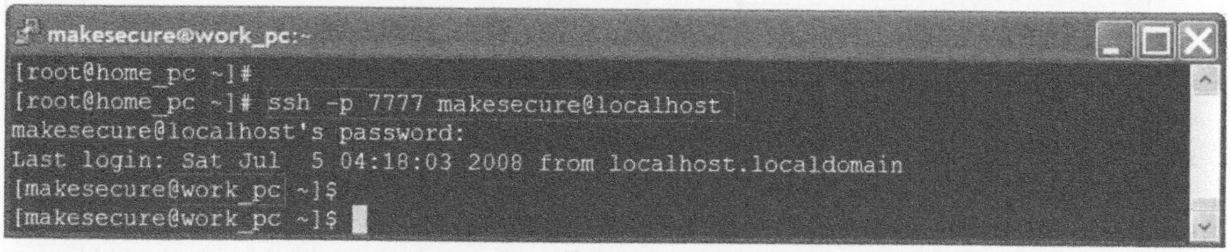

```
 makesecure@work_pc:~                                              _ □ X
[root@home_pc ~]#
[root@home_pc ~]# ssh -p 7777 makesecure@localhost
makesecure@localhost's password:
Last login: Sat Jul  5 04:18:03 2008 from localhost.localdomain
[makesecure@work_pc ~]$
[makesecure@work_pc ~]$
```

Using SSH SOCKS Proxy –D To Tunnel Your HTTP/DNS Traffic

In this section we'll explore the –D option of SSH protocol and its capability to create a SOCKS proxy in which you have the ability to tunnel protocols such as HTTPS and DNS over to the remote system. This is a fun feature of SSH port forwarding as it allows you to surf the Internet undetected from your corporate eyes. Perhaps you want to surf the Internet undetected or perhaps you are a consultant that goes to many customer locations and do not want to leave any trace of your Web surfing. As described above, always make sure that you are following your company's security policy and always check with your security department if you are not sure that what you're doing is allowed or not.

Figure 13.18 displays a typical corporate office where your work PC or laptop is plugged behind a firewall and some type of URL filtering server. URL filtering servers usually block unauthorized Web sites such as chat rooms and e-mail sites as well as monitor all user browsing. The next section will explore how to bypass this URL filtering server and freely browse the Internet.

Figure 13.18 Corporate Office with URL Filtering

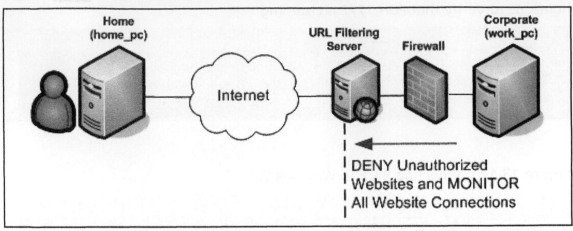

In order to avoid the URL Filtering Server from blocking your connection or monitoring your browsing habits, we must create a SSH port forwarding tunnel with a remote PC which we will use as a jumping point to surf the Internet. All HTTP traffic will then be forwarded inside the SSH tunnel which is encrypted and undetected by the filtering server over to the remote PC and then the remote PC will browse the Internet on your behalf and forward any responses back to you over SSH. We will use the –D feature of SSH to create a SOCKS proxy on the local machine that will tunnel our Web requests. Figure 13.19 displays the main page for SSH –D option, notice that currently SOCKS 4 and SOCKS 5 protocols are supported.

NOTE

Your remote PC (home_pc) in this case does not need to have anything else configured but SSH and Internet access. As long as your remote PC is able to browse the Internet all we need is SSH access to it.

Figure 13.19 SSH –D Option from Help Pages

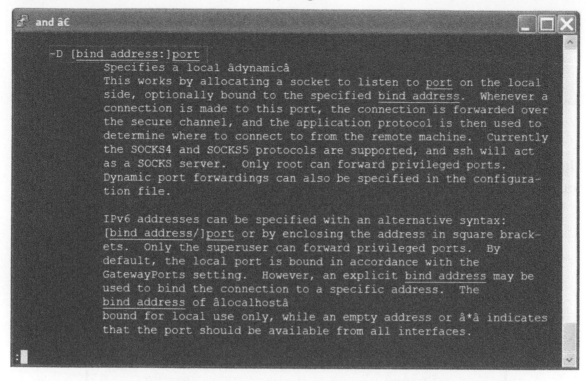

Figure 13.20 displays the SSH –D command we will use from our work_pc to open up our SOCKS proxy over to our home_pc. The command ssh makesecure@home pc –D 8080 creates port 8080 SOCKS on the local host (work_pc). After we create our proxy, all that is left for us to do is to configure our browser on our work_pc with the proper SOCKS Proxy (see Figure 13.21) and then we are off browsing and undetected from the corporate eye via our home PC.

Tɪᴘ

By default SSH will only open up access to your forwarding port from your localhost. If you want to have all of your friends on the same subnet access this port that you've set up, you can use this command as an example:
  ssh makesecure@home –pc –D 192.168.1.0:8080
  This command will allow anyone on the 192.168.1.0 network to access your localhost on port 8080 and surf the web via your SOCKS proxy just as you can. You can apply the same concept to all of our previous examples within this chapter.

Figure 13.20 Using SSH –D Command to Create SOCKS Proxy

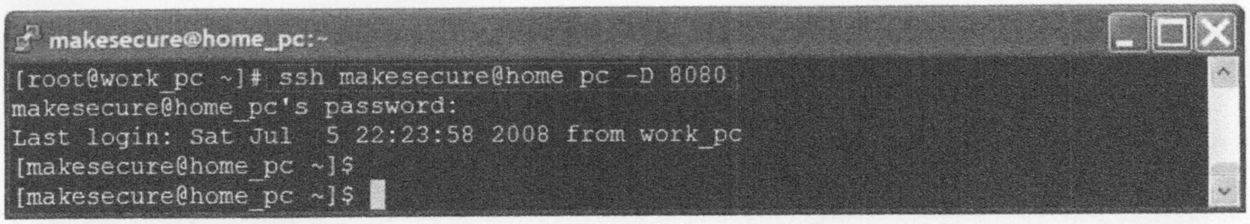

Figure 13.21 Client Browser Configuration
for New SOCKS Proxy (Firefox Browser)

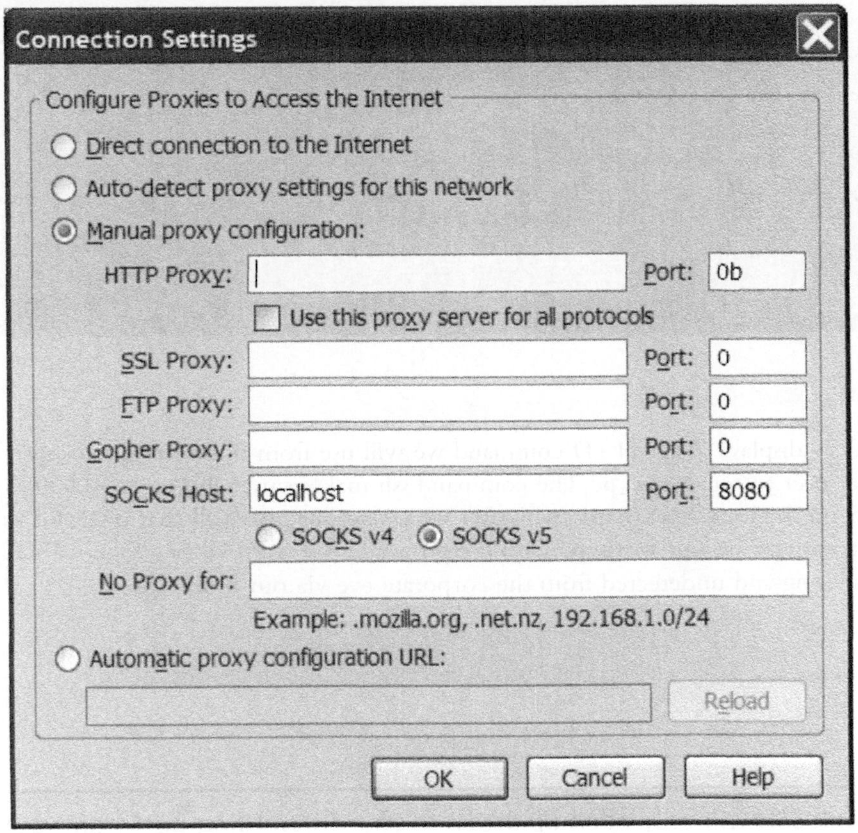

To verify our traffic connections let us take a look at Figure 13.22. After configuring our browser on work_pc to point to port 8080 I've tried surfing to www.google.com. In Figure 13.22 we are using the tcpdump utility on our home_pc to capture traffic related to google.com. As you can see, we are receiving DNS and HTTP traffic from our work_pc via SSH that is then sent out to the

Internet and back via SSH tunnel to work_pc. This verifies our SOCKS tunnel via SSH and we are now surfing the Internet undetected from our corporate eye!

Figure 13.22 A tcpdump from home_pc
Verifying HTTP/DNS Throughput from work_pc

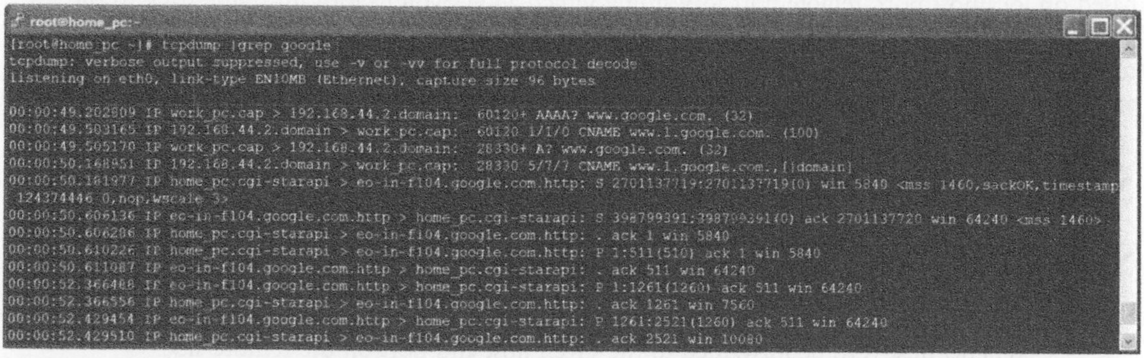

```
root@home_pc:~
[root@home_pc ~]# tcpdump |grep google
tcpdump: verbose output suppressed, use -v or -vv for full protocol decode
listening on eth0, link-type EN10MB (Ethernet), capture size 96 bytes

00:00:49.202809 IP work_pc.cap > 192.168.44.2.domain:  60120+ AAAA? www.google.com. (32)
00:00:49.503165 IP 192.168.44.2.domain > work_pc.cap:  60120 1/1/0 CNAME www.l.google.com. (100)
00:00:49.505170 IP work_pc.cap > 192.168.44.2.domain:  28330+ A? www.google.com. (32)
00:00:50.168951 IP 192.168.44.2.domain > work_pc.cap:  28330 5/7/7 CNAME www.l.google.com.,[|domain]
00:00:50.161977 IP home_pc.cgi-starapi > eo-in-f104.google.com.http: S 2701137719:2701137719(0) win 5840 <mss 1460,sackOK,timestamp
124374446 0,nop,wscale 3>
00:00:50.606136 IP eo-in-f104.google.com.http > home_pc.cgi-starapi: S 3987993391:3987993391(0) ack 2701137720 win 64240 <mss 1460>
00:00:50.606286 IP home_pc.cgi-starapi > eo-in-f104.google.com.http: . ack 1 win 5840
00:00:50.610226 IP home_pc.cgi-starapi > eo-in-f104.google.com.http: P 1:511(510) ack 1 win 5840
00:00:50.611087 IP eo-in-f104.google.com.http > home_pc.cgi-starapi: . ack 511 win 64240
00:00:52.366488 IP eo-in-f104.google.com.http > home_pc.cgi-starapi: P 1:1261(1260) ack 511 win 64240
00:00:52.366556 IP home_pc.cgi-starapi > eo-in-f104.google.com.http: . ack 1261 win 7560
00:00:52.429454 IP eo-in-f104.google.com.http > home_pc.cgi-starapi: P 1261:2521(1260) ack 511 win 64240
00:00:52.429510 IP home_pc.cgi-starapi > eo-in-f104.google.com.http: . ack 2521 win 10080
```

Summary

SSH port forwarding or tunneling allows you to forward otherwise unsecure TCP traffic inside a secure SSH tunnel. Protocols such as FTP, POP3, SMTP, HTTP, TELNET and others can all be forwarded inside this encrypted SSH tunnel, providing increased security features such as encryption and authentication that may not otherwise be supported. Throughout this chapter we have explored three different scenarios where port forwarding can be used: Local port forwarding which forwards based on localhost port, remote port forwarding which allows you to forward traffic back to the initiator, and SOCKS proxy that will allow dynamic protocols such as HTTP and DNS to be tunneled through. You should now have a good overview of what SSH port forwarding is all about and the capabilities it offers. I hope that it will guide you in your solution requirements.

Solutions Fast Track

SSH Port Forwarding Commands

- ☑ The -L [bind_address:]port:host:hostport] command specifies that a given port on the local (client) host is to be forwarded to the given host and port on the remote side.

- ☑ The –R [bind_address:]port:host:hostport] command specifies that a given port on the remote (server) host is to be forwarded to the given host and port on the local side.

Securing E-mail with SSH Local –L Port Forwarding

- ☑ E-mail protocols such as SMTP, POP3, and IMAP can be secured inside an SSH tunnel.

- ☑ Command *ssh -L 4444:mailserver.com:25 user@mailserver.com* will open port 4444 on the local machine and forward all traffic directed to it over to mailserver.com port 25 via SSH tunnel.

- ☑ SSH server listens on TCP port 22 by default but can be reconfigured to listen on other ports as well.

Bypassing Firewalls with SSH Remote –R Port Forwarding

- ☑ SSH port forwarding can be used to bypass firewalls and their restrictions.

- ☑ Command *ssh –R 7777:localhost:22 user@home_pc.com* will allow you to SSH in to port 7777 from home_pc.com and it will connect you back to the server you initiated this command from on port 22.

- ☑ The "-N" option will prevent execution of commands on the remote host.

Using SSH SOCKS Proxy –D to Tunnel Your HTTP/DNS Traffic

☑ SSH Version 2 supports SOCKS4 and SOCKS5 protocols.

☑ The –D option with SSH is used to create a SOCKS proxy on the local machine that can then be used to surf the Internet undetected from your corporate URL filtering servers.

☑ Use the man ssh command from your *nix command prompt to view detail help pages on SSH and its options.

Frequently Asked Questions

Q: Where can I find more help documentation on SSH and its port forwarding capabilities on Unix?

A: The help pages under Unix can be accessed with the "man" command. Within your command prompt type in *man ssh* for a full help page on SSH and all of its options.

Q: Our corporate firewall blocks all outgoing SSH traffic—is there a way around this to get to my home PC?

A: One of the things you can try is to reconfigure your SSHD at your home PC to listen on a port other than 22, perhaps port 80 that is used for HTTP. This will work and bypass many firewalls.

Q: My client is Windows based and I do not have OpenSSH, what else is out there?

A: You can install VMware player and download one of the UNIX images all for free—my favorite is CentOS and it is what we have used in this chapter. There is also SecureCRT but that is commercial software. Cygwin is another open source project that will work.

Q: What can I do to prevent my users from being able to port forward?

A: First, block port 22(SSH) out to the Internet. Second, you'll need an application inspection program such as IPS (Intrusion Prevention System) that will know the difference between HTTP and SSH protocol if your user decides to move SSH protocol up to port 80(HTTP).

Index

Printed and bound by CPI Group (UK) Ltd, Croydon, CR0 4YY

03/10/2024

01040343-0011